THE GREAT SIBERIAN MIGRATION

The Great
Siberian Migration

Government and Peasant in
Resettlement from Emancipation
to the First World War

DONALD W. TREADGOLD

Princeton, New Jersey
Princeton University Press
1957

Copyright © 1957 by Princeton University Press
London: Oxford University Press
All Rights Reserved
L.C. Card No. 57-5482

DONALD W. TREADGOLD is Associate Professor of Russian history at the University of Washington in Seattle. He is the author of *Lenin and His Rivals: the Struggle for Russia's Future*, and a contributor to various journals in the field of Russian history. He visited the U.S.S.R. in the summer of 1956.

Printed in the United States of America
by Princeton University Press, Princeton, New Jersey

For

Alva

NOTE

The writer wishes to acknowledge the financial assistance received from the Russia in Asia Project of the University of Washington, as well as the suggestions of colleagues there. I am particularly indebted to Professor Franz Michael of the Far Eastern and Russian Institute and to Miss Gladys Greenwood, assistant editor of Institute publications, for their thoroughgoing and helpful comments. Professors Michael Karpovich of Harvard University and Marc Szeftel of Cornell University read the entire manuscript, and I profited a great deal from their criticism. My wife assisted me in the work of writing and revision with patience, persistence, and unfailing good sense. The defects of the finished product are my own responsibility.

The system of Russian transliteration used is that of the Library of Congress, unless the word in question has passed into common English usage in a different form. In proper names I have deviated from the system to render final ый and ий by English "y," and ь by English "i" or have omitted it.

Equivalents of Russian measures: 1 desiatina = 2.7 acres; 1 verst = 0.66 mile; 1 pood = 36 pounds; 1 sazhen = 7 feet.

Equivalents of certain Russian terms: *guberniia* = province; *uezd* or *okrug* = county; *oblast'* = region; *khutor* = farm (enclosed plot with house on it); *otrub* = farm (enclosed plot with house in village).

CONTENTS

CHAPTER IV. The Migrants Enter Siberia

PART THREE. THE TRANS-SIBERIAN

RAILWAY, 1892-1906

CHAPTER V. Kulomzin and the Committee
on the Siberian Railway

CHAPTER VI. The Migrants Move by Rail

PART FOUR. STOLYPIN AND THE

DUMA, 1906-1914

CHAPTER VII. Stolypin and Siberia

CHAPTER VIII. Migration, the Intelligentsia,
and the Duma

TABLES

ILLUSTRATIONS

PLATES (following page 130)

Nos. 1, 2, 4, and 6 are from Volume 1 of *Aziatskaia Rossiia*, St. Petersburg, 1914; Nos. 3, 5, and 7 from the second edition of *Siberia and East Central Asia*, by John Bookwalter, New York, 1899.

MAPS

THE GREAT SIBERIAN MIGRATION

"The peasant is wise, but the commune is foolish."

"Where our feet are, there are our heads [and destinies] also."

—RUSSIAN PROVERBS

Russian and American Frontiers

Siberian migration was one aspect of a broader process at work in Russian society during the nineteenth and early twentieth centuries, a process by which the formerly legally stratified society was being replaced by one of legal equals, in which economic opportunity was increasingly accessible to all on equal terms. An important early landmark in this process was the Great Reforms of Alexander II (1855-1881), which freed the serfs and gave them land, created multiclass local self-government, reformed the judicial system, and made military service an obligation of all classes. During the reign of Alexander III (1881-1894) the operation of these reforms was restricted. Under Nicholas II (1894-1917) some of the limitations were in turn removed, and under revolutionary pressure in 1905 a national legislative assembly was created for the first time. Such political changes were paralleled by a diversification of economic activity, a growth of industry, and a notable broadening of the base of Russian culture through increased public education, expansion of the press, and a proliferation of the arts. One vital aspect of the whole process involved the agricultural population, which was numerically nearly the whole of the Russian people. Like other groups, the peasantry was moving in the direction of legal and economic equality, at a level where the individual and family were able to count for more than they had ever done in Russian history. All such changes were far from complete when the First World War broke out, but the degree to which they had made themselves felt deserves to be better understood.

Siberian migration affected, and was in turn influenced by, changes in population density, communal institutions in the village, land tenure and land use, the pattern of production, consumption, and trade, the use and payment of peasants for part-time industrial labor, the legal status of the peasant, his political rights, and many other developments in the homeland west of the Urals. Siberia had its own social, economic, political, and legal problems. Siberian migration was a phenomenon which thus involved European Russia, Asiatic Russia, and the Empire as a whole, and in particular its agriculture and its peasantry.

The Great Siberian Migration was an agricultural movement

which led to greater social equality than had existed earlier. In this respect it readily suggests similarity to the American westward migration. My study was begun, in fact, with the aim of comparing the American and Siberian frontier movements.[1] Turner declared, "The existence of an area of free land, its continuous recession, and the advance of American settlement westward, explain American development." This was the core of his frontier hypothesis, which he formulated with reference to the United States alone. He later went on to suggest that comparison with "Russia, Germany, and the English colonies in Canada, Australia, and Africa" would yield similar results. Such comparative studies may well someday serve as a basis for a general theory of frontier movements in modern times. Such a theory, however, ought to be worked out in full consciousness of the different geographical, intellectual, and institutional contexts of the countries which have known great migratory movements. Turner believed that the American frontier had certain clear effects, including the emergence of a "composite nationality," nationalism, sectionalism, democracy, and individualism. Some critics have indicated that certain elements of each "effect" either existed prior to the westward movement or owed something to other factors besides colonization. Evidence of that sort does not vitiate Turner's findings, although it shows that he ought to have been more careful in what he claimed as the overall significance of the frontier. He should have expressed more clearly an awareness of cultural heritage and institutional origins. He might have thereby avoided implying that America was made only by Americans—or worse still, only by American pioneers. Furthermore, like any other student of mass movements, he would have done well to remember more often that the story of a mass movement is far from the whole story of the thousands or millions of individual men and women who make it up. Anyone studying migration in some country other than the United States—not to mention today's students of the American frontier—would profit by examining very carefully the work of Turner and his school, then setting it aside to embark upon the study itself. In order to understand the ways in which the applicability of Turner's theory may be limited in areas outside America, it is well to have in mind the differences between the foreign movement studied and the main characteristics of the American frontier.

[1] My article, "Russian Expansion in the Light of Turner's Study of the American Frontier," *Agricultural History*, October 1952, was written at the start of this study.

4

Russian and American migration may be compared briefly for the period beginning around 1800. American migration can be traced back to Jamestown, Russian migration to the settlement of the primitive Slavs in the Dnieper valley, in the early centuries of the Christian era, but a more restricted period may be more fruitfully used for comparison. By 1800 Russia had acquired substantially the same boundaries she kept until 1917 (the main exception being Central Asia, in most of which Russian migration was of lesser significance). The United States then had only a fraction of the territory she was to acquire through expansion. Therefore Russian migration proceeded almost wholly into areas already under Russian control, either to the Black Sea region, much of which was in 1800 newly acquired, or to Russian Asia, most of which had flown the Tsar's flag since the seventeenth century. In contrast, American migration had both to settle and annex new territory, beyond the land purchased as "Louisiana" in 1803.

The physiography of the two countries had similar and dissimilar features. Russia's mountains were mainly along the southern border, keeping out the warmth of the south and allowing Arctic cold to range freely over the land. Much of the climate was more comparable to Canada's than to that of the United States. The areas of tillable land in Asiatic Russia lay chiefly in one fairly long belt around 300 miles wide, running from the Urals to the Altai, between latitudes which were too cold or too dry for ordinary farming. America's farm land covered a vast area of a thousand miles square. Yet from the viewpoint of the pioneer there was something in common. The Russian crossing the Urals faced first the fertile farmlands of Western Siberia, then some wooded and mountainous terrain near Lake Baikal, and beyond it a small area of good land on the Pacific Coast north of Vladivostok. The American crossing the Appalachians found a great tillable Middle Western area, then the Rocky Mountains, then good land on the Pacific Coast (and, in addition, near the Rockies, a great desert, whereas Russia's Asian desert ran east and west, to the south of the migrants' route).

The institutional patterns were quite different. In 1800 Russia possessed the governmental institutions of bureaucratic absolutism, and manorial landownership accompanied by serfdom (replaced in 1861 by state-fostered communal landownership among the freed peasantry). America was a free republic, and landed property was allodially held (the slave system disappeared after 1863, though the problem of property was not solved for the freed slaves). Russia had the reputation abroad—especially from the reign of Nicholas I (1825-1855)—of being a land of political repression as well as geographical inhospitableness, while America enjoyed widespread renown in Europe as the Utopia of the Western world; as Goethe said, "America, you have it better."

Thus American migration had two related but not identical aspects. One was the mass introduction of foreign-born into the country; the other was the winning of the West. There was some difference in the motivation of the two groups of settlers. The immigrant came to escape political oppression or poverty, and was convinced that better things awaited him across the Atlantic. The native-born or Eastern-acclimated pioneer was a free man to begin with; he also sought economic opportunity in the West, though it was seldom because he was a pauper.

Russia knew nothing similar to the Atlantic migration, but its eastward movement was in many ways comparable to the winning of the West. Her settlers were initially serfs fleeing oppression and poverty, and even after 1861 the freed peasants were often escaping legal restrictions and economic want. At the beginning of the nineteenth century they were coming to feel that a better life could be found in Siberia, but this was quite a new notion. There is a Russian proverb, "Even in Siberia people live," reflecting the old idea that Siberia was chiefly a frozen land and that to live there was in itself a punishment for exiles. However, there is also another proverb: "Siberia is said to be terrible, but those who live there live better than we do." This proverb probably mirrors an early stage of rosy rumors about a rainbow's end in the east, when such reports still sounded surprising.

Russians had more to escape from than Americans (and more than many of the Atlantic immigrants to America), and less to escape to. Nevertheless the Siberian settlers, like the American pioneers, voluntarily risked all they had and left accustomed surroundings to go into a wilderness in search of a better life. They knew hunger, disease, storm and drought, deprivation, homesickness, and loneliness before they succeeded in building new homes, planting new fields, making new neighbors, and finally gaining a new prosperity and a new happiness. Some died, some returned, some gave up after a year. The overwhelming majority stayed and survived.

Siberia lacked a number of features of the American frontier. The natives there were less of a problem than the American Indians, partly because the Russians treated their natives better, partly because the natives were seldom as warlike as the Indians, partly because they were not mainly in the agricultural areas where settlers headed at first (though when the Russians penetrated the Central Asian steppe, something very like an Indian problem arose, which erupted in a great Kazakh revolt in 1916). Siberia had no cowboys, for cattle were raised as part of peasant farming rather than as a prime product for market. Rail travel played a more prominent part in Siberian migration, partly because much of the American West was settled by the time the transcontinental railways were completed; when the Trans-Siberian was built, the bulk of the migrants were still to come. Siberian colonization lacked much of the local color which attended Wild Bill Hickok and Buffalo Bill, partly because of different cultural traditions, partly because the Siberian migrants were almost entirely family groups; much of the "wildness" of the American West was the work of bachelors. As a result of its less dramatic or dramatizable character Siberia's story was not carried to Europe, as the story of the Wild West was to the court of Queen Victoria and elsewhere. In Siberia there was no political slogan akin to "Fifty-four Forty or Fight." Even if Russian Tsars had had to win elections as American presidential candidates did, there might not have been any such slogans. No one had to suggest that it was "manifest destiny" for Russia to have Siberia because she had it already. Finally, Siberian settlers did not take up legally allodial holdings, and legally could undertake migration only with the government's consent, in return for which state aid was provided. This would appear to be a fundamental contrast; in actual fact it made much less difference than one might suppose.

With all its contrasts with the American movement, Siberian migration produced a society much more like that of America than was the Russian society from which it stemmed. The American historian, John D. Hicks, declares that Siberia "shows more similarities with the American frontier than with any other area."[2] This study provides considerable evidence which might support that statement.

Siberian migration resulted in the creation of a new Siberian society which had a higher level of prosperity and a greater degree of social flexibility than European Russia. The life of the new Siberian peasantry suggested both to officials and to peasants themselves, what the Russian peasantry might become. The departure of

[2] In a review of Walter Prescott Webb's *The Great Frontier*, in *Saturday Review of Literature*, December 27, 1952.

7

millions from congested European Russia was one factor enabling the peasants who remained to move nearer that goal. An important aspect of domestic improvement was the progress of "land settlement" (*zemleustroistvo*), the emergence of the legally independent farmer on a consolidated holding. Land settlement had its own European roots, and was developing independently of any direct or indirect relationship between the homeland and Siberia. Toward the end of the period in question, however, certain officials of the Tsar perceived the actual and potential link between Siberian migration and land settlement in European Russia and the way in which they complemented one another. Especially under the ministry of Stolypin, the government came at last to an active sponsorship of both movements. A paradox thereupon emerged. Though still a despotism, the government had accepted and championed what appeared to be a progressive movement among the agricultural population. The revolutionary intelligentsia, although consciously dedicated to progressive political and social change, opposed this same movement with vigor, partly because the Tsarist government which was now supporting it was their sworn enemy, but chiefly because they feared that it would lead to property relationships and attitudes which would prevent the attainment of some variety of socialism. One section of that intelligentsia, the Communists, finally seized power amid the governmental collapse which was hastened by the First World War. After a period of concessions to the peasantry, which was by that time close to independence, the Communists reduced the peasants to a state of legal and economic subjection far more rigorous than before.

Part of the story of the Siberian migration is not to be found in this study. The rise of the Siberian sectional feeling, changes in Siberian administration, and the growth of the cooperative movement are topics which are treated briefly or not at all. Certain aspects of the migration itself are not treated at length. Chiefly they are the role of differing religious beliefs (the Old Believers were prominent in a number of localities) and of national origins among the migrants. The migrants were almost wholly Great Russians, Ukrainians, and Belorussians, whose languages make up the Eastern Slavic linguistic group. The official reports and private accounts I have used almost never distinguish among the three. Therefore the reader must often interpret the word "Russian" as used in the study to render *rossiiskie*, inhabitants of the Empire, rather than *russkie*,

Great Russians.[3] The sources make it unlikely that any investigation will ever succeed in clarifying in detail this vexed question.

This study deals chiefly with the peasants and the central government, that is, the actual migrants and the state power which had to be either satisfied or eluded if migration took place. The intelligentsia, who were mainly interested bystanders, and the Duma, during the period of migration legislation, played an important role, but briefly. It was the peasants, in spite of or with the aid of the government, who made the Great Siberian Migration.

[3] See W. Kubijowytsch, *Siedlungsgeschichte, Bevölkerungsverteilung und Bevölkerungsbewegung der Ukraine*, Berlin, 1943, for an attempt to treat Ukrainian migration to Asia from Tsarist statistics. His only means of doing so is to add the totals from the provinces of predominantly Ukrainian-speaking population. Not all the inhabitants of those provinces spoke Ukrainian, but some who did speak it came from adjoining provinces, and probably the figures are quite accurate as far as they go. Kubijowytsch thus derives the following percentages of total Asiatic migration from Ukrainian provinces: from 1891-1900, 36%; 1901-1910, 49%; 1911-1914, 60%; 1924-1928, 24%; overall, 45%. By the same method one could obtain Belorussian figures by adding the relevant provincial totals. However, such tabulations merely beg the question of "nationality." How far had the idea of being a Ukrainian or Belorussian national, or even the consciousness of speaking a separate language rather than dialect, spread among the migrants from the provinces in question? These matters are most difficult to study.

PART ONE

THE COLONY AND THE HOMELAND

CHAPTER I

The Origins of the Great Siberian
Migration

"Every time I went to the village of Griaznukha, in a corner of the thick forest, I experienced a peculiar feeling which it would be hard to describe: that this was the edge of the world, a completely separate universe, a page from Russian history of the seventeenth century. Somewhere far off men were creating the wonders of civilization, building great industrial centers, discovering new routes, making great discoveries, causing fearful bloodshed, but Griaznukha remained the same Griaznukha, foreign to wonders, discoveries, and bloodshed."— D. N. Mamin-Sibiriak's story, *Glavnyi barin*.

Russian Resettlement Invades the Old Siberia

The crossing of the Urals by some 7,000,000 Russians during the last century of Tsarism was surpassed in magnitude by only one other recent migration, and equalled by perhaps two others. In the mighty Atlantic migration, the greatest of all historic time, which "overshadows all other population movements in peace or war," some 35,000,000 people came from Europe to America in a century.[1] From the 1880's until about 1930 several million Chinese entered Manchuria, though the movement has not yet been studied thoroughly enough for the details to be clarified.[2] The wave of resettlement most similar to the Siberian in size, and also in geographical conditions, was that which gave Canada a total of 8,000,000 inhabitants after a century of free colonization ending in 1914.[3]

The social scientist may justifiably consider the Great Siberian Migration as a single phenomenon. The historian may see in it the

[1] Marcus Lee Hansen, *The Atlantic Migration, 1607-1860*, Cambridge, Mass., 1945, p. 11.

[2] See C. Walter Young, "Chinese Immigration and Colonization in Manchuria," *Pioneer Settlement*, New York, 1932.

[3] Vladimir Sineokow draws this parallel with some care in his *La Colonisation Russe en Asie*, Paris, 1929, p. 212. It seems to have been French travelers, perhaps mindful of their country's role in Canada, to whom this comparison suggested itself most frequently. See Pierre Leroy-Beaulieu, *The Awakening of the East*, translated by Richard Davey, New York, 1900, p. 3ff.; Claudius Aulagnon, *La Sibérie Économique*, Paris, 1901, Ch. x.

latest stage of a much larger process within the Russian Empire. It was a stage in the forward movement of the line of more or less continuous settlement (or "frontier") which began with the dawn of history in the mixed forests of the upper Volga basin. The first scattered settlements in Russia's Asiatic possessions, which lay far ahead of the frontier of settlement, were established three hundred years before the frontier crossed the Ural Mountains.

The causes of the Siberian migration as well as of the previous movement within European Russia must thus be sought in the homeland. But its course and its effects depended in part on the nature of the old Siberia, for three centuries a scantily inhabited fur colony and the domain of settlements like Mamin-Sibiriak's Griaznukha. When the frontier crossed the Urals in the nineteenth century, the old Siberia was swallowed up by a new society, different both from that of the old fur territory and that of the contemporary homeland.

The Advance of the Frontier in Europe

The persistence of colonization as a central feature of all Russian history has attracted the notice of the most outstanding of the men who studied Russia. The greatest of Russian historians, Vasily O. Kliuchevsky, was also the first to make the assertion, in his *Course of Russian History*, that "Russia's history, throughout, is the history of a country undergoing colonization. . . . Migration, colonization constituted the basic feature of our history, to which all other features were more or less directly related."[4] Kliuchevsky's most gifted pupil, Paul Miliukov, observed to an American audience in 1903: "Both Russia and the United States have been colonized . . . in recent historic times. Hence the settlement and the exploitation of the natural resources of . . . [their countries] form the very warp of their historical texture. Most of the important features of their economic, social, and political development must be referred to this process of colonization."[5]

The same sort of observation has been made by foreign interpreters of Russia. B. H. Sumner, perhaps the best of them, wrote at the start of his *Survey of Russian History*, "throughout Russian history one dominating theme has been the frontier," and he wrote the first section of his topically organized book around this very theme.[6]

[4] V. O. Kliuchevsky, *Kurs russkoi istorii*, Moscow, 1937 (reprint, Ann Arbor, 1948), Vol. v, pp. 20-21.
[5] P. N. Miliukov, *Russia and Its Crisis*, Chicago, 1905, p. 5.
[6] B. H. Sumner, *Survey of Russian History*, 2d ed., London, 1947, p. 9.

The process of Russian colonization in historic times began with the settlement of the Eastern Slavs in the mixed-forest region extending from the upper Dnieper to the upper Volga. The eleventh-century Grand Princedom of Kiev, the first great state of the Eastern Slavs, opened on the rich agricultural land of the southern steppe, and it is likely that many farmers ventured into its northern fringes, where there were no trees to be cleared off and the soil was richer. The steppe, however, was then and remained for centuries longer the preserve of mounted nomads. Hazardous for scattered squatters, agriculture was impossible for a compact population. Incursions by Avars, Magyars, Pechenegs, and Polovtsy denied the black earth to the Kievan people and undermined the security of the Kievan state. Under the Mongol onslaught of the thirteenth century Kiev foundered completely.

Whether or not the mass of the people then fled northward to the region of Moscow, as Kliuchevsky suggested, in any case previously existing settlements there served as the basis for a slow and difficult building up of a new center of power in the principality of Vladimir. The cluster of towns in this district was gradually taken over and consolidated by the princes of Moscow, whose followers were also penetrating the forests and waterways of the northeast, in part under the leadership of the missionaries and monasteries of the Orthodox Church. Meanwhile near the Baltic Sea the trading city-state of Lord Novgorod the Great (*Gospodin Velikii Novgorod*) was acquiring a vast pioneering empire in the northeastern hinterlands.

By the later fifteenth century the Moscow princes were strong enough to throw off the last vestiges of Mongol suzerainty, and once more an independent Russian state stood on the line between forest and steppe. Almost simultaneously Moscow completed the process of subjugating all other Russian principalities, nearly the last of which to lose its independence was Novgorod. The Tsars, as the princes of Moscow now styled themselves as a sign of their new independence from the Mongols, strove to centralize the control of their large forest domain by building up a new class of nobles who were granted portions of the newly annexed lands as a pledge of their loyalty. By the sixteenth century the Muscovite state was sufficiently consolidated to attempt with success the conquest of the Mongol succession states of Kazan, Astrakhan, and Sibir, all three of which adjoined Moscow's southeastern boundary.

The successful partnership between the Tsar of Russia and his new servitor class produced casualties in the realm of the rights of other groups. Gone were the earlier power and privileges of the ancient hereditary nobility or boyars, as well as the freedom which the peasant previously possessed to arrange his relationship with the lord of the land which he tilled on a contractual basis and, if worse came to worse, to flee his dwelling-place without penalty. Russia had become a state where all were politically subject to an autocracy, a society where a growing proportion of the common people were bound by serfdom.

Discontented peasants, oppressed by the exactions of such a harsh regime, fled in large numbers toward the Black Sea from the sixteenth to the nineteenth century. In the southern steppe, subject to the ruler of no state, those peasants formed bands of "Cossacks," who practiced the occupations of soldier, pirate, hunter, and, later, farmer. From this anarchic region many a great uprising, from Bolotnikov in 1606-1607 to Pugachov in the 1770's, welled up and flowed back on the enserfed and autocratic center, only to be broken on its ramparts. As the frontier of settlement moved forward into the Ukraine and the lower Volga valley, the military lines and outposts of the state crept along in its wake. Both the settled and wilder portions of the steppe were still at the mercy of raids by outlaws and the Crimean Tartars. Their state, the last survival of the Mongol Empire in Russia, had been preserved by the opportune rise of a new protector in Ottoman Turkey for two centuries before Catherine the Great was able to weaken the Turks sufficiently to destroy their Crimean satellite. Tartars or no Tartars, there was in southern Russia free land in abundance until the middle third of the nineteenth century, at the disposal of those serfs who could escape the hand of the Russian Tsar. Only then did the frontier close up to the Black Sea and the foothills of the Caucasus and cross the Urals, but there had for centuries been settlers far ahead of the line of settlement, both in the south and in Siberia.

The Conquest of Siberia

The town and tiny khanate of Sibir, which gave the whole region its name, first appeared on a Russian map in 1367 and again on one of 1459.[7] From the fifteenth century onward, the phrase "the

[7] See S. M. Seredonin, "Istoricheskii ocherk zavoevaniia Aziatskoi Rossii," in *Aziatskaia Rossiia*, St. Petersburg, 1914, Vol. 1; Vsemirnaia Vystavka v Parizhe. Komitet Sibirskoi Zheleznoi Dorogi, *Kolonizatsiia Sibiri v sviazi s obshchim pereselencheskim voprosom*, St. Petersburg, 1900, Ch. 1.

land of Siberia" (*Sibirskaia zemlia*) is used in the Russian chronicles. The city of Novgorod had established a loose sort of control over a wedge of territory across the Urals by the twelfth century, and by 1364 Novgorodians were roving through the valley of the lower Ob. It is reported that after Novgorod fell to Ivan III a century later, many of its citizens fled over the Urals in order to escape Moscow rule. This was the first milestone in the kind of migration which was to populate so much of Asiatic Russia.

The wedge of trans-Ural territory called Iugria (*Iugurskaia zemlia*) was annexed along with its mother city of Novgorod, and in 1488 Ivan III first officially claimed Siberian territory for the Moscow Tsardom by adding to his title the phrase "prince of Iugria" (*Kniaz' Iugorskii*). His son Basil III extended the claim a trifle by adding *Kondinskii* and *Obdorskii*. However, the type of control which Moscow exerted over these regions was still of the very loose and nominal type which Novgorod had exercised earlier. Tribute was gathered from the natives, but the Russian population in the area remained negligible. Moscow's annexation of the northwest tip of Siberia was merely part of the annexation of Novgorod and was not intended as the beginning of an advance to the Pacific.

Only after another century had elapsed did Moscow launch an offensive to the east. In 1554 Ivan IV used the title "ruler of Siberia" (*povelitel' Sibiri*) in a document sent to Edward VI of England, but Sibir was in fact still one of the independent Tartar succession states. Thirty years later Cossack bands under the fabled adventurer Yermak, supported by the merchant family of the Stroganovs, engulfed the little state ruled by Khan Kuchum, and the title was made good in practice.

After overwhelming three Mongol khanates, Ivan IV was less concerned with the possibility of pushing farther eastward than with the danger from the fourth khanate which remained in the Crimea. He did not, however, feel strong enough to attack the Crimea, whose khan was protected by Turkey. Instead he turned to the Baltic to fight the long Livonian War. While the armed forces and financial resources of the Muscovite government were deeply embroiled in the Livonian war effort, private adventurers and entrepreneurs soon discovered that after the capture of Sibir the Tartar crust which edged the Russian borders had been broken clear through, and that what lay ahead was open territory. Whereas the Central Asiatic steppe was still held by the Kazakhs and other Turkic peoples, loosely organized but strong and often warlike, the Siberian forest was empty of all but scattered and weak native tribes. Cossacks and adventurers moved rapidly across northern Asia, headed for the Pacific, followed by officials and soldiers. Under Boris Godunov the outpost of Tara became the center for Russian relations with the steppe. During the Time of Troubles that center moved to Tomsk, founded in 1604. By the 1610's the Cossacks were on the Yenisei in force, and Yeniseisk was founded in 1618. During the 1630's they advanced to the valley of the Lena. In the next decade expeditions went ahead toward the Pacific in two directions, north to the Anadyr and south to the Amur.

The southern prong of conquest stopped when strong resistance was met from the Chinese at Albazin in 1650, and after some fighting the border with China was amicably fixed by the Treaty of Nerchinsk in 1689. In contrast, the northern prong of Cossack advance continued. Around 1700 Atlasov penetrated Kamchatka, which was to provide a base of operations for the great sea voyages of Bering and others a few decades later. Six of the Aleutians were annexed in 1766, Kodiak Island in 1784, and in 1804 Novo-Arkhangelsk was built on Sitka Island. The Russo-American Company had begun operating in 1798, chiefly in Alaska, but after enjoying a period of success during the Napoleonic Wars the company began to decline.[8] In 1867 Russia sold its North American possessions to the United States and retreated to the Asiatic mainland. Two centuries after China had stopped the southern advance, America had checked the northern.

The three hundred years which had passed since the time of Yermak had been in large part an era of exploitative commerce, in which fur was the chief commodity. Like the Spanish search for gold in the southern plateaus of America, the Russian quest for furs was not at first bolstered by dense enough settlement to support the thinly scattered outposts. Neither Spain nor Russia could withstand the solid financial and naval strength of Britain or the United States which challenged them in the New World by the nineteenth century. Spain could not turn to agriculture for an alternative source of wealth, but Russia found that the land of the steppe, as it ceased to be an empty and treacherous haven for marauding nomads, yielded rich returns.

About the time that the fur-trading frontier faded and came to an end, the Asian steppe began to be cultivated on a significant scale. As the Russian adventurers had swept through the Siberian forests, their

---

[8] See S. B. Okun, *The Russian-American Company*, ed. by B. D. Grekov, translated by Carl Ginsburg, Cambridge, Mass., 1951.

flank had been protected by extensions of the lines of border outposts (*cherta* or *liniia,* singular) which it had long been a practice to maintain in European Russia against raids from the open steppe. By 1800 Russia had reached the Black Sea and the lines disappeared, but in Asia Russian possessions still did not extend beyond the northern end of the Caspian. The conquest of central Asia took most of the rest of the nineteenth century, but much of the remaining land annexed either was desert or was already tilled by settled Turkic peoples. By the beginning of the nineteenth century the great latitudinal black-earth zone was clear for Russian settlement from the Prussian and Austrian borders to where it narrowed into insignificance near Lake Baikal, just north of Mongolia.

The Development of Siberian Administration

The Russians crossed the Urals in the 1580's and reached the Pacific in the 1640's. Since Siberia was thus acquired all at once, so to speak, it was natural that the St. Petersburg government should try to treat it as a unit. It was as a single fur colony that it was regarded economically, and as a single unit that it was governed politically.[9] From the sixteenth century until 1763 (except for a twenty-year hiatus from 1710 to 1730), there existed a Siberian *prikaz,* or bureau, the chief governmental office for trans-Ural affairs, first in Moscow and then in St. Petersburg after Peter the Great transferred the capital there. The administrative center of Siberia very early became Tobolsk, and it remained so as long as the unity of the Siberian domain was preserved. It was Tobolsk which became the capital of the province (*guberniia*) when in 1710 Peter the Great made Siberia one of the first regular administrative subdivisions Russia had ever known. The *Sibirskii prikaz* was simultaneously abolished.

The creation of a Siberian province coordinate with those of European Russia indicated that St. Petersburg thought it could already dispense with exceptional administration for this vast wild region and bring to an end what would today be called territorial or colonial government. The attempt shows more about prevailing political theory in St. Petersburg than about the realities of Siberia. The distances were too great. In 1730 the *Sibirskii prikaz* was reestablished.

The next developments came soon after the accession of Catherine

[9] See S. G. Svatikov, *Rossiia i Sibir'. K istorii sibirskogo oblastnichestva v XIX v.,* Prague, 1929.

the Great some thirty years later. Siberia was now designated as the "Siberian realm" (*Sibirskoe tsarstvo*). It was urged that Siberia should not any longer be considered a Russian colony, dependent on the homeland, but a colonial empire capable of supporting itself as well as of rendering tribute. That is, Siberia should not be a "Canada" to Russia's "England," but rather an "India." Whatever Catherine and her advisers had in mind when using such terminology, the difference was that India was inhabited by a population of an advanced civilization different from that of its mother country, and Siberia was not. Catherine did not attempt to give the new designation of "realm" any particular content, for she was busily engaged in partitioning Poland and in conquering and peopling the last of the Black Sea steppe. During her reign, in any case, Siberia was for the first time subdivided administratively. Two districts (*namestnichestva*) were established, with centers in Tobolsk and Irkutsk respectively. The government was beginning to recognize in practice that West Siberia, which adjoined the homeland, was developing faster than the distant east.

As he did with so much of his mother's legislation, the Emperor Paul promptly nullified her subdivision of Siberia, thus returning to her earlier conception of Siberian unity. There matters rested when in 1801 Alexander I undertook for the first time to dispatch a trusted official to the Siberian scene with instructions to report on how best the question of Siberian administration might be solved.[10] The journey of Privy Councillor Selifontov was the first in a series of notable inspection trips by Tsarist officials which continued through Speransky to Stolypin a century later, aimed at discovering how the changing conditions of Siberia were affecting its administrative requirements.

Selifontov's report resulted in the creation of a unified governor-generalship for the whole of Siberia, and Selifontov himself was given the post in 1802. However, administrative subdivisions were restored and increased in number. In 1804 Tobolsk province was divided into a smaller Tobolsk and a new Tomsk, and these two provinces retained the same boundaries down to the Revolution. In 1805 Yakutsk was also given a separate administrative status as a special region (*oblast*).

The governor-general of such a gigantic area as Siberia could not, without an army of officials which he did not have, affect very deeply

[10] See Marc Raeff, *Siberia and the Reforms of 1822*, Seattle, 1956.

the lives of many of the Tsar's subjects within his jurisdiction. However far his writ ran, it was, under the corrupt and absentee administration of Ivan B. Pestel (1805-1819), often a calamity to those whom it did touch. The Siberians themselves now found voice to demand justice for their own region, and in 1813 the Committee of Ministers responded to their protests by setting up a special Committee on Siberian Affairs. But this committee produced no perceptible results, and the real reexamination of the administrative problems of Siberia began only when Michael M. (later Count) Speransky replaced Pestel as governor-general in 1819.

Speransky's solution, as expressed in the legislation of 1822, was to retain a degree of central policymaking in St. Petersburg, placing it in the hands of a second Siberian Committee which replaced the one of 1813, while at the same time carrying further the process of local administrative subdivision and decentralization of responsibility. In 1822, as a result of Speransky's recommendations, based on his own observations in Siberia, the region was separated into two governor-generalships. Within the west with its center at Tobolsk (later Omsk) there was set up a new Omsk region. Within the east with its center in Irkutsk, there was created a new Yeniseisk province. All the older subdivisions were retained in both west and east.

The East Siberian governor-generalship lasted until 1917. The West Siberian was eliminated in 1882 as the advance of Russian settlement within its borders made "territorial" government no longer necessary. Although Speransky's Siberian Committee lasted only until 1838, it was then superseded by a Bureau for the Administration of Siberian Provinces (*Uchrezhdenie dlia upravleniia sibirskikh gubernii*) which continued to exist up to the Revolution.[11]

Siberia was not greatly affected by the Great Reforms of Alexander II in the 1860's, for it was not thought appropriate to extend their application to Siberia. The Reform laws had aimed at restricting landlordism, but the gentry was still left an important social and political role to fulfill, and it was given a leading part in the newly created institutions of local self-government known as zemstvos. If there was to be a Siberian zemstvo, the government must either create a Siberian gentry artificially or accept local peasant self-government. This dilemma remained unsolved to the last. However, the 1870 reform of municipal government was extended to several Siberian

[11] The Siberian Committee was temporarily reestablished from 1852 to 1864, when it was finally absorbed by the Committee of Ministers.

cities (Tomsk and Krasnoiarsk in 1871; Tobolsk, Irkutsk, Semi-palatinsk, Tiumen, and Tara in 1872; Omsk, Petropavlovsk, and Ishim in 1873; and others), and in 1896 the legal reform of 1864 was introduced in Siberia with certain limitations.[12]

During the reigns of Alexander II and Alexander III a number of new administrative subdivisions were established as the population grew in number and as problems became more complex throughout Asiatic Russia. By 1867 the advance into Central Asia had proceeded far enough for the creation of a separate governor-generalship of Turkestan. The southern steppe was the target of Russia's advance in Asia, and her declining preoccupation with the northern forest was indicated by the sale of Alaska in the same year. In 1882 a new governor-generalship of the steppe was created out of portions of both West Siberia and Turkestan. Also in 1882, the West Siberian governor-generalship, as already mentioned, was abolished and the Tomsk and Tobolsk provinces came directly under the jurisdiction of the Interior Ministry in St. Petersburg, like the other Russian provinces. Two years later the East Siberian governor-generalship was stripped of the Russian Far East, consisting of Transbaikalia, the Amur, the Maritime Province, and Sakhalin. These four districts became the new Amur governor-generalship. In 1882 there had been only two major subdivisions of Asiatic Russia, directly under St. Petersburg; in 1884 there were six—Tobolsk and Tomsk provinces and the governor-generalships of the Steppe, Turkestan, East Siberia, and the Amur.

In 1887 the East Siberian governor-generalship was renamed the governor-generalship of Irkutsk. Thereupon, as Svatikov points out, the very name of Siberia vanished from the administrative nomenclature of the region.[13] It had disappeared as the gradual and irregular advance of Imperial arms and of Russian settlers had proceeded to the east and south of the Asian possessions of the Empire. The

---

[12] Jules Legras, who was present at the ceremony of 2 July 1897 in Irkutsk when Minister of Justice Muraviev formally inaugurated the judicial reform in Siberia, reports that Muraviev declared " 'que, jusqu'à présent, la Sibérie était en proie au régime de l'arbitraire, et qu'on voyait des exemples de révoltante iniquité' "—strong words for a minister. (Legras, *En Sibérie*, Paris, 1899, pp. 259-60.) The reform was treated as the event of the year in the preface of W. A. Dolgoroukoff, *Guide à Travers la Sibérie et les Territoires Russes en Asie Centrale, Année Troisième*, Tomsk, 1898-1899.

V. G. Korolenko's story, *At-Davan*, depicts the cruel arbitrariness of a Siberian official, modeled after an aide to the governor-general of East Siberia active during the 1880's. This was the period of Korolenko's own exile in Yakutsk, and the period which Muraviev no doubt had especially in mind in making his speech.

[13] Svatikov, *op.cit.*, p. 77.

regional evolution of Siberia from an administrative point of view was proceeding rapidly, and it was becoming possible to link Asiatic Russia ever more closely with the homeland. On the 300th anniversary of the "conquest of Siberia" by Yermak, Alexander III expressed to the East Siberian governor-general his hope that "the vast and rich Siberian region, already for three centuries forming an *indivisible part* of Russia, will be in a position *indivisibly* together with it to enjoy similar institutions of state and society, the benefits of enlightenment, the increase of industrial activity to the general good and the glory of our beloved fatherland."[14] Peter the Great had tried in vain to integrate Siberia with European Russia by administrative fiat; Alexander III observed the process of integration taking place more or less spontaneously, as a result of the advance of settlement toward the east. At the same time he recognized the likelihood that Siberia might develop regionalist sentiments, and thus his italicized "indivisibles" in the above statement.

The Early Colonization of Siberia

The Soviet economist Liashchenko sums up the place of Siberia in the life of the Russian Empire as follows: "Even during the twentieth century Siberia represented for Russian Tsarism a place of exile and partly a source of income from the 'cabinet' factories [owned by the Tsar personally], while for capitalism it represented as before a commercial base for obtaining agricultural raw materials and for selling industrial products, chiefly those of light industry."[15]

Liashchenko's Marxist categories prevented him from correctly evaluating or even mentioning the role that Siberia played in the life of the Russian peasantry. The assumption that underlies the whole quotation is that Siberia had a colonial type of economy, chiefly exploited by outside forces, and lacking any significant sector independently developing enough strength to satisfy human wants on a large scale. Liashchenko's dictum is a ludicrous distortion of the position of Siberia in the twentieth century. It is partly accurate if applied to the seventeenth, though it still does not improve very much on the widespread Western misconception that the bulk of Siberian settlers were exiles or forced laborers.

It is of course true that Siberia, like some colonies of Britain and France, became a place of exile in the seventeenth century, and that this characteristic persisted in Siberia after it had become insignificant

---

[14] Quoted *idem*.

[15] P. I. Liashchenko, *Istoriia narodnogo khoziaistva SSSR*, 2 vols., Moscow, 1948, Vol. II, p. 532.

in America or Australia or the French West Indies. The Kolomenskoe rebels in the reign of Alexis, the Cossack followers of Stenka Razin, the *strel'tsy* under Peter the Great, the Polish rebels of the 1830's and the 1860's—all paid for their revolutionary deeds with Siberian exile. The exiles were often political offenders who had the best sort of educational background and a strict code of ethics, and down into the nineteenth century some of these elements contributed a great deal to the building up of the region. As early as the reign of Michael (1613-1645), orders had been issued for the freeing and rehabilitation of exiles in Siberia, and this proved the easier to carry out owing to the well-known Russian attitude of commiseration and forgiveness for the convict. As the Russian official Kulomzin wrote, "L'exil en Sibérie, en raison du caractère désert de cette contrée, conserva jusqu'au début du xixe siècle son caractère colonisateur; à partir de ce moment, il n'offrit plus qu'un caractère purement pénal."[16] While the size of the permanent Siberian population and the numbers of the migrant influx were growing steadily, the number of exiles also increased sharply. From 1823 to 1862, 356,000 exiles crossed the Urals, many of whom had participated in the Decembrist uprising or the Polish revolt.[17] It was only then that antagonism and tensions between exiles and settlers became a problem.[18]

A second element in early colonization was made up of various kinds of compulsory colonists. There were sent to Siberia "by summons and by selection" (*po vyzovu* and *po priboru*) a number of officials and others from the serving class who were to administer the colossal domain and act as agents of Imperial policy. Localities and administrators in European Russia were also required to send certain numbers of peasants to colonize Asiatic Russia. In the east these people paid dues or rendered state service of some kind, but in return state assistance and certain exemptions were provided for them.

Often the exiles were men who hated the regime, and while most of them probably would not have gone willingly to Siberia in any

---

[16] A. N. Koulomzine, *Le Transsibérien*, translated by Jules Legras, Paris, 1904, p. 182.

[17] *Kolonizatsiia Sibiri*, Ch. 2; V. K. Kuznetsov, "Russkie starozhily v Sibiri i Srednei Azii," in *Aziatskaia Rossiia*, Vol. I.

[18] In Mamin-Sibiriak's story, *Klad*, the following exchange occurs between a convict and a freeman (the period is the 1880's, the locale the Ural region):
" 'Oh, you Siberian convicts!'
'And how did you get to Siberia, grampa?'
'I? I came a different way. I came on my own hook, not by the help of the whip. I'm going to die in *Russia*. I'm sick of the sight of you convicts!' "

circumstances, they certainly did not want to go there under sentence. The compulsory colonists had a greater or lesser degree of loyalty to the regime, but usually did not want to go to Siberia either. However, according to Lantzeff, the "bulk of the permanent Russian population in Siberia" even as early as the seventeenth century was not made up of those two groups, but rather of "peasants who went there to seek free land, to escape creditors and government regulations, to be free from the menace of servitude."[19] The vagabond *guliashchie liudi*, the disinherited individuals known as *izgoi*, and the Old Believers who fled the persecution of the Regent Sophia furnished some of these, but many were ordinary Russian ploughmen who crossed the Urals of their own volition in search of a better life.

As early as the seventeenth century the departure of free (the Russian word was *samovol'nye*, people who went "by their own will") migrants had an impact on the homeland. Provincial governors cited the flight of the peasants as the reason for their inability to furnish army recruits; on the report of one governor to this effect, Peter the Great himself noted sarcastically that "not all the peasants have fled to the Don and Siberia!"[20] Miliukov estimated that the taxed population of central Russia diminished by 20 per cent during the last quarter of the seventeenth century, owing to military levies and flight to the borderlands taken together.[21] Once the peasant had escaped serfdom and military service, it proved very difficult to locate him; and in Siberia, even if he were found, he might not be sent back. The local Siberian authorities needed colonists, and they often hid the fugitives they were supposed to return. According to one writer, many officials felt that without a broad wave of migration it was impossible to settle and hold Siberia, yet it was impossible to open the dike for such a wave as long as the system of serfdom prevailed in European Russia and not in Siberia.[22]

Why did Siberia escape serfdom? Serfdom grew as a function of the government's need to satisfy its creature and bulwark, the gentry class. The government needed the gentry to administer civil affairs, but in the early modern period much more to lead and man its army against the dangers of the Tartars and Turks in the south and their occasional Polish and Swedish allies in the west, who came during

---

[19] George V. Lantzeff, *Siberia in the Seventeenth Century*, Berkeley, 1943, p. 155.
[20] Quoted in *Kolonizatsiia Sibiri*, p. 28. In 1714, on a report of the governor of Archangel.
[21] P. N. Miliukov, *Ocherki po istorii russkoi kul'tury*, 4th ed., St. Petersburg, 1900, Pt. 1, p. 26. The exact time interval referred to was from 1678 to 1710.
[22] *Aziatskaia Rossiia*, Vol. 1, p. 444.

the eighteenth century to overshadow the horsemen of the steppe in power and peril. In Asia the dangers were by comparison minimal. The Central Asian Turks might harass the Siberians, but they were not particularly warlike, and there was practically no armed friction with China once the border was fixed. The gentry did not wish to leave the amenities of the capitals for the valleys of the Yenisei and the Lena, and fortunately the military needs of Siberia could be cared for without them, by Cossacks and small regular detachments.[23] Siberia escaped the gentry, and so it escaped serfdom. From the very first it was an area of greater freedom than European Russia. Although it was controlled by St. Petersburg for centuries in which the Black Sea steppe remained a no man's land, Siberia had no serfs either before or after Catherine the Great handed the south over to the gentry and serfdom. Thus Siberia received a steady trickle of discontented men and women from west of the Urals long before the frontier of settlement began to advance into it. Compulsory colonization of Russian Asia limped along feebly. Free colonization moved steadily, and the government could not and did not try to check it entirely. Often compulsory colonists fled back to Russia, meeting en route free colonists escaping from Russia![24]

In the seventeenth century the government made some desultory efforts to bring back the voluntary colonists. Yet during the eighteenth, "political colonization yields to economic colonization, and there is already less worry about free migrants,"[25] who could be useful in settling Siberia as long as serfdom was not infringed in principle. From 1700 to 1800 the Russian population of Siberia is estimated to have increased from 200,000 to 500,000. "This considerable growth of the Siberian population in the eighteenth century," stated the Committee on the Siberian Railway, "cannot but be ascribed chiefly to the colonization of the country by free migrant elements."[26]

The Search for a Migration Policy: Speransky and Kiselev

A Russian official writes, "There runs like a red thread throughout the history of migration, above all, the failure of attempts to confine this advancing movement of the people within the limits of any definite formal plan."[27] When the line of settlement was advancing within European Russia, the government had no such thing as a

---

[23] See Seredonin, *loc.cit.*
[24] *Aziatskaia Rossiia*, Vol. i, p. 444.
[25] *Ibid.*, p. 449.
[26] *Kolonizatsiia Sibiri*, p. 44.
[27] "Krest'ianskoe pereselenie i russkaia kolonizatsiia za Uralom," *Aziatskaia Rossiia*, Vol. i, p. 450.

migration policy. The peasant was either a serf or state peasant; if he escaped he ought, if possible, to be brought back. There had been from earliest times in Siberia an official effort to colonize by compulsion, but since that effort was unsuccessful, there was also a willingness to wink at illegal flight which brought people in to settle voluntarily.

From the beginning of the nineteenth century there began to be attempts to bring the realities of migration and the laws into some semblance of harmony. In 1799 a ukase of the Emperor Paul on the settlement of Transbaikalia showed an intention of the government not only to accept the status quo as regards the free colonists in the east but to attempt to utilize them for state ends. Alexander I in 1806 tried to set up general rules for Siberian colonization by state peasants, by which migrants might be coaxed into moving under state permission and control. Then rather abruptly came a law of 1812 which forbade the migration of state peasants, and although certain exceptions were made—for example, for the southern district known as New Russia—the prohibition was extended to Siberia.[28]

Michael M. Speransky, when entrusted with evaluating the whole problem of Siberian policy, was struck by the futility of relying exclusively on compulsory colonization. In his report of 1821 to the Siberian Committee, Speransky declared that the Senate ruling of 1812 had been extended to Siberia only through misunderstanding, since it made no sense to prohibit free migration while simultaneously spending money to colonize that region. Speransky pointed to the "tendency which had been observed among peasants of certain provinces of European Russia to migrate to Siberia, where they expected to find greater land space than at home,"[29] and the persistence of the same motive supporting the smaller-scale resettlement which had been going on from Tobolsk province to Tomsk. He contended that free migration of peasants to Siberia had two positive advantages to the state: first, it served to settle that vast underpopulated domain, and, second, it furnished the land-hungry peasants of the homeland with the abundance they needed. The upshot of Speransky's report was, among other things,[30] the ukase of Alexander I of 1822 which granted permission to all state peasants to migrate to Siberia, or within Siberia, provided certain conditions were satisfied.[31]

[28] I *Polnoe sobranie zakonov*, 25, 150.

[29] Paraphrase of Speransky in *Kolonizatsiia Sibiri*, p. 62.

[30] See Raeff, *op.cit.*, for discussion of the administrative changes concerning Siberia which resulted from Speransky's recommendations.

[31] I *Polnoe sobranie zakonov*, 28,997.

One of the most important prerequisites to the success of that or any other state-sponsored migration plan was the actual allotment of suitable land in Siberia. Surveying of such lands had from 1714 on moved slowly by fits and starts, uncoordinated with any consistent policy for the utilization of areas deemed fit for settlement. Actual State Councillor Zaveleisky was sent to Siberia in 1835 in order to examine surveying conditions, and he reported that about 1,000,000 migrants could be accommodated in Western Siberia and Yeniseisk province.[32] But the magnitude of the tasks involved in surveying and allotting land for so many people, not to mention the possible social consequences of a movement of such scale, cooled the interest of Zaveleisky's colleagues, and nothing came of his report. In general the St. Petersburg bureaucracy cannot be charged with underestimating the hatred of the regime and the economic discontent which would swell the dimensions of migration if given free rein. It is said that official fears that New Russia would actually be emptied of its population lay behind a ukase which specifically denied its inhabitants the benefits of the migration law of 1822.[33]

However, certain elements in the Imperial government were convinced of the need for a sound policy which would permit peasant self-improvement, including the possibility of resettlement. The urgency of reforms which would deal at least with the needs of the state peasants, who had no gentry overlords to object, was sharpened by uprisings along the west slope of the Urals, in Perm and Orenburg, in 1834-1835.

The formulation of a new policy was entrusted to Count P. D. Kiselev, who took over the new Ministry of State Domains in 1837. He was a capable and conscientious officeholder. Although a Soviet scholar charges that in his views Kiselev "did not go beyond the limits of the feudal world," he still admits that "such a position did not prevent Kiselev from subjectively feeling himself to be a defender of the peasantry, a fighter for truth and justice, just as it did not prevent his contemporaries and liberal admirers from extolling him as a prophet of humaneness and freedom."[34] This is powerful testimony from a later beneficiary of the miseries which Kiselev sought to reduce.

Kiselev tried both to improve the condition of the state peasants

[32] *Kolonizatsiia Sibiri*, p. 70.

[33] *Ibid.*, p. 65. The ukase of 1823 referred to excepted Kherson, Ekaterinoslav, and Tavrida from the law of 1822.

[34] N. M. Druzhinin, *Gosudarstvennye krest'iane i reforma P. D. Kiseleva*, Vol. I, Moscow-Leningrad, 1946, p. 278.

of European Russia and to establish the prerequisites for a stable migration policy. First of all, the earlier sporadic methods of locating suitable lands were discarded, and in 1837 a special organization was established called the Siberian Survey (*Sibirskoe mezhevanie*). The Survey was authorized to operate on the basis of a norm of 15 desiatinas of land per adult male "soul." From the holdings of the long-established residents of Siberia, or "old-settlers," the organization was entitled to "cut off" surpluses above that norm to be allotted to new migrants. Or, if water scarcity or other factors made the cutting-off process unfeasible in a particular locality, the migrants would be introduced into old-settler villages.

Kiselev set about to broaden the scale of legal migration, both from European provinces to West Siberia and from West to East Siberia. The first objective was sought by the rules of 1843 which allowed state peasants to migrate from villages which were "exceptionally short of land," granting on arrival to each family which was judged to satisfy this requirement 35 desiatinas of land, monetary aid, and freedom from all obligations, including military recruitment.[35] Under this legislation, about 350,000 state peasants resettled in Siberia up to the 1860's. For the most part these migrants came from the central and southeastern provinces and went into West Siberia. In Tobolsk 8,400 males were settled in 1845-1847; by 1851 the total reached 19,503; in 1852-1854, 24,990 arrived. From 1852 to 1863 Tomsk received 18,340, and the Ministry of State Domains also supported some migrants who went to Yeniseisk province.[36]

Kiselev also sought to facilitate resettlement from West to East Siberia, because the number of migrants into West Siberia was exceeding the supply of lands which could be surveyed and allotted for them in time. During the 1840's migrants were already entering in force, areas in which insufficient land had been set aside, and then were often seeking to move out again. In 1846 legislation tried to stop this process—ineffectually, for in the 1850's the influx of migrants was again inundating the surveyors. In order to try to keep the migrants moving east if necessary in search of land, general rules of resettlement from Yeniseisk to Kamchatka were issued in 1852, though apparently they were not extensively used.

For the first time, Kiselev had managed to inaugurate a migra-

---

[35] See *Kolonizatsiia Sibiri*, pp. 73-75.

[36] *Ibid.*, pp. 76-81. The Committee on the Siberian Railway termed the overall progress of the settlement of the 1840's and 1850's "very satisfactory," on the basis of data of the 1890's showing Kiselevian villages solidly established after half a century.

tion policy liberal enough to induce a sizable number of settlers to move under the requirements of law. One of his stated purposes— that of relieving overcrowding and land hunger in European Russia —was of course served every time a single peasant migrated, legally or illegally. His second aim—that of reducing the scale of "irregular" (that is, illegal) migration, which threatened law and order on both sides of the Urals—was not achieved. Although a third of a million state peasants took the "regular" road opened by Kiselev's policy, irregulars did not diminish at all in number, and their total remained almost equal to that of the regular migrants.[37] One government report spoke of the "almost principled refusal of the people to use government aid" which the continued flight of free settlers indicated.[38]

Why did they refuse? Undoubtedly because they understood that government aid was coupled with government obligations. Whether or not the obligations, in reality or in erroneous anticipation, out-weighed the aid, many evidently thought they did or would. Men willing to leave their homes behind by thousands of miles were insistent not merely upon a change of landscape or even more land but upon freedom even at the price of rejecting the state largess furnished under the Kiselev policy. It is to the credit of Kiselev that there was nevertheless no attempt to bring back the irregulars. To return the free settlers would be inconvenient and useless; it "would reduce them to complete ruin, under such circumstances bringing no benefit to the state." Thus by 1842 one finds 842 irregular migrants from Smolensk being allotted migrant portions along with the regulars, even though the former received no loans or exemptions.[39] In 1843 the Committee of Ministers made the decision to leave such people alone in their new homeland, only compelling them (if possible!) to pay their obligations and furnish recruits. There appears to have been some attempt, in lieu of returning irregulars to European Russia, to compel them to resettle in the Kirghiz steppe as enrolled Cossacks, but the extent to which this was actually done is doubtful.[40]

By the end of the 1850's the number of migrants under the Kiselev policy had ceased to be significant. Perhaps this was because a sweeping peasant reform was already being discussed and the villagers wanted to wait and see what changes it would bring before trying their luck across the Urals. Thus came to an end, on the eve

[37] *Aziatskaia Rossiia*, Vol. 1, p. 449.   [38] *Idem.*
[39] *Kolonizatsiia Sibiri*, p. 82.   [40] *Ibid.*, p. 85.

of Emancipation, the first government attempt at a migration policy which had any visible degree of success in persuading colonists to conform to law. Of course the policy applied only to state peasants, and private serfs still had to flee illegally if they were to reach Siberia.

By freeing the serfs, Emancipation at last removed, from the path which led to the free land of the south and east, the basic obstacle confronting the hardest-pressed and most wretched of the Russian people. Migration policy had to be reexamined and reconsidered in its fundamentals if the Great Reforms, though not legally applied to Siberia, were not to lead directly to revolutionary social changes there and indirectly to upheavals in European Russia as well. Thus far the government had substantially failed to harness a movement much smaller than the one in prospect bade fair to become. As an official report puts it: "All . . . changes in state policy . . . in fact were only very imperceptibly reflected in the main movement of the people —the free migration of the unfree peasants."[41]

For three centuries Siberia had been legally a freer country than European Russia, and in fact the possibilities of evading all laws and all officials, as will be noted later, were great. Those who chafed under the political and economic oppression in European Russia had known or suspected Siberia's "Utopian" qualities. By the time of the mid-nineteenth century there was added a growing number of settlers whose chief source of dissatisfaction was not the political police nor serfdom but "land hunger." When, two or three decades after Emancipation, it became no longer possible to find free land in the southern steppe, the old Siberia became the sole hope of the land-hungry. "With its 'magic charms,' " as Lozovoi wrote fifty years later, "Siberia has lured and irresistibly attracts the masses of people of central Russia, all those to whom the European portion of Russia has become a 'stepmother.' "[42] The consequences for government policy, Siberia, and the homeland were tremendous.

The Scale of Siberian Migration

The extent to which the Great Migration transformed the old Siberia can be best understood by a glance at total population figures (see Table 1).

Thus the Siberian population, while remaining less than a million from the time of conquest until the beginning of the nineteenth cen-

[41] *Aziatskaia Rossiia*, Vol. I, p. 450.

[42] Lozovoi, "Voprosy pereseleniia i kolonizatsiia Sibiri," *Vol'naia Sibir'*, III, 1928, p. 129.

TABLE 1

Growth of Siberian Population, 1622-1921[43]

	Natives	Russians and Foreigners	Total
1622	173,000	23,000	196,000
1662	288,000	105,000	393,000
1709	200,000	229,227	429,227
1737	230,000	297,810	527,810
1763	260,000	420,000	680,000
1796-1797	363,362	575,800	939,162
1815	434,000	1,100,500	1,534,500
1858	648,000	2,288,036	2,936,036
1897	870,536	4,889,633	5,760,169
1911	972,866	8,393,469	9,366,335
1921	——	——	11,070,000

tury, increased by roughly ten times in the hundred years that followed, and the growth of population from 1897 to 1921 exceeded the entire number of inhabitants of the former year.

The figures just cited include both migrants and the natural increase of the old-settlers (*starozhily*, as they were called to distinguish them from the newly arrived *novosely* or "new settlers" who began arriving toward the latter part of the nineteenth century). The migrants themselves numbered as in Table 2.

The total of exiles is probably more or less accurate. Since their numbers depended entirely on governmental action, one could record with certainty how many were exiled, even if some escaped en route or eluded official surveillance in Siberia. The figures for the peasants are on the contrary often incomplete and inaccurate. Even taking the figures as given, however, we can observe that the proportion of exiles to the total seems to change abruptly in the 1880's and rapidly becomes insignificant.

During much of the post-Emancipation period, yearly figures are available (see Table 3).

Thus peasant migration to Siberia remained at a low level during the first half of the nineteenth century, rose somewhat during the 1850's, stayed steady in the 1860's, declined a little in the 1870's jumped significantly in the 1880's, continued to climb rapidly to the

[43] Table from Arved Schultz, *Sibirien: eine Landeskunde*; Breslau, 1923, p. 167. Figures do not include Central Asia.

TABLE 2

Russian Migrants Reported as Settling in Asiatic Russia (1801-1914)[44]
(In thousands)

	Peasants	Exiles, Prisoners	Total	Annual Average
1801-1850	125	250	375	8
1851-1860	91	100	191	19
1861-1870	114	140	254	25
1871-1880	68	180	248	25
1881-1890	279	140	419	42
1891-1900	1,078	130	1,208	121
1901-1910	2,257	25	2,282	229
1911-1914	696	27	723	180
TOTAL	4,708	992	5,700	

Estimated total of unreported migrants, not more than 700,000.

peak years of 1908-1909, then decreased slightly and remained steady at about 300,000 annually until the war.

The aggregate size of the Siberian migration is difficult to determine with precision. Table 2, taken from Obolensky-Osinsky, gives a total of 5,700,000 migrants and exiles for the whole period 1801-1914 and notes that probably an additional 700,000 were not tabulated, making a total of 6,400,000. The total of exiles and prisoners is 992,000. Many of these people were actually able to settle and live more or less normal lives even while under sentence; many remained when their sentence expired and became free Siberians. In contrast, many were either detained in prisons or used (before 1861) as serf labor in Nerchinsk and in other government enterprises. If we estimate that half the exiles were in fact also settlers, then our total of settlers comes to approximately 5,900,000. However, Table 3, which is constructed from different sources (indicated in footnote), yields a total of migrants (and scouts) of 5,375,353 for the period 1887-1913 alone. If we consider half the exiles as settlers, the total is raised to around 5,875,000. Adding Obolensky-Osinsky's figures for 1801-1880 (398,000) brings the figure to about 6,275,000. Subtracting Table 3 figures for 1887-1890 from Table 2 figures for 1881-1890, we arrive at about 130,000 for our still missing years 1881-1886, and when

[44] V. V. Obolensky (Osinsky), *Mezhdunarodnye i mezhdukontinental'nye migratsii v dovoennoi Rossii i SSSR*, Moscow, 1928, p. 84.

TABLE 3

Migration to Siberia, 1887-1913[45]

	Total Migrants and Scouts	Per Cent of Irregulars	Returners
1887	25,137	—	1885-1893
1888	35,848	—	2,302 families
1889	40,195	—	3.6% of total
1890	48,776	—	
1891	87,432	—	
1892	92,146	—	
1893	64,321	—	
1894	65,500	—	—
1895	120,000	—	—
1896	190,310	38.4	29,915
1897	86,676	38.9	35,990
1898	202,720	39.8	56,053
1899	223,209	45.5	65,605
1900	219,265	30.0	89,666
1901	120,125	33.2	54,796
1902	110,930	34.5	47,870
1903	125,500	32.8	44,041
1904	46,732	81.7	15,597
1905	44,029	92.6	11,524
1906	216,648	50.8	46,262
1907	567,979	19.7	117,518
1908	758,812	47.7	121,204
1909	707,463	47.9	139,907
1910	353,000	(est. 20%)	(70,000)
1911	226,100	—	(64,000)
1912	259,600	—	(34,000)
1913	327,900	—	(23,000)
TOTAL	5,375,353		

[45] Table gives figures for 1887-1895 from A. A. Kaufman, "Pereselenie," *Entsiklopedicheskii Slovar'* (Brockhaus-Efron), Vol. XXIII, p. 271; for 1896-1909 from I. I. Popov, "Pereselenie krest'ian i zemleustroistvo Sibiri," in A. K. Dzhivelegov and others, eds., *Velikaia Reforma*, Vol. VI, 1911, p. 255; figures for 1910-1913 from Antsiferov, *loc.cit.*, p. 324, except that figure for 1910 returners comes from V. P. Voshchinin, *Pereselencheskii vopros v Gosudarstvennoi Dume III sozyva*, St. Petersburg, 1912, p. 45. Figures for the years 1910-1913 are probably considerably too low; for example, a report in the authoritative periodical, *Voprosy Kolonizatsii*, No. 9, 1911, pp. 458-59, gives the number of migrants settling in Asiatic Russia in

we add this the total becomes 6,400,000. Our two methods of arriving at a total are thus about 500,000 apart. This statistician's nightmare can scarcely be pursued further with profit, for the individual constituent figures of the tables contain much conjecture and even during the later years of migrant registration we cannot be certain of how many eluded the registry. My own estimate (based on the amount of evidence which I have encountered indicating that the statistics are incomplete) is that the whole movement of settlers from 1801 to 1914 was somewhat under 7,000,000.

The regional increase of population was incomparably higher in Siberia than in any other part of the Empire. While the total number of inhabitants of what became the U.S.S.R. rose by 34.7 per cent from 1897 to 1923, the rate of 74 per cent was registered from Siberia and the Russian Far East.[46] When one finally learns from the 1926 census that 23 per cent of the Siberian population in that year was not born there—and this percentage would not include most of the children and grandchildren of the migrants of the peak years—the impact of the Great Migration becomes dramatically clear.

1910 as about 465,000 rather than 353,000. In general the table probably underestimates reality, and the individual figures should be treated with caution.

Figures of returners in parenthesis do not include scouts, whose return movement accounts for a large percentage of all other returner figures. For example, out of the 117,518 who returned in 1907, 90,323 were scouts; out of 121,204 for 1908, 76,102; and so on. Thus the peak of the return movement of the direct migrants was attained, not in 1907, but in 1910, and it declined thereafter.

[46] See Frank Lorimer, *The Population of the Soviet Union: History and Prospects*, Geneva, 1946, Ch. IV.

CHAPTER II

The Peasant in the Homeland

"And if we now observe, in the agricultural reality which surrounds us, that small farming enterprise not only is not dying out, but during the last decade actually has been strengthening its position, then the explanation lies by no means in its technical superiority, but in economic and social circumstances which result from the nature of a private enterprise in which production is carried on by the family without employing wage labor."—Alexander Tschajanow, *Die Lehre von der bäuerlichen Wirtschaft*, Berlin, 1923, p. 6.

Regional Development in Russian Agriculture: Siberia and the Center

According to Geroid T. Robinson, "among the peasants west of the Urals, Siberia was regarded as a kind of Utopia,"[1] and this attitude was increasingly translated into action at the turn of the twentieth century. While parts of Siberia were in fact more like a Utopia than like a frozen waste (contrary to the usual Western conception, which persists to this day), they offered rigors enough. Still, the severity of climate, the distance from loved ones and accustomed institutions, the difficulty of supply and the distance to markets—all might seem to the migrant minor hindrances compared with the pressures of his former situation in the homeland.

In the 1870's the agriculture of European Russia, by which nine out of every ten Russians lived, went into a prolonged depression. There had long been an agrarian problem in Russia, but all its facets had never been so sharply etched in public consciousness. The peasant seemed powerless to solve by his own initiative the problems created by the sheer numbers of his village neighbors, the ancient modes of land tenure and land use, the changing conditions of the market for farm produce, and the weight of his financial obligations. The socio-political institutions to which he was subject limited more or less severely his capacity to deal with all of these hindrances. The village commune had an important role in determining the peasant's financial obligations, land tenure, land use, and the degree to which he felt the pressure of population density (by prescribing conditions of with-

[1] Geroid Tanquary Robinson, *Rural Russia under the Old Regime*, reprint, New York, 1949, p. 251. This had not always been so; cf. Foreword.

36

drawal from or accession to membership). Local governmental units, such as province, county, and township, had varying degrees of authority over financial exactions and conditions of movement. The Imperial central government, with its multitude of subsidiary agencies, determined policies in regard to movement of population, monetary levies, and the legal status of the land. The peasant might persuade, evade, or escape the hand of authority in this or that instance, but the only way he might hope to make a clean break with his manifold problems was to emigrate from his village. No wonder Siberia appeared to him as a Utopia.

On looking closely at the agricultural geography of Russia, one will discover that there was nothing magic about the line of the Ural mountains, whose modest slopes formed the boundary between European Russia and Siberia. On both sides of the Urals the peasantry constituted the overwhelming majority of the population, lived in communes, ate rye bread, worshipped in the Russian Orthodox manner, and acknowledged the same Tsar, who in St. Petersburg was almost as far away from Sevastopol as from Tobolsk. Yet Siberia had some regional characteristics peculiar to it. Throughout its vast expanses, which like some areas of northern European Russia had never known serfdom, there was only the pale shadow of a ruling class in the shape of officialdom. The large landowners who were so powerful west of the Urals were virtually absent to the east.[2]

The Russian Empire may be divided into several socially homogeneous regions, of which Siberia was but one. From the standpoint of agricultural development, these regions, Chelintsev argues, represented successive "phases of agrarian evolution."[3] After reaching the Dnieper valley, perhaps in the seventh century A.D., Eastern Slavs settled down and turned to agriculture in the Central Agricultural Region, centering on the midpoint of the line which ran roughly from Lvov to Kazan, which separated the mixed-forest from the rich

[2] Golovachev asserts that there were some 3,700 serfs in Siberia, of whom 2,800 were peasants and the rest household serfs. The 2,800 were distributed on 36 estates, of which 28 were in Tobolsk, 6 in Tomsk, and 2 in Yeniseisk province. ("Chastnoe zemlevladenie v Sibiri," *Sibirskie Voprosy*, St. Petersburg, 1905, Vol. I, pp. 133-34.) Alexander Michie, a British traveler, reported that Siberia had only one noble serf-owner, a certain Rodinkoff, vice-governor of Yeniseisk province. His grandfather had received from Catherine the Great a grant of land and peasants in Siberia under the terms of Russian serfdom. Michie wrote that Rodinkoff did not try to exercise his rights; his brother had tried to do so by levying contributions on "his" peasants, and had been promptly murdered in consequence. (See Michie, *The Siberian Overland Route from Peking to Petersburg,* London, 1864, p. 324.)

[3] A. N. Chelintsev, *Sel'sko-khoziaistvennye raiony Evropeiskoi Rossii, kak stadii sel'sko-khoziaistvennoi evoliutsii*, St. Petersburg, 1910.

steppe land to the south and east. As time passed, settlement thickened and expanded in all directions, though most persistently and steadily southward and eastward toward the fertile steppes. Beginning in the center, the original crude methods of clearing new land by felling trees or burning undergrowth followed by steady cropping yielded to more regular types of exploitation. In the more densely settled areas, fallowing began to be adopted, and a three-course system of winter grain, spring grain, and fallow spread in the villages of the center.

Here the village commune, the precise circumstances of whose origins are still uncertain, first made its appearance. It provided a rough kind of mutual security against intruders and distributed equally the obligations which government or serf-owner managed to impose. In the seventeenth century the commune acquired the custom of periodical redistribution of land, providing an economic basis for the sharing of both financial and military obligations. In 1719 Peter the Great introduced the "soul tax" and legislated joint liability of the commune for taxation and recruitment.

The commune was the fundamental social institution of those who tilled the soil—both the serf of central Russia (and later of the south as serfdom crept toward the Black Sea) and the "state peasant" of the north and Siberia. Serfdom and the legal status of state peasant were institutions which by the end of the seventeenth century included virtually the whole peasant population. But neither serfs nor state peasants were exclusively agriculturists; there were some household and industrial serfs, and a few state peasants ascribed to state factories, while those who did till the soil were not constrained to do so in any particular manner. The regulation of the actual process of agricultural production was the function of the commune, which, owing to the division of redistributed land into strips of nominally equal worth, had come to govern the crop cycle, although the actual farming unit was the peasant household rather than the commune.

The vigor which remained in communal institutions by the middle of the nineteenth century is in dispute. In any event, the commune was preserved and given new powers by the Emancipation laws, which vested in it a joint liability for the redemption payments owing for the land allotted the peasantry in 1861. Despite the legal strengthening of the commune, it appears that its agricultural functions were already withering. Although the beginnings of population pressure had helped to create the commune in the first place, the high degree of overcrowding prevalent by the middle of the nineteenth century seemed to be undermining it. As every foot of ground became more precious, there was less eagerness among both ex-serfs and ex-state peasants to acquiesce in redistribution of land or to disturb the precariously small holdings in any way. So there came about a crisis in the communal system in central Russia even before the depression of the 1870's.

If the same evolution, from squatting and clearing to communally regulated three-course farming to a crisis in the latter system, had been repeated at the same rate beginning with every extension of the area of settlement, then of course there would have been no discernible agricultural regions at all except in the physiographic sense. Every mile would be at a different stage from the one which lay between it and central Russia, and from the one beyond it. Actually the evolution was not so regular, steady, or spontaneous. Regions developed their own common characteristics under a variety of pressures outside the seemingly "elemental" (*stikhiinyi*) process of expanding settlement.

The degree of effective political control exercised by Russia and other nations which controlled Russian population (for example, Lithuania or Poland), or the absence of any control over tillable areas (as in the southern steppe); the wars in progress or threatening to break out; the latter-day growth of urban industry, providing a new outlet for discontented rural dwellers and significantly altering the conditions of the market; the recent acquisitions of ports on the Black Sea—any or all of these might and did divert or delay the direction of expanding settlement and the course of agricultural evolution in general. The result of discontinuities owing to such factors was that agrarian regions came into being as the line of farms advanced—for example, the Ukraine, the lower Volga region, the northern Caucasus, and Siberia, each of which possessed some common and distinctive features.

The nodal area of the "agrarian problem" remained in the geographical source of the expanding settlement. No matter how rapidly peasants left the central region, the natural growth of population kept pressing on its resources. This was the region where at the time of Emancipation farming was most highly developed and land prices highest—and therefore landowners' demands for reduction of allotments to the ex-serfs the sharpest. The center had long been the stronghold of the commune and the strip system with three-course rotation. Since no grass crops were grown in that rotation, it was of grave moment to the freed serf that perhaps the greatest economic defect of the Emancipation land settlement was its failure to provide him with sufficient pasture land. Nowhere was this lack felt more keenly than in central Russia. The pre-1861 weaknesses of the region had become intensified. Thus the center was the area of greatest suffering during the depression of the 1870's and the focus of peasant revolt beginning in 1902.[4]

The government response to the crisis was to found the State Peasant Bank in 1882, reduce redemption payments still owing for the allotments granted the ex-serfs after Emancipation, and repeal the soul tax. When in 1891-1892 a famine swept the still stricken countryside, the government was prompted to reduce interest rates and reorganize the Peasant Bank thoroughly. These were useful, but still only superficial and piecemeal measures.

If one asked a peasant leaving, say Kiev or Chernigov province, why he wanted to abandon his homeland to seek his fortune elsewhere, he was likely to reply, "There was not enough land." This peasant level of understanding of the agrarian problem was never really transcended by the revolutionary parties which had appeared by 1900. To the last they all couched their agrarian programs in terms of immediate expropriation of non-peasant lands for the benefit of the peasant.[5] Actually a more than superficial study of the straits into which the villager had fallen was bound to show that it was not simple insufficiency of land which lay at the root of the problem. It was rather that the manner in which the land was usually held and cultivated prevented many peasants, especially in central Russia, from producing enough to maintain a decent level of consumption.

It had not yet occurred to the peasant, to any influential bureaucrat, or to the revolutionaries, to pass beyond palliatives, applied or proposed, to an examination of whether the prevailing modes of agricultural production and consumption remained (if they had ever really been) workable, given the increasing population density and shortage of land. No one failed to realize that the situation was worst in central Russia, but few seemed to conclude from this that the

[4] The best discussion of the economic situation in the pre-Revolutionary Russian village is to be found in George Pavlovsky, *Agricultural Russia on the Eve of the Revolution*, London, 1930. For convenient general treatments, see also Robinson, *op.cit.*; Alexis N. Antsiferov, Alexander D. Bilimovich, and others, *Russian Agriculture during the War*, New Haven, 1930; Vladimir P. Timoshenko, *Agricultural Russia and the Wheat Problem*, Stanford, 1932; Naum Jasny, *The Socialized Agriculture of the USSR*, Stanford, 1949; and Launcelot A. Owen, *The Russian Peasant Movement, 1906-1917*, London, 1937.

[5] See my *Lenin and His Rivals: the Struggle for Russia's Future, 1898-1906*, New York, 1955.

introduction of a new type of farming was most urgently needed precisely in that region.

The swift industrial development from 1880 onward was helping, as Lenin noted, to create a wider domestic market. The new urban consumers were taking more peasant produce at higher prices, but this did not in itself affect peasant productivity. The beginnings of a solution to the agrarian problem must be traced, not in the coming of the Industrial Revolution to Russia, but in the first signs of a new stage of agricultural development, which was making its appearance in the west and was moving rapidly in the direction of expanding settlement toward the south and east. This stage was one of independent, individual family farming. It has been variously described since then, as found in Russia and elsewhere, as *trudovoe khoziaistvo* (literally, "toiling economy," the enterprise of the man who is both manager and laborer on his farm), "die bäuerliche Wirtschaft," "family farming," "not capitalism, not socialism."[6] Its emergence may be traced in three main aspects: land tenure, land use, and market conditions.

Land Tenure: Weakening of the Gentry and the Commune

When traveling in the south-central steppe of Russia in 1926, Geroid T. Robinson came upon a wrecked manor house. "Prowling among these architectural bones, one could imagine anything: troikas at the door; bearded servants bowing and scraping; harpsichords and hunting feasts; the gossip of St. Petersburg and Paris; hoopskirts, silks and sabres; medalled dignitaries with powdered wigs, or the mutton-chop whiskers of a later day; daughters in French gowns, home from the Riviera; sons in the Guards' uniform of the Napoleonic Wars or the Great War—all musty and remote, buried more deeply by these last ten years than by the ten decades that went before. . . ."[7]

Actually the "burial" of gentry farming and the colorfully rich gentry society which it supported began shortly after Emancipation. By 1916 90 per cent of the crop area was farmed by the peasants, before the "ten years" of which Robinson speaks had begun. Even half a century before, as Pavlovsky points out, "the landed property of the gentry was in course of almost feverish liquidation."[8] If large

[6] The last phrase is David Mitrany's in his *Marx against the Peasant*, London, 1951, Ch. VIII.

[7] Robinson, *op.cit.*, pp. 1-2.

[8] Pavlovsky, *op.cit.*, p. 190.

landholding was the chief culprit of the agrarian problem, then the Revolution may have killed it, but it was already dying. The problem of land tenure was by no means the sole or even fundamental one which the peasant faced, but it is worth careful attention—in part because the peasant himself often thought it was, but also because the revolutionary intelligentsia tended to agree.

Even if the solution was to be sought in the extension of tenure, there was a good deal of unused land available aside from what might be expropriated. In the category of "land reserve" (state-owned), the land census of 1905 listed 74,400,000 desiatinas in European Russia, whereas competent authorities estimated that over 600,000,000 desiatinas in Asiatic Russia were fit for cultivation.[9] However seriously one should take these figures, Antsiferov justifiably concludes that "as regards Asiatic Russia the tillage of cultivable land had only been begun. In this respect Russia stood far behind all other countries in Asia, Europe, and America." However, let us examine not the potential but the actual pattern of tenure.

It is to the everlasting credit of the authors of the Emancipation legislation that they gave the serfs not only their freedom but also land, which was not secured to the freed American slaves. Abundant and careful attention has been devoted to the defects of the Emancipation land settlement, perhaps less to the subsequent developments in land tenure which the Emancipation made possible. In 1861 there were 8,450,782 peasant households in fifty provinces of European Russia. They received "allotments" (*nadely*) of 111,600,000 desiatinas from land which had been previously owned by the gentry but actually tilled by the communal peasants and physically separate from the manorial lands. There are no comparable figures available for the land then possessed by other social classes. For 1877-1878 and 1905, however, comparison is possible (see Table 4).

The figures show clearly that the peasant holdings were increasing rapidly, both absolutely and relative to those of other classes, from 1861 to 1917. Since 1877-1878 the peasants had increased the area of their holdings from 121 to 185 million desiatinas, or by about 50 per cent; their share of the total had risen from 32 per cent to 47 per cent.

Now let us survey the change in size of holdings within the peasantry (figures are available only for holdings of allotment land, not for privately owned peasant land). See Table 5.

[9] Antsiferov, *op.cit.*, pp. 17-18, citing the American Investigation Society of Siberia.

Notice that the number of peasant holdings, which had been about eight and a half million in 1861, rose steadily. At the time of the land census of 1916 (in 48 provinces) it had reached 15,712,000. Throughout that period the growth in the number of households was largely a product of the rising birth rate. But in addition young people

TABLE 4

Changes in Land Tenure in Russia[10]
(millions of desiatinas)

Groups Holding Land	1877-1878	1905	1917
State, public institutions	166.3	154.7	147.2 (37.3%)
Peasants:			
1. allotments	116.7	133.8	
2. privately owned	5.0	24.7	
	121.7 (32.2%)	158.5 (40.1%)	185 (46.8%)
Gentry	73.2	58.2	42.5
Other social groups	15.8	23.8	20.5
			63 (15.9%)
TOTAL	377.0	395.2	395.2

TABLE 5

Changes in Peasant Allotment Tenure in Russia[11]

	1877-1878 (40 provinces)		1905 (50 provinces)	
Size of holdings	No. of holdings	% of total	No. of holdings	% of total
Under 2 des.	375,000	4.4	580,200	4.7
2-5 des.	516,400	6.2	2,276,700	18.6
5-20 des.	7,533,600	77.8	8,123,600	66.1
Over 20 des.	972,300	11.6	1,294,500	10.6
TOTAL	9,397,300	100.0	12,275,000	100.0
			23,000 (unknown size)	
			12,298,000	

[10] Figures for 1877-1878 and 1905 from census of Central Statistical Committee, cited in "Rural Economy," in Antsiferov and others, *op.cit.*, p. 20. Figures for (1 January) 1917 from Antsiferov's own estimate in *ibid.*, pp. 22-23, based on work of D. I. Pestrzhetsky.

[11] Table from *ibid.*, p. 31.

more frequently were establishing separate homes and farms, as shown by the fact that the number of households rose faster than the total population. This was one reason for the increasing individualization in Russian agriculture.

While the number of peasant holdings rose markedly, the striking fact which emerges from the last table is that the overall pattern of peasant land tenure did not change significantly. Both extremes of peasant landholding remained stationary, while only slightly over a tenth of the holdings slipped from one intermediate category to the next lower one—from the 5-20 to the 2-5 desiatina group. In other words, the increased population had not been thrown into the agricultural laborer category, but had had to be satisfied with slightly smaller holdings. If the current trend continued, a considerable proportion of family holdings was going to grow still smaller. The peasant was threatened by the increase of his own numbers. The chief social institution which underlay this threat was the commune.

As Pavlovsky correctly pointed out, the main indictment against the commune was that it relieved the individual peasant of the responsibility for the excessive increase of his family, since the commune had to find room for new members who appeared in its midst.[12] If individual tenure should supplant communal tenure, the family would limit its growth, since it could no longer hope that the commune would gratuitously allot it more land. That individual tenure, coupled with division of inheritance, would have such an effect had been demonstrated in France. By the time of Napoleon there had existed individual tenure, and the Code which he issued had only to prescribe division of inheritance to reduce the birth rate. In Russia there already existed division of inheritance, but there was as yet no individual peasant tenure. It was this sort of reasoning which was employed by Pavlovsky and others, including the Danish economist Carl Andreas Koefoed when he wrote: "There are countries where 150 years ago the people died by the thousands from hunger and where now, thanks to the transfer of the peasants to [individual] farms, three times as many people as before live in complete sufficiency, and have no side employment, in such prosperity that the last village *batrak* [poorest peasant] lives better than the rich peasant of Russia."[13]

In other words, the problem was not, as the peasant so often conceived it, lack of land, but the way in which the land was used. It

[12] Pavlovsky, *op.cit.*, p. 83.
[13] A. A. Kofod, *Khutorskoe razselenie*, St. Petersburg, 1907, p. 6.

was unlikely that there would for some time be too many people for Russia to feed, but even the existing population could no longer be fed by the old farming methods. Koefoed suggested that agricultural productivity could be raised by passage from the strip system to many-field rotation with the inclusion of grass crops. In order to alter the prevailing methods of land use, land tenure must first be reformed—not simply by giving the peasant more land to be held in strips, whether by purchase or rental or expropriated grant, but by consolidation of the existing strips into one holding, or "enclosure."

Whatever the desirability of enclosure, there is evidence that it was already being adopted in Russia. It had begun to be introduced, following the nearby Prussian example, in the Russian-administered Kingdom of Poland during the 1820's. In the 1860's it had begun to spread in Suwalki province, in the 1870's in Kovno. German colonists who migrated from Poland to Volhynia during the same decade practiced enclosure, and their Russian neighbors had started to follow their example. Latvian and Estonian migrants into Pskov, Vitebsk, Mogilev, and Smolensk provinces had done likewise, and enclosure was thus appearing in Belorussia. Enclosure had invaded eight Russian provinces of the northwest before Stolypin ever thought of legislating in favor of the process.[14]

Koefoed had noticed enclosure taking place when traveling in his capacity as assessor of the Gentry-Bank of Mogilev in 1903-1904. Once his attention was caught by the phenomenon, he studied it widely in Russia and traveled in Western Europe to compare conditions there with what he had seen in the East. He came to know A. A. Rittikh, director of the Department of State Domains in the Ministry of Agriculture and "one of the ablest of the younger officials," and through him managed to meet Stolypin for the first time in 1906. He put the case for enclosure before the minister, and found that he was able to appeal to Stolypin in terms of the latter's own experience. Stolypin was, as Pares says, "no theorist, but a common-sense country gentleman, with estates in two parts of Russia —Kovno, where the separation movement onto farms had proceeded without legislation, and Saratov, where the disadvantages of the communal system had been particularly evident and there had been the most widespread agrarian riots. He had no special expert knowl-

---

[14] *Ibid.*, Ch. 2, and A. N. Chelintsev, *Sel'sko-khoziaistvennaia geografiia Rossii*, Berlin, 1923, pp. 118-19.

edge; but, as in other questions, he had the pluck to seize the obvious, and to act accordingly."[15]

In order to support enclosure, the government had to assault the commune frontally. The "allotment" land distributed to the peasants by Emancipation remained legally in the disposition of the commune. Thus enclosure of the strips of land under control of the peasant at a given moment had to be preceded by withdrawal from the commune and confirmation of title (*ukreplenie*) to those strips as private property.

Both steps—confirmation of title and enclosure—had already become possible under the terms of the General Statute of Peasants of 1861. It provided that any village with repartitional tenure could by a two-thirds majority convert itself into one with hereditary tenure. Furthermore, in a village which had cleared itself from the redemption payments, any individual could claim withdrawal from the commune. By the Statute of Redemption, any individual could by paying his share of the redemption payments ahead of time claim withdrawal forthwith. It was under these statutes that the enclosures reported by Koefoed had been carried out—presuming that the laws were observed, which was as regards the Russian peasantry a presumption of fair magnitude.

Pavlovsky concludes from an examination of these statutes that "from the start, communal tenure was treated . . . as an intermediate stage in the development of peasant landownership, rendered necessary, primarily, by the need of adequate security for the redemption credits."[16] Such seemed clearly the intention of certain officials of Alexander II's government; the eventual objective was full ownership, and withdrawal from the commune, by each peasant family on payment of the redemption debt. However, even in the 1860's other bureaucrats had wished to preserve the commune, out of a Rousseauist-Slavophile belief that it was a "natural" and indigenous institution, as well as from an administrator's conviction that the commune was a reliable instrument to ensure peasant loyalty to the regime.

During the reign of Alexander III, the two opposed viewpoints clashed. At first the adherents of the original objectives of Emancipation prevailed. In 1882 the State Peasant Bank was established to assist peasants in obtaining land. In 1885 the poll tax was abolished.

---

[15] Bernard Pares, "The New Land Settlement in Russia," *Russian Review* (London), 1912, Vol. I, No. I, p. 65.

[16] Pavlovsky, *op.cit.*, p. 118.

The State Council recommended that the obligation of joint responsibility, which had been introduced at the time of Peter the Great's establishment of the tax, and the passport system, which assured the commune's ability to fulfill that obligation, should in consequence also be terminated. At this point, however, the opposed viewpoint won the ascendancy. Count D. A. Tolstoy and other ministers announced the policy of "tutelage by the village commune" and retention of "allotment" tenure as a type of dependent landholding under which the peasant could not alienate his lands. Several laws restricted the existing or prospective freedom of the peasantry. In 1886 the system of redemption payments was extended to cover the former state peasants as well as the ex-serfs, placing a heavy burden on a group which had seemed to be moving rapidly toward economic independence. In the same year Tolstoy, against considerable opposition from his colleagues, brought about issuance of a law on division of large households. By its provisions the power to approve separation into smaller family groups was taken away from the household elder and assigned to the village assembly, which must sanction each separation by a two-thirds vote. In 1889 the rural justices of the peace were replaced by Land Captains (*zemskie nachalniki*), who not only tried local cases as judges but were given administrative supervision over peasant self-government. In 1893, a law prohibited the sale of communal land by village communes without higher administrative consent, as well as the mortgaging of allotment land, and repealed the Emancipation provision that permitted a family which had paid its redemption debt to withdraw from the commune and receive a land title in full ownership. Such withdrawals were also to depend upon the approval of the village assembly. Finally, in the same year the Land Captains were ordered to encourage the resumption of land redistribution, a practice which had fallen into disuse in a large proportion of communes. The policy of the government had come to be one of preventing the growth of individual ownership and of keeping the commune alive.

However, the debate between advocates of communal tutelage and peasant independence continued in official circles. The peasant riots of 1902 hastened a reconsideration of the old policy of Alexander III's government. Nicholas II placed Sergei Witte at the head of a committee on agricultural needs which set up several hundred local subcommittees. Witte, formerly a defender of the commune, emerged from this investigation as a convinced opponent of it, and he was supported by a large number of the local committees in his recommendation that it be abolished. Nicholas II hesitated to take any sweeping action, but he did consent to the termination of the fiscal reasons for the continued existence of the commune. Joint communal liability for state obligations, including redemption payments, was abolished in 1903; the remaining redemption payments were reduced by half in November 1905 and finally cancelled in January 1907.

The way had accordingly been prepared for a direct assault on the commune by Peter Stolypin, who became Prime Minister in the middle of 1906. The Stolypin agrarian legislation was the most radical body of laws since the Great Reforms. By the ukase of 9 November 1906, approved by the Duma as the law of 14 June 1910, and completed and codified by the law of 29 May 1911, new rules for confirmation of title and enclosure were set forth.[17]

For villages with hereditary tenure, which were found mainly in the western provinces, *confirmation of title* was made unnecessary. All their allotments were proclaimed to be private property, and any peasant under hereditary tenure was enabled to proceed forthwith to enclosure. To this category were added, by the law of 1910, those communes which had not carried out a general redistribution of land since 1887. All such communes were thereby blanketed into the hereditary-tenure classification.

From the repartitional-tenure type of commune, any head of a peasant family could at any time obtain confirmation of title to his share of allotment land as private property, retaining the right to use meadows and forests which belonged to the village. Private holdings which emerged from either type of tenure were considered the property not of the whole household but of the head of the household personally.

From 1906 on *enclosure* was possible, under whatever tenure the commune operated, by a two-thirds vote of the village assembly. By the 1910 law this provision was changed so that while the repartitional-tenure communes still needed two-thirds, the hereditary-tenure communes could proceed to enclosure by a simple majority vote. The 1911 law went further in setting forth conditions of enclosure. For the first time it required that enclosure proceed simultaneously with confirmation of title, which had previously been considered an independent step preliminary to enclosure. By the law of 4 March 1906 there had been established local District Land-Settlement (*zemleustroistvo*) Commissions, which were authorized to aid in the work

---

[17] Texts of the three laws in *Polnoe sobranie zakonov Rossiiskoi Imperii, Sobranie tretie*, St. Petersburg, 1885-1916, Nos. 28528, 33743, and 35370 respectively.

of title confirmation and consolidation. The expense of surveying was borne chiefly by the central government.

The painful and slow work of enclosure on the basis of the Stolypin legislation actually began in 1907. Russia's peasants numbered 11,864,641 households, possessing 118,721,024 desiatinas of land.[18] Of these households, 2,752,596 were under hereditary tenure. Of the remaining 9,112,045, there were 3,489,989 households which had not carried out general redistribution for some time, and so were automatically converted by the law of 1910 previously mentioned.

The results were as follows. By 1 January 1916, confirmation of title (from the repartitional-tenure type, no such action being necessary for the hereditary-tenure communes which had become private property in 1906) was completed on the part of some 2,000,000 households, and many others were in the process of doing so. Thus far we have, in round numbers, the following picture. Out of a total of 12,000,000 peasant households, the 2,800,000 hereditary-tenure ones by general law, plus 2,000,000 repartitional-tenure ones by individual action, had become private property via the Stolypin laws, while during the same period some 130,000 communes were converted under the old provisions, making a total of almost 5,000,000. To this figure must be added the automatic conversions of the law of 1910. Bilimovich[19] and Pavlovsky tend to take seriously the effect of this blanket provision, while Robinson believes that only some 2,100,000 (the 470,000 households which received official certification of conversion plus an estimated 1,700,000 where conversion was applied in practice, throughout villages some of whose members had obtained certificates) should be counted as having undergone conversion.[20] At any rate, a figure somewhere between 2,100,000 and the 3,500,000 covered by the blanket provision of the 1910 law should be added to the total of 5,000,000. Thus somewhere between 7,100,000 and 8,500,000 holdings—approximately two-thirds of the peasant households of all Russia—had been converted into private property in the decade from 1906 to 1916 (in only eight of which years work was actually going on).

The process of enclosure, which was the final objective of the whole Stolypin agrarian policy, was naturally more gradual. While confirmation of title was a legal action involving no actual transfer or reshuffling of holdings, enclosure entailed the complex and difficult

---

[18] Pavlovsky, op.cit., Ch. 5. There is a minor discrepancy between these figures and those of Antsiferov.

[19] Bilimovich, "The Land Settlement," in Antsiferov and others, op.cit., p. 335.

[20] Robinson, op.cit., pp. 212-16.

business of reallocating strips on the land. Nevertheless by 1916 enclosure embraced 1,228,964 households, over one-tenth of the peasant families of European Russia.[21]

The percentage of holdings enclosed reached the highest point in the southern and eastern parts of the black earth belt. The percentage in New Russia was 27.2, in Samara 28.1, in Saratov 22.1, compared with an overall percentage in European Russia of 10.7.[22] The western provinces, where the example of enclosed farms in neighboring districts had led to the beginning of the whole process in Russia, had enclosed only 16 per cent of their holdings. Enclosure thus proceeded most rapidly in the regions of most recent settlement rather than in the west, where it had first been introduced.

The Stolypin laws had produced a revolution in land tenure. The role played by peasant attitudes in this phenomenon is evaluated differently by scholars who do not challenge the sort of statistical picture just given. Robinson, although he writes, "There was no mistaking the *trend* toward individual property and independent farming,"[23] is inclined in general to minimize the possible effect, had not war and revolution interrupted the operation of the Stolypin policy. He feels particularly strongly that "the part played by official compulsion" in producing enclosure was too great to support the conclusion that the peasant response was fully sympathetic. Bilimovich, on the other hand, asserts, "The enormous scale on which land settlement was effected cannot fail to convince the student that it was a genuine popular movement."[24] This writer is convinced that the peasants, once the possible benefits of individual tenure were made clear by explanation and example, responded widely and enthusiastically.

The regional evolution of Russian agriculture as a whole, and especially the crisis in the communal central area, had reached a point wherein the proposal of a new system was bound to evoke a favorable reaction. Those who were not interested in migrating were forced to seek a less drastic solution which could be carried out on the spot. The question is not whether the peasant, if left alone, would have conceived the idea of enclosure by himself. The man deeply involved in his own problems is seldom the best author of their solution. The example of agricultural improvement via enclosure which was available in the west would probably not have been imitated so rapidly,

[21] See table in Pavlovsky, *op.cit.*, p. 135.
[22] *Ibid.*, p. 139.   [23] Robinson, *op.cit.*, p. 264.
[24] Bilimovich, *loc.cit.*, p. 341.

however, nor would enclosure under the Stolypin laws have spread like a prairie fire, if the need for a fundamental and creative change had not been felt.

Land Use: Decline of the Three-Course System

Like the inhabitants of most agrarian countries, the Russian peasant lived chiefly on grain. Hence the importance of grain harvests and prices, and the other matters pertaining to bread which have confused the more fortunate among urban dwellers ever since Marie Antoinette probably did not, but might well have, asked why people clamoring for bread did not eat cake. There were four chief grains produced in Russia: rye, which was par excellence the home staple; oats which was likewise home-consumed; and wheat and barley, which were mainly cash grains and those exported.[25]

According to the land census of 1916, given the average number of persons per Russian peasant household as 5.3, the area normally required to be under cereals in order to feed a household of average size was 2.28 desiatinas. Out of the average peasant holding of 11.9 desiatinas, 4.1 were actually under crops, while over half were allowed to lie fallow.[26] The difference between 2.28 and 4.1 ought to have permitted a fair nutritional margin. Such a margin may have existed for some families, but many had to sell so much in the market in order to meet their obligations that they had no surplus at all.

The usual manner of using the land was to grow predominantly the four cereals on an extensive basis, by way of the three-course strip system imposed by communal arrangement. One of the facts brought to light during the agrarian slump of the 1870's was that those who deviated from the norm of land use and diversified their production were sometimes spared disaster regardless of the size of their landholdings. The former state peasants, who had generally higher allotments, suffered gravely. Yet in the western provinces many ex-serfs with smaller holdings, partly because of the spreading cultivation of sugar beets and other industrial crops, were affected much less seriously.[27]

[25] The depression had not slowed export of grain to world markets. The annual cereal export in the 1860's averaged 110 million poods; by the 1890's the average reached 442 million and continued to increase. The origin of the export grain is not quite certain. A frequent assumption has been that large gentry farming produced "an exportable surplus" (Pavlovsky, *op.cit.*, p. 221), but the simultaneous decline of large farming and the rise of grain export seem to indicate that the answer was not that simple, and that fair-sized amounts of peasant production found their way abroad.

[26] Antsiferov, *loc.cit.*, p. 23.   [27] Bilimovich, *loc.cit.*, p. 307.

The grain-growing norm of cultivation was best represented by the central region, in which the suffering was most acute. During the depression the area under the chief crops actually diminished in the center. From 1881 to 1893 it grew only very slowly, then began to accelerate somewhat, and finally tapered off again. According to Timoshenko, the situation in the center finally reached an impasse in which further expansion of the cropped area could take place only if the three-course system was abandoned.[28]

Abandonment of three-course rotation, in favor of diversified farming and the development of livestock industry, began during the 1880's and 1890's, but not in the center. As in the case of enclosure, this development started in the western provinces, once more apparently under the influence of the example of Russia's neighbors. In the period just after 1900, diversification of farming began to spread into the Central Agricultural Region, measured by the growth of the area under the four chief grains as compared with the increase of the total area under crops.

If expansion of the crop area under the old system of farming became impossible in the center, it soon became difficult in the south as well. "The free land on the southern Ukrainian steppes and on the steppes of Lower Volga was all taken up during 1881-1899, and further expansion of agricultural production was checked."[29] The frontier of settlement was moving across the Urals, leaving European Russia with the choice of changing its agrarian methods or accepting a stationary level of production for a rising population. Whereas from 1903 to 1913 the area under crops increased more than 50 per cent in the north Caucasus, 59 per cent in the Central Asian steppe, and 81.5 per cent in Siberia, the increase in 42 provinces of European Russia averaged a mere 8.2 per cent. The special characteristics of the southeast, including its especially favorable climatic conditions for spring wheat and the nearness of the Black Sea ports which pressed the demand for export grain, contributed to a considerable absolute and relative increase of the crop area in the two cash grains, wheat and barley, during the same period. While rye had held first place in Russian grain production in 1901-1905, by 1913 wheat had replaced it, so it appears that it was not only in the south that more cash grain was being raised. But the dominant position which grain of all kinds had long held in Russian agricultural production was weakening. The peasant was producing less rye, in part because he

[28] Timoshenko, *op.cit.*, p. 138.
[29] *Ibid.*, pp. 140-41.

was eating other foods besides bread. The diversification of farming results not only in greater economic resilience in relation to the market, but improved diet and better health.

Timoshenko concludes: "The degree of diversification of farming in the black-soil zone, as we have seen, diminishes from west to east and to the southeast. These variations in some degree accord with the density of population and correspond to the time of colonization of different regions of the zone, for colonists came from the northern and northwestern areas and moved toward the south and east."[30]

Diversification was the latest phase of the evolution of land use which had begun in central Russia with the so-called *perelog* or *zalezh* system, wherein large areas were left fallow for several years and then used for pasture. This system had disappeared in central Russia centuries ago in favor of the three-course system, which was now beginning to yield to the diversification of farming as it spread from the west. In the region of latest settlement, Asiatic Russia, *perelog* was still to be found here and there. In the Black Sea steppe the *perelog* system had already collapsed as settlement thickened, but instead of evolving into three-course rotation, it had been replaced by a new type of land use peculiar to the region, known as the *pestropole* system. Under the latter, there was no regular rotation and land was sowed for several years running before it was left fallow. The spread of this system of exploitation could be explained by the ease of export by sea. Nevertheless this system too appeared to be merely transitional. Timoshenko saw signs of the evolution of *pestropole* in the direction of diversification, for as a result of the work of some local agricultural experimental stations, there had been introduced into the crop cycle some leguminous hay and corn.[31]

Thus while peculiarities of a given region might occasion deviations, the usual evolution in land use was proceeding at different rates in different regions from *perelog* to the three-course system, which was giving way in turn to diversified farming. The west and center of Russia had taken centuries to pass through these successive stages, and only following the end of serfdom had there been any signs of progress in the central region. But on the southern frontier and, as we shall observe, in Siberia, these stages were being traversed in a matter of decades.

The Changing Market

If it is true that the newest stages of agrarian evolution in Russia

[30] *Ibid.,* p. 197.   [31] *Ibid.,* p. 201.

included the decline of communal tenure and the spread of diversified farming, it may well be asked why in the late nineteenth and early twentieth centuries the passage from one stage to another was so much more rapid than before. Equally swift and more obvious were economic developments of another sort, in which, many scholars have contended, lay the causes of the changes in Russian agriculture. Those developments included the growth of machine industry and the spread of railway transportation. New groups of urban consumers were growing and needed a larger food supply, while the railways could carry it much faster and more safely to the industrial centers. The expansion of the home market, and the increased exports which the railways helped make possible, stimulated the demand for agricultural produce. The new market likewise entailed a greater use of money. All these factors certainly influenced peasant farming. But exactly how?

Pavlovsky concludes his excellent book on Russian agriculture thus: "It was the commercialization of Russian farming, indeed, that was the keynote and the mainspring of its progress on the eve of the war; and to it have been due all those changes in the Russian agricultural industry, its geographical distribution and its output, with which I have had to deal in the preceding chapters."[32] The importance of "commercialization" cannot be challenged, but to ascribe to this single cause the latest changes in Russia's agrarian evolution is unwarranted. For centuries Russian peasants had been migrating, establishing new settlements, exchanging one type of tillage for another, in region after region. The new freedom and mobility which resulted from the Great Reforms made possible a notable acceleration in the social changes which were slowly transforming the Russian village. Likewise Russia's rapid industrial growth owed much to the free movement and greater opportunities for investment which attended the undermining of the old social stratification. "Commercialization" as well as the readjustment of the ex-serf to living and farming independently were both consequences of the new freedom, and each powerfully influenced the other. The new industrial capitalist could hire workers more easily; the newly emancipated villager could sell his produce more readily.

The peasant was being drawn into the orbit of the new market. Observing the impact of capitalist industry on agriculture, many investigators drew the conclusion that the peasant would become a capitalist (or proletarian) as well. The Russian village would produce

[32] Pavlovsky, *op.cit.*, p. 321.

for profit; it would divide into agricultural employers and agricultural laborers. So it seemed to the economists and politically-minded intellectuals who were impressed by the way Karl Marx had transformed his description of English economic development into a forecast of development elsewhere. Decades passed, and the peasantry did not split into capitalists and proletarians, but many of the intelligentsia continued to feel it would happen soon.

However, some of the best economists were mulling over the data gathered by the zemstvo statisticians, who intensively studied the local conditions of peasant economy for forty years prior to the war, and came up with facts inconvenient to Marxist expectations and hopes.[33] Deferring our examination of how this minority of economists attempted to theorize on the basis of zemstvo data, let us note two important consequences of "commercialization" which appeared from these data. Commercialization raised grain prices, from which the peasant benefited absolutely, and it also raised land prices, from which he benefited more than other social groups.

Whether peasants benefited from lower or higher grain prices had been the subject of an argument which raged bitterly in the 1890's among Russian economists and politicians. It was then a moot question because certain peasants, especially in the north, had to buy bread at least for certain months of the year, and as consumers desired low prices. But the rest of the story was that though some of them bought grain in the winter, they might still sell it in the fall, and to the extent they did so, they desired high prices. The northern peasants were in any event not typical. Because of the thin, infertile land which they occupied, they had long supplemented their farm earnings by home crafts or other means in order to survive. In Russia *as a whole*, the peasants were turning more and more to production for market as grain prices advanced. As Oganovsky points out, peasant enterprise characteristically produces both for market and for home use. Insofar as a particular farm produces for market, under capitalism its owner strives for high prices; insofar as he produces for home use, he attempts to extract the maximum produce from the land *regardless of its market price*.[34]

If, then, the peasant is the beneficiary of high grain prices, how do high land prices affect him? The fact was that he could pay the *highest* prices for land, since, as Brutskus noted, it was the peasant

[33] See pp. 57-59, below.
[34] N. P. Oganovsky, *Individualizatsiia zemlevladeniia v Rossii i eia posledstviia*, Moscow, 1917, Ch. 1.

55

who secured the most from the land that he already held, and who could expect to secure the most from that which he undertook to buy. "None can extract money from land better than the peasantry."[35] According to Oganovsky, given conditions of private property, the peasant is "the unconquerable competitor of all other classes on the land market."[36] He cites statistics indicating that in future "the peasants as before will buy much of the land of others, but will sell little of their own, and the mobility of their holdings will remain three or four times less than that of large holders. . . ."[37] Of course the peasant did not like to pay high prices for land, but was nevertheless in a position to outstay all bidders. The precise explanation will be suggested shortly, but it is to be sought not in any technical superiority of small farming, but, as Tschajanow (Chaianov) says, in the "economic and social circumstances which result from the nature of a private enterprise in which production is carried on by the family without employment of wage labor."[38]

The increase of extra-allotment renting of land and the rise of land prices showed a fairly regular regional variation, with the areas of most recent settlement once again exhibiting the most rapid rate of change. As of 1890, the map of extra-allotment renting was one in which the rental area of the average holder decreased from west to east and from north to south, whereas the size of allotment ran in the reverse direction.[39] Once more the exception was the Black Sea area, where rentals though frequent were not of the peasant-producer type common to other areas but of an entrepreneurial kind, producing for the export market.

The overall rise in land prices was sharp. Oganovsky computes that although the productivity of peasant tillage rose steadily from 1861 to 1910 (from 29 to 43 poods per desiatina), land prices rose 18 times faster (from 1863 to 1909, from 17 r. 40 k. to 101 r. 50 k. per desiatina).[40] The increase was greater, for the period 1910-1914 at least, the nearer to the southern and eastern borders. In Oganovsky's opinion this indicated, first, the greater rise of population in the east, and, second, "the resettlement of peasants seeking land from west to east."

Peasant farming was thus successfully adapting itself to a capitalist

[35] *Ibid.*, quoted from B. D. Brutskus on p. 84.
[36] *Idem.*
[37] *Ibid.*, p. 40.
[38] Alexander Tschajanow, *Die Lehre von der bäuerlichen Wirtschaft*, Berlin, 1923, p. 6.
[39] Oganovsky, *op.cit.*, p. 47.   [40] *Ibid.*, p. 62.

THE PEASANT

market—without itself becoming capitalist. Antsiferov states, "There is no doubt that peasant farming was more successful [than private estates] in adapting itself to the new conditions of the market and especially of the foreign market upon which Russia was dependent"[41] —understanding by "Russia," of course, large private traders and the Imperial budget rather than the peasant producer, whom even the collapse of foreign trade in World War I could not shake.

The Theory of Peasant Enterprise

We have seen that the latest stage of development of the Russian peasantry was the nascent emergence of independent, individual family farming. We saw that certain investigators managed to chart the appearance, region by region, of new features in peasant land tenure, land use, and adaptation to the new market. Following the Revolution of 1905, a number of younger Russian economists made the complex of these new features the subject for what we may call the theory of peasant enterprise, a phrase reproducing in English the sense of the Russian term *trudovoe khoziaistvo*.

These economists were chiefly four: V. A. Kosinsky, whose book *K agrarnomu voprosu. Krest'ianskoe i pomeshchich'e khoziaistvo* was published in 1906; A. N. Chelintsev, whose *Sel'sko-khoziaistvennye raiony Evropeiskoi Rossii kak stadii evoliutsii sel'sko-khoziaistvennoi evoliutsii* appeared in 1910; N. Makarov, and A. Chaianov. B. D. Brutskus and A. A. Chuprov, as well as a few others, made contributions.

Kosinsky, who was the pathfinder of the new school, declared that peasant enterprise was "sharply differentiated from capitalist enterprise in that in *trudovoe khoziaistvo there are not the two classes of capitalist economy*—there are neither entrepreneur-employers, nor hired laborers, but there is only *one class*—of *toiling entrepreneurs*" (emphasis in the original).[42] Thus, he argued, it made no sense to try to analyze farm income into the equivalent of profit on capital, rent on land, and wages for labor. If profit was absent, then the "law of equality of profits" would not operate; if rent was lacking, then "land" would not be valued according to the standard of capitalized rent but in another way. The toiling entrepreneur, Kosinsky asserted, treated his own labor as a capitalist would his capital, and tried to maximize the return per unit of labor expended. Given the deter-

[41] Antsiferov, *loc.cit.*, p. 293.
[42] V. A. Kosinsky, *Osnovnyia tendentsii v mobilizatsii zemel'noi sobstvennosti i ikh sotsial'no-ekonomicheskie faktory. Mobilizatsiia zemel'noi sobstvennosti*, Prague, 1925, p. 245.

mination of the peasant to obtain maximum return on his labor, he is found to calculate the value of the land by capitalizing its "toiling yield," a sum greater than the capitalized rent. The upper limit the peasant is willing to pay for land is determined in this manner, while the upper limit the capitalist will pay will depend on capitalized rent. When demand is intense, land prices will continue to rise toward the maximum "toiling" valuation. Thus Kosinsky attempted to explain both the increase in Russian land prices (or an aspect of it) and the puzzling phenomenon by which the peasant proved himself the "unconquerable competitor" for the purchase of land.

Chaianov argued along similar lines, and summoned his fellow economists to develop a system of national economy whose subject would be enterprise from which hired labor is absent. "Such a theoretical system," he declared with a flourish, "would have a relationship to our classical economics similar to the geometry of Lobachevsky to that of Euclid . . . it must be granted that the manner of thinking of many modern economists, in which the entire economy appears *exclusively* in the categories of capitalist economy, also is an abstraction and corresponds just as little to reality; for the present-day world economy is a conglomeration of economic formations, in which capitalistic forms are intermingled with all sorts of other ones."[43]

As with any creative innovation in thought, this theory was capable of being carried to the point of exaggeration and oversimplification. Though Makarov sharply dissociated himself from those "who attempted to present their own socialist ethical viewpoint as a socio-psychological feature of the toiling peasantry," he warned his readers against making their concern for the fate of the peasantry an excuse for sentimental distortion.[44] Kosinsky, writing in 1925, feared that Chaianov, Chelintsev, and Makarov himself had gone too far with the theory of peasant enterprise, and cautioned in particular that if *all* land went into peasant hands it would be necessary to import food from abroad—presumably to feed the cities. Still, he ended his book with a resounding: "One cannot deny that *trudovoe khoziaistvo* values land *more highly* than capitalistic economy; one cannot deny the undermining influence of *trudovoe khoziaistvo* on extensive, capitalist forms; one cannot deny the genuine absence of two classes in the makeup of *trudovoe khoziaistvo.* . . ."[45]

[43] Tschajanow, *op.cit.*, pp. 130-31.
[44] N. Makarov, *Krest'ianskoe khoziaistvo i ego evoliutsiia*, Vol. I, Moscow, 1920, p. v.
[45] Kosinsky, *op.cit.*, p. 305.

Unfortunately, the Communist victory put an end to this new but promising line of investigation and reflection in Russia. The men referred to were damned as "ideologists of the kulaks," and so forth, and not many outside Russia paid any further attention to their work.[46]

The Attitude of the Intelligentsia

If the recent agricultural history of Russia was roughly as we have sketched it, and there was developing under conditions of the new capitalist market a type of agriculture which was also new, but not capitalist, it was by no means certain that such trends would be self-completing or that they would inevitably triumph.

In an autocratic country the peasants would not be asked what sort of agrarian order they preferred, and in a country of rare literacy their answers might be insufficiently sophisticated to be immediately translatable into public policy. It is not fair to say that the wishes of the peasants were ignored by the government, but it would be inaccurate to assert that even the enlightened bureaucrats of the last years of Tsarism acted primarily out of a wish to satisfy those desires. A man cannot wish for what he has never seen or but dimly knows about, but that does not mean he will not choose something new when it is offered and explained. The least that can be said is that Stolypin, Krivoshein, Gurko, and other officials were sufficiently empirical in their *economic* views to be guided by the actual position of Russian agriculture and the real psychology of the peasants in offering new institutions and techniques which were beginning to travel softly and gradually into Russia from the West on the strength of willing acceptance.

The same degree of empiricism was lacking among the Russian intelligentsia. If we mean by that term the politically interested and educated men and women from all social classes, they were for over a century prior to 1906 deeply concerned with political ideas without

---

[46] For example, the article on A. N. Chelintsev in the *Bolshaia Sovetskaia Entsiklopediia*, 1st ed., Moscow, 1934, charges that the "objective role" of his theories "was reducible to ideological masking, in the interests of the capitalist [*kulak*] group of households, of the enormous contradictions" in the village.

Chelintsev and Chaianov are both vigorously criticized by G. A. Studensky, professor in the Moscow Agricultural Academy, in "Die Ökonomische Natur der bäuerlichen Wirtschaft," *Weltwirtschaftliches Archiv*, 28. Band, Heft 2, October 1928, pp. 318-39. See also A. Skalweit, "Die Familienwirtschaft als Grundlage für ein System der Sozialökonomik," *Weltwirtschaftliches Archiv*, 20. Band, 1924, p. 231ff., as well as Chaianov's reply in same journal, 22. Band, 1925, ii, pp. 1ff. The Skalweit article has not been available to me. Skalweit gives a brief counterreply at the end of Chaianov's last-mentioned article.

having any need or opportunity to assume responsibility for their implementation. No one could maintain that these men and women failed to display a profound and emotional attachment to the welfare of the peasantry, a feeling of shame for the muzhik's misery—for which the gentry class which fathered the intelligentsia was regarded as chiefly responsible—or that they failed to take account of the full extent of peasant suffering, from the contemplation of which they derived great vicarious pain.

But the struggle which the intelligentsia conducted throughout the period of the revolutionary movement was aimed at the government, and its attitudes toward officialdom helped fix some of its attitudes toward the peasantry. By its nature the intelligentsia was anti-official above all else, and accordingly fostered the notion that the guilt of priest, bureaucrat, and industrialist was so deep and their power so great that the peasant himself was a helpless, passive victim of history, incapable of either achieving or suggesting solutions. Because the intelligentsia felt that the educated intellect was the crucial and indispensable weapon in the revolutionary arsenal, they not only dismissed the opinions of the unlettered peasant, but also neglected his deepest attitudes. The intelligentsia were, more often than not, positivist or materialist in their philosophy, socialist in their political aims, while the peasants were Christian in their outlook and oriented toward the family and the individual in their mode of life and aspirations. In the judgment of the intellectuals, the peasant's attitudes were not so much wrong as childish. They were not merely expressions of false propositions about the nature of the world and the social order, but they represented primitive beliefs or superstitions which it was the intellectuals' duty to change through "education." In many tangible ways the Russian people were in fact backward in relation to some of their neighbors, but the term "backward" is employed in countless books on Russia, both scholarly and popular, to imply in addition that the peasant's attitudes were "primitive" in exactly the same sense the Russian intellectuals thought. This is not surprising, since the attitudes of the Russian intelligentsia were held by many of the intellectuals of the Western world, from whom the Russians often derived them.

The whole populist tradition in all its manifold and divergent forms had been originated and developed by men who had a tendency to "represent their own socialist ethical viewpoint as a socio-psychological feature of the toiling peasantry"—as Makarov says, rightly implying that it was no such thing.[47] If the ethics of the intelligentsia led them to accept socialism in one or another variant before and after Marxism came to Russia, then their economics was classical in the sense which applies to both Ricardo and Marx, in which as Chaianov says "the entire economy appears *exclusively* in the categories of capitalist economy."

Such tendencies were limited neither to Russia nor to the early twentieth century nor to economic analysis. Let us take the example of Max Laserson, a careful scholar who is representative of this kind of thinking, when he writes: "Russian capitalism, unable to mature under governmental pampering and governmental control, produced an unripe ideological socialism untempered by extended experience with legal trade unionism. The old structure, deprived of an influential middle class, simply could not stand up."[48] Here one finds the categories of "capitalists," "government," "working class," expressed or implied but no mention of the 85 per cent of the Russian population which was rural in 1917.

It is of course true that percentage of population is no reliable indication of the influence or importance which a group may have in a society, especially in one like Tsarist Russia. As Wladimir Weidle says, "In Russia the people itself can never be seen in action, except in great inarticulate movements: the peasant colonization, the growth of the Cossack community or sporadic risings against law and order. . . ."[49] Yet Weidle recognizes that migration was an action of the peasantry, and one may add that the less obvious agrarian developments in the direction of individual family farming thus far outlined also represented peasant action. Unfortunately for the peasant, his economic actions could not secure for him freedom and security permanently, because of events in the political realm which eluded his comprehension and control. Those events were the result of revolution which brought to power men who were benevolent and undogmatic, in the Provisional Government, and then finally men who were fanatical and unyielding, in the Bolshevik Government, both groups sharing lack of belief in the economic viability or ethical desirability of independent farming.

[47] See note 44.

[48] Max M. Laserson, *The American Impact on Russia, Diplomatic and Ideological, 1784-1917*, New York, 1950, p. 421.

[49] Wladimir Weidle, *Russia: Absent and Present*, transl. by A. Gordon Smith, London, 1952, pp. 15-16.

Conclusion

In the words of Antsiferov, "at the end of the nineteenth and the beginning of the twentieth centuries all agricultural development was in the direction of the improvement and extension of peasant farming."[50] In this light, migration, during the period to be treated, appears less as a flight from grinding misery than as one facet of an overall adjustment in Russian agriculture which gave promise that it might be achieved with success. The peasant who arrived in the free lands of the Siberian frontier might quickly become prosperous enough to be wasteful—it is said that Siberian steppe farmers sometimes burned grain for fuel simply because wood was distant and bread plentiful. The peasant in the homeland might also become prosperous, but only at the expense of the difficult and complicated processes of enclosure and diversification of farming. Whether by way of migration or individualization ("land settlement"), the Russian peasant was finding a diminishing number of impediments on the road to a better and happier future.

The intelligentsia for the most part regarded these social changes with profound skepticism. The economists who developed the theory of peasant enterprise were in a tiny minority among their own colleagues, and insignificant beside the much larger group of politically minded. For example, Kaufman, the great student of migration, minimized the significance of what it could do for Russian welfare.[51] Oganovsky, investigator of the process of individualization in agriculture, emphasized its difficulties and disadvantages.[52] Foreign scholars then and since have often adopted a similar viewpoint. Max Laserson did not feel that the role of the peasant required any place at all in his analysis of Russian society, while Geroid T. Robinson, although filled with commiseration for the peasant, treated the Stolypin reforms critically and with great reserve. These men, Russian and non-Russian, wished the peasant the best in the world. The Russians mentioned believed that only sweeping political changes could solve his problems, and thus Oganovsky ends his book on individualization with a sentence on "the great Russian revolution" which is unrelated to anything he has previously said yet serves as the logical conclusion of his whole argument, which has ruled out peaceful evolution.

The issue is not raised here as to whether broad political changes

[50] Antsiferov, *loc.cit.*, p. 25.
[51] See A. A. Kaufman, *Pereselenie i kolonizatsiia*, St. Petersburg, 1905.
[52] Oganovsky, *op.cit.*

were both likely, given the state of educated opinion, and desirable, considering the manner in which the Tsarist government had often discharged its political functions and obligations to the people, even after creation of the Duma. Moreover, one may accept the judgment that neither land settlement nor migration offered any panacea for Russia's agrarian difficulties.

The peasant in the homeland often found himself encumbered by myriad problems whose solution seemed utterly beyond his powers. The "relative overpopulation" which stifled his efforts may be defined as meaning that the ratio of the labor force (remembering that most of it consisted of laboring enterpreneurs) to the land occupied, under existing forms of land tenure and use, was too high to assure a decent livelihood to the occupants. As a remedy Lozovoi suggested aiding the peasant to do three things: to progress toward better forms of agriculture, to find work outlets in nearby industry, and to migrate to underpopulated regions.[53] The three parts of this remedy were solely dependent neither on governmental decision nor on peasant initiative. They were rather evolving and mutually dependent aspects of peasant action which state policy could restrict, accelerate, or otherwise influence if it chose. At home the muzhik could improve his methods and increase his holdings and earnings, at the cost of great effort. On the frontier, he could do the same with relative ease; the effort required was to get there and establish himself. Our concern will be with the peasant on the frontier.

[53] Ia. G. Lozovoi, "Voprosy pereseleniia i kolonizatsii Sibiri," *Vol'naia Sibir'*, III, 1928, p. 121.

63

PART TWO

THE FRONTIER CROSSES THE URALS,

1861-1892

CHAPTER III

Migration Policy after Emancipation

The Consequences of Emancipation

According to a recent writer, "Migration to Siberia was at first discouraged by the government. At the end of the eighties this policy changed, largely for reasons connected with the new expansionist policy in the Far East."[1] Underlying this statement is the traditional interpretation of Siberian resettlement, in which migration is assumed to have depended largely on government policy. Such a presumption can scarcely be supported by the evidence. It is also doubtful whether the Russian "expansionist policy in the Far East," which did not move into high gear until the weakness of China was revealed in the Sino-Japanese War of 1894-1895, was responsible for the shift of migration policy during the 1880's. It is true that the shift was a significant one, but its explanation must be sought in the course of migration itself following Emancipation.

If serfdom had meant any one thing to the Russian peasant on gentry lands, it had been that he was not free to move if he wished. Though it was only rather late that the lord acquired effective power to dispose of the serf's person as a chattel, for the entire two centuries of the legal existence of serfdom the peasant had been bound to a certain plot of land. To put it very mildly indeed, serfdom had been "an independent cause of the unequal distribution of the village population throughout the territory of European Russia."[2] Emancipation in 1861 removed the legal bar to migration along with personal servitude. Legally the serf was no longer bound to the land nor to the whim of his lord, but both legally and economically movement was still difficult and hazardous for him.

The Emancipation Act of 19 February 1861 did not deal specifically with migration at all. It did set forth, under Article 130, conditions by which a peasant desiring to move might obtain a certificate of discharge (*uvol'nitel'nyi prigovor*) from his commune and thus be in a position to petition for enrollment in the commune of his destination. Those conditions were that the peasant be not currently liable for military service, have no arrears in state or communal levies, pay

---

[1] Hugh Seton-Watson, *The Decline of Imperial Russia, 1855-1914*, New York, 1952, p. 112.
[2] *Kolonizatsiia Sibiri*, p. 97.

his taxes through 1 January of the following year, have no private obligations recorded against him at the township office, and present in advance a certificate of admission (*priemnyi prigovor*) from the commune to which he planned to migrate. As Voroponov charged, such rules constituted simply a "prohibitory system in relation to migrants."[3] Such a procedure could be followed only by a peasant who was sufficiently prosperous that he would probably not need to migrate in any case.

It appears that some of the liberal officials who authored the Emancipation legislation were saying, at least privately, that their work was not finished with the promulgation of the laws of 1861. In the words of Prince Vasilchikov, they contemplated "that after nine years there would be granted to the peasants another right, just as substantial as that of holding land, the right of *free removal*" (emphasis in the original).[4] Even if the attempt on the life of Alexander II in 1866 and the other developments which led to constriction of the policy of Great Reforms had not occurred, however, there were attitudes among influential people which would have opposed such a law, whether or not successfully. There was a widespread fear that giving the ex-serf the right to migrate would generate "harmful mobility and vagabondage among the village population."[5] The harm alluded to would be the creation of a scarcity of wage-laborers and renters of land for the gentry,[6] who had now either to employ their ex-serfs for wages or rent lands to them if

---

[3] F. Voroponov, "Vopros o krest'ianskikh pereseleniiakh," *Vestnik Evropy*, January, 1876.

[4] Quoted by I. I. Popov, *loc.cit.*, p. 250.

[5] Quoted in *Kolonizatsiia Sibiri*, p. 97. Quotation is not identified; context indicates a government report, in any case undoubtedly reflects attitudes of many officials.

[6] Eastern employers in the United States were likewise concerned about the effect of migration on wages and the availability of laborers. There were no existing legal restrictions on the right to migrate, except for the slaves, and none could be imposed. It was hoped that setting high prices by law for the western lands (which were, like Siberian land, owned by the national government) would limit migration, and the history of early land legislation reflects continual tension between Easterners who wanted to raise, and Westerners who wanted to lower, land prices. In early decades the system was one of auction of new lands at any price above a fixed minimum, which was altered several times. It was only in 1862 that the Homestead Act was passed, providing 160 acres of free land for every settler proving five years of continuous residence and cultivation. However, the desired effect was not achieved. As before, both settlers and speculators (virtually absent from Siberia, where the land was not openly sold) circumvented the intent of the law. "The sad truth was that the vast bulk of western land was never homesteaded, and that the part of it which was entered under the homestead act was seldom farmed by the original entrant. In fact only about a third of the homestead entries between 1862 and 1882 were ever made final." (Robert E. Riegel, *America Moves West*, New York, 1947, p. 574.)

their own estates were not to lie idle. Certain groups of gentry, such as those of Riazan, defended the need of the peasant to migrate. Other, apparently more influential, circles cited the "dangers" involved.[7] The consequence was that the mass of ex-serfs had no legally established method of migration. It was true that nothing stopped them from liquidating under often unfavorable circumstances in order to go to cities as laborers, or simply going physically while remaining legally in their old commune, but this road had been open even before Emancipation, with the consent of many serf-owners.

The state peasants were not much better off than the ex-serfs with respect to resettlement. Their fairly extensive use of the Kiselev regulations of 1843 has already been mentioned, though during the late 1850's those rules fell into disuse. Kiselev had left the Ministry of State Domains in 1856, and soon afterward the forthcoming general peasant legislation was being bruited about and debated. By the law of 24 November 1866, the state peasant of European Russia, though not of Siberia or the Caucasus, was given his own land under a complicated redemption scheme.[8] Almost immediately afterward, however, credits for the migration of state peasants were cut off by the decree of 15 December 1866.[9] In 1870 the government restored the exemptions of 1843 for the benefit of settlers, but since the allotment of state lands for migration had ceased and since irregular migrants were not eligible for such exemptions, the enactment remained a dead letter. As Iadrintsev points out, the aim of the government of Alexander II was to free the state peasant from bureaucratic domination and put him on his own.[10] Yet to achieve that objective the government had to go farther than it was willing to go in the 1870's. Kulomzin states bluntly that the laws of the 1860's and 1870's were "directement opposés à l'émigration des paysans,"[11] whether formerly subject to landlords or to the state.

Special Treatment for the Amur and the Altai

Although no general migration legislation would be forthcoming until the 1880's, certain areas were treated as exceptional and their settlement was permitted. These were chiefly the Amur region, ac-

---

[7] See "Krest'ianskoe pereselenie i russkaia kolonizatsiia za Uralom," *Aziatskaia Rossiia*, Vol. I, p. 451.

[8] 2 P.S.Z. 43,888. See Robinson, *op.cit.*, pp. 89-92.

[9] 2 P.S.Z. 43,987.

[10] N. Iadrintsev, "Polozhenie pereselentsev v Sibiri," *Vestnik Evropy*, August 1881, p. 615.

[11] Koulomzine, *op.cit.*, p. 183.

quired only in 1858 by treaty with China (the Ussuri followed in 1860), and the Altai district.[12]

Immediately following the annexation of the Amur, a fund of 150,000 rubles was established to furnish state aid to Russian immigrants willing to settle there. A law of 26 March 1861 (to run for twenty years, and later extended by enactments of 26 January 1882 and 18 June 1892, each time for a further ten-year period) abolished the newly established system of state aid, but instead granted the migrants exemptions: from the soul tax permanently, recruitment for ten levies, land rent and taxes for twenty years, and so forth. The size of allotment was set at 100 desiatinas per family—a handsome portion indeed. After an interval of twenty years, communes and families were authorized to purchase this land for 3 rubles per desiatina; in practice it was individual householders rather than communes who most frequently took advantage of that provision. From 1863 to 1868, 6,400 immigrants arrived; from 1869 to 1882 the influx almost ceased; then from 1883 to 1893, 13,000 came in. When migration to West Siberia was halted in 1892, settlers who had received permission to settle in the Amur somehow managed to stop en route in the temporarily forbidden west and failed to appear at their supposed destination.

Many of the Amur settlers came not from Europe but from other parts of Siberia. The Ussuri region also attracted few from European Russia, but some who went first to the Amur then moved south to the Ussuri in search of a better climate. Since the overland trip took two years, the government gave up the struggle to make the Ussuri attractive enough for migrants to continue their journey beyond the rich lands of West Siberia, and organized migration by sea from Odessa. The Siberian Railway was to affect settlement in the Far East much more than it did that in the west. Once reaching the Pacific became a matter of but a few days more by rail, and as good land became harder to find in the west, the Far East received more migrants. In 1907, 20.1 per cent of all who crossed the Urals went there; in 1909, the number of migrant plots registered for occupation in the Amur and Ussuri regions together was greater than for any other single migrant region. In the last years before the World War there was an organized effort by leaders of the Old Believers—mem-

[12] Kaufman, "Pereselenie," in *Entsiklopedicheskii Slovar'* (Brockhaus-Efron), provides a convenient summary of policy in relation to the Amur and Altai regions. On the Old Believers in the Far East, see *Voprosy Kolonizatsii*, No. 7, 1910, pp. 541-42.

bers of a group which had gone into schism with the Russian Orthodox Church in the seventeenth century—to settle in the Russian Far
East. Many came from the southwestern part of the Russian Empire,
and in 1908-1910 almost 5,000 were granted permission to come
from Rumania and Austria-Hungary. If we take the period of the
Great Migration as a whole, however, we find that the Amur and
Ussuri regions played but a minor role in the process of Asiatic settlement.

Those seeking the legal route might also go to the Altai mountain
region (*gornyi okrug*) of Tomsk province, in west-central Siberia.[13]
By an act of 30 June 1865, the Emperor's own (*Kabinetskie*) lands
there were opened under certain limitations. While the relatively few
settlers who went to the Russian Far East did so as a result of
strenuous efforts on the part of the government, the Altai colonization owed little to government initiative. Immediately after Emancipation, irregular migrants appeared in the rich lands of the Altai,
sometimes with the consent of local authorities, sometimes not. By
1865 the number of new settlers was over 4,000, and only then did the
local administrators take the initiative in persuading St. Petersburg
to legislate on the subject. By the resulting law of 30 June, peasants,
with the permission of the administration of the Altai *gornyi okrug,*
could settle either in old-settler villages or on special migrant allotments, in new areas receiving 15 desiatinas of land per male "soul"
—the norm, apparently originating with the 1837 charter of the
Siberian Survey, which came to be used for all Siberia.[14] For this
land they had to pay dues to the Cabinet of His Majesty (*Kabinet
Ego Velichestva*). As in the case of the 1861 law on the Amur, no
monetary aid was granted to the Altai migrants.

Under the provisions of the 1865 law, 3,691 persons were enrolled
in the Altai from 1866 to 1871. From 1872 to 1877 there were 4,288;
in 1878-1883, 9,727. Meanwhile the irregular migrants increased
sharply. In 1876 there came 1,765; in 1882, 17,942; in 1884, 30,544.
From 1884 to 1889 the annual number of total immigrants—both
regular and irregular—rose from 12,000 to 19,000, and for the six-
year period the total was 96,331. In 1890-1894 over 160,000 came.

[13] See V. V. Sapozhnikov and N. A. Gavrilov, "Zemli Kabineta Ego Velichestva," *Aziatskaia Rossiia,* Vol. 1.

[14] The "15-desiatina norm" had been used on an Empire-wide basis in the
legislation of 1866 on state peasants. Under its provisions, if the land had not
been definitely demarcated, the peasant could keep up to 15 desiatinas per male
"soul" where state lands were plentiful, or 8 desiatinas where they were not.

Most of these people were entering the rather small steppe area of the Altai, chiefly its western portion.

At first the migrants seemed to prefer to enroll in old-settler villages, but that pattern soon changed. In 1884 those taking up new lands made up 16 per cent of the total, and by the mid-1890's they reached 75 per cent. The reason for this was the rapid filling up of old-settler villages in the rather small region. For the certificate of admission required, the fee in the 1870's and 1880's was usually 5 to 10 rubles, but in the early 1890's it rose to 50 or 100. Some old-settler villages not only ceased to enroll any newcomers, but began to expel those inhabitants who were not formally enrolled.

At this point the Emperor's Cabinet instructed the Altai administration not to permit enrollment of any more migrants until the governor of the province of their origin gave approval. But the wave still continued and in 1896 the number of irregulars rose to nearly 100,000. The government attempted to meet the crisis by the Imperial order of 27 April 1896. By its provisions, previous irregular migrants were to be enrolled and settled on portions of 15 desiatinas per male soul, with full freedom from dues for three years and half-exemption for three more. Settlers in the future were to be installed without hindrance on free lands, and were extended the same privileges as migrants to state (not Imperial) lands had received under the law of 1889, which will be discussed shortly. The order of 1896 was simultaneously aimed at restoring order out of the chaos produced by the flood of irregulars who had already come, and at persuading would-be migrants to the Altai to use legal channels in the future.

The attempt was unsuccessful. In the autumn of 1897 the Minister of the Imperial Court, under whose jurisdiction the Cabinet lands lay, flatly prohibited the sending of "scouts" into the Altai. It was a frequent and most advisable precaution for would-be settlers to send scouts in advance to inspect their intended destination and lay a claim for the land they desired to occupy.[15] In this and other cases, however, the effect of the prohibition of scouting was so minute that it seemed more like a governmental disavowal of responsibility than an effective regulator of migrant conduct.

The richness of the Altai lands made them the initial and most

[15] Scouting in this sense was often practiced by the American pioneer, but neither law nor custom provided for any such formal designation. "Possibly friends or relatives had moved earlier and had found a desirable region or else the father or an older son would make a preliminary tour." (Riegel, *op.cit.*, p. 72.)

sought after target of the Great Siberian Migration. From 1885-1890, 48 per cent of all migrants went to the Altai, in 1892, 69 per cent. During the 1890's, however, the percentage declined slowly. The railway served that region quite as well as others, but the available lands were diminishing. The Altai's percentage of the total was 42 per cent in 1899, 27 per cent in 1901, and only 17 per cent in 1902.

If the trickle into the Far East was in large part artificial, with the number of settlers falling far behind the government's desires and plans, the movement into the Altai was of a directly opposite nature. The Altai region was the scene of a sort of dress rehearsal for the coming flood of largely spontaneous Siberian migration. It provided a glimpse of the manifold problems ahead for both the settlers and the government, and set the pattern of migration policy in which St. Petersburg was forever scrambling to keep up with the actual course and character of migration, but never quite succeeding in doing so.

The Legislation of the Eighties

While during the later 1850's many peasants had shelved thought of resettlement in the hope that Emancipation would solve their problems, during the 1860's they often continued to hope that the Emancipation would not be the last measure to promote agrarian improvement. However, others continued to move, simply ignoring the legislative restrictions which Article 130 of the Emancipation Act had placed in the way of individual migrants (by making it necessary for each to settle with both his old commune and his intended new one in a manner usually beyond his powers). Those restrictions were in effect nullified by a rather hasty circular which the Minister of Interior, with the consent of the Minister of State Domains, put out on 3 April 1868. Its terms permitted the migration of entire communes of peasants of all categories, thus making arrangement between the individual and the commune unnecessary. At once some 30,000 peasants from the central provinces applied for the right to migrate, and interest was also shown in the provinces of Lithuania, Belorussia, and the Ukraine.[16] Alarmed, the government issued another circular a month later, on 4 May, placing severe restrictions on such movement. Large parties of migrants from the Ukraine and Belorussia were returned en route, and this ill-conceived venture in the field of migration policy collapsed.

The only laws on migration (except the abortive circular of 1868)

[16] See Kaufman, *loc.cit.*

which were passed during the 1860's and 1870's were those which confined themselves to recognizing the *fait accompli* of irregular settlement. In those decades the geographical center of gravity of migration lay in the southeast of European Russia. The total of migrants to the Orenburg-Ufa region, according to Kaufman, reached 100,000 by the end of the 1870's. Laws of 6 April 1869, 6 February 1871, and 28 January 1876 sanctioned the enrollment of migrants into Orenburg, Ufa, and Samara, and one of 21 November 1876 did the same thing for irregulars in Tobolsk and Tomsk. The government in those decades considered migration not so much criminal as simply extra-legal. Such movement was rightly regarded as carrying some of its own factual penalties. However, its growing dimensions were constantly forcing the government to issue laws which in effect freed irregulars from those very penalties by allowing them to regularize the position they had reached by flaunting authority.

Much of the negative attitude exhibited by the government in the realm of migration policy from the Emancipation up to the 1880's may be traced to P. A. (later Count) Valuev, Minister of Interior from 1861 to 1868 and Minister of State Domains from 1872 to 1879. During the 1870's thousands of petitions from ex-state peasants were piling up in his office, but Valuev simply refrained from acting on most of them.[17]

By the 1870's the population pressure in the swollen black-earth provinces had become great enough to alarm the zemstvos. Since the central government appeared unwilling to act on its own initiative, some of the zemstvos tried to prod it into action. In 1879, for example, the zemstvo of Chernigov, one of the provinces where the situation was worst, petitioned the Committee of Ministers, begging it to change the general regulations on migration for Chernigov so that all peasants of the province would be granted the right to take up state lands in Orenburg and Ufa. Minister of State Domains Valuev replied sullenly that it was necessary to act with caution "in order to impress on the population the fact that the government, once having settled the land order of the rural population, does not consider itself obliged to continue this settlement and to give out valuable state lands for the satisfaction of temporary and accidental needs."[18] After Minister of Interior Makov expressed agreement with this point of view, Valuev emphasized that he regarded the government's decision as especially important "in view of the state

[17] *Aziatskaia Rossiia*, Vol. I, p. 453.
[18] *Kolonizatsiia Sibiri*, p. 105.

of mind observed on all sides among the village population, which on the basis of false rumors and malicious gossip is everywhere expecting a new division of land in the form of addition to the allotments." The request of the Chernigov zemstvo was accordingly refused.

Notwithstanding Valuev's obstinacy, events were fast making his stand untenable. By the end of the 1870's the coincidence of two developments rendered impossible the postponement of the formulation of a rational migration policy. A severe agricultural depression was creeping over the country, and the frontier of settlement was nearing the boundary of European Russia. As Bilimovich points out, migration to the southeast and the Caucasus could proceed at a fair rate without any state aid, but when "in the eighties the stream of emigrants reached the Ural Mountains," government support became "absolutely essential"[19]—at least, it was needed much more than before. Since free and fertile land in European Russia was almost gone, the distant Asian lands could be reached by those suffering most from the slump only by means of government aid.

In 1880 there came to the fore in the government a man who was prepared to act boldly to deal with peasant problems, General Count M. T. Loris-Melikov. He became head of the extraordinary "Supreme Commanding Commission" on 12 February 1880 and on 6 August of the same year was appointed Minister of Interior. In a memorandum on the needs of agriculture he listed three measures as essential: first, the reduction of the redemption payments; second, credit assistance to peasants who desired to purchase land; third, the facilitation of migration and assistance to peasants wishing to move out of thickly-settled regions.[20]

Thus Loris-Melikov was from the start favorable to a new migration policy. When Alexander II received a report on conditions in Orel for 1880 which presented views opposed to the Valuev position on resettlement, he wrote on the document that Loris-Melikov ought to give it serious attention,[21] and there seemed every reason to expect a broad-gauged reexamination of agrarian problems.

However, in March, Alexander II was assassinated, and only a few weeks after the accession of Alexander III, Loris-Melikov was forced out of office. His successor, Count N. P. Ignatiev, nevertheless

[19] Bilimovich, loc.cit., p. 309.
[20] Article "Loris-Melikov," in Entsiklopedicheskii Slovar' (Brockhaus-Efron), paraphrases the cited memorandum, a portion of which is to be found in Trudy moskovskago obshchestva sel'skago khoziaistva, Moscow, 1882, Vol. XI, pp. 8-9.
[21] Aziatskaia Rossiia, Vol. I, p. 453.

pursued some of the same objectives. Together with the Minister of State Domains, he brought about the promulgation of "temporary rules" on migration on 10 July 1881.[22] Since it was considered desirable "to satisfy, without special publicity, demands expressed by certain groups of the agricultural classes" that they be granted permission to migrate, these rules were not published. They provided that it was no longer necessary to show evidence that the commune of the migrant's destination consented to his arrival, and whereas previously his obligations up to the following January had had to be discharged before departure, they were now deferred for several years after he reached the new settlement.

The "temporary rules" further established the first agencies to assist the actual movement of settlers, in the form of special offices along the most frequently traveled routes. These were entrusted with the function of furnishing information and certain kinds of material aid and medical assistance. The first such "migrant point" was set up at Batraki in Simbirsk province, though it was soon moved to Syzran.

The "rules" affected only the peasant class (*soslovie*), and to the last the government's view of migration as a matter pertaining exclusively to the peasantry provoked mutterings of dissatisfaction among other social groups. Three years later, by the decree of 17 February 1884, the government was prodded into extending the "rules" to cover those who were legally townsmen though factually agriculturists of long standing. But it would not retreat further. Certain officials, including those most influential under Alexander III, did not want geographical mobility to become confused with social mobility, and keeping the peasant "loyal" was thought to mean keeping him a communal peasant under state tutelage, and certainly not allowing him or others to become pioneers free of class restrictions.

Simultaneously the "temporary rules" charged the Ministry of State Domains with the organization of migrant allotments within European Russia, specifically in Kherson, Ekaterinoslav, Samara, Taurida, Orenburg, and Ufa. In the provinces named, from 1881 to 1893 there were allotted 288,000 desiatinas, on which 63,687 people were settled. The greatest number, 36,971, went to Kherson; the next largest, 9,347, to Samara. In the 1880's two other districts were filling up rapidly: the Don region, where during the mid-1880's "strong measures" were taken to halt irregular migration, and the

---

[22] Summarized in *Kolonizatsiia Sibiri*, p. 110ff.

Kuban in the north Caucasus. Whereas 30,000 settlers entered the Kuban in 1870, the number rose to 237,000 by 1881, by the mid-1880's to 300,000, by 1900 to 800,000.[23] The southern steppe was thus being settled by irregulars faster than the government could bring into effect its belated attempt at organizing regular migration.

After the "temporary rules" were issued, Ignatiev set up two committees to consider the draft of a general migration law. One was a special commission in the Ministry of Interior under the chairmanship of Privy Councillor P. P. Semenov; the other was a council of "informed men" (*svedushchie liudi,* that is, men from outside the government who had special competence or experience). Ignatiev was thus endeavoring to apply the principle of non-bureaucratic consultation in law-making which Loris-Melikov had advanced. The result, however, was not harmonious.

The Semenov commission concluded that the migration movement had exhibited particular strength in the late 1870's and the year just past, 1880, and that it represented a natural movement prompted by economic distress, chiefly lack of land, which was concentrated in the black-earth provinces. Such movement, it was decided, ought to be supervised by the government from beginning to end. The council of "informed men," on the other hand, opposed the concept that migration should be confined to bureaucratic control. It suggested that the elected zemstvos should supervise the departure of migrants, migrant offices, their journey; and officials in charge of peasant affairs, arrival at their destination. The council believed that migration ought to be open to all rural inhabitants, but distinguished two types of prospective migrant. In its opinion, the neediest peasants ought to be extended state aid for resettlement in suitable areas closest to the overpopulated provinces, while economically better-off villagers should be permitted to move, without any government assistance, to distant Siberia, Central Asia, and the Caucasus.

The problem was also put up to provincial governors for comment. Count D. A. Tolstoy, who had become Minister of Interior in 1882, reported the governors' reactions to Alexander III. In so doing he interpreted them as evidence that difficulties and disorder would be provoked by the publication of a law which provided general assistance to peasants desiring to migrate. Tolstoi concluded that a real demand for migration existed only in twelve provinces of the north and center of the black-earth zone.[24] No doubt the demand was most

[23] Kaufman, *loc.cit.*
[24] *Kolonizatsiia Sibiri,* p. 111.

77

urgent there, where "land hunger" was sharpest, but the indications were that the government was retreating in the direction of the negative Valuev position on migration. Regulations issued by the Ministry of Interior in May 1884 embodied the recommendation of the Semenov commission that migration was to be entirely directed by the central government, though they delegated to the provincial governors—who were appointed by St. Petersburg—discretionary powers to prohibit migration entirely within their jurisdiction.

Another special commission was now established, this time under the chairmanship of Privy Councillor Viacheslav von Plehve, later to be assassinated while Minister of Interior, which was to give further consideration to a general migration law. In 1884 funds allotted for aid to migrants totalled only 40,000 rubles, and in succeeding years the sum fell to 20,000. There was grudging acknowledgment of the need when in 1886 special officials were appointed to assist migrants in Ekaterinburg, Orenburg, Zlatoust, Tobolsk, and Tomsk.

However, by the time Plehve's commission reported, the need was thought to have lessened. It was piously hoped that the activities of the Peasant Bank, founded in 1882, and other factors alluded to vaguely, would reduce the cases of real hardship which did exist. We do not have the full text of the commission's report; at any rate, nominally on the basis of its recommendations, a general migration law was finally issued on 13 July 1889.[25] This law has been called one of the two "last echoes of the program of 1880"[26]—that is, of Loris-Melikov's policy. We do not know whether any of his followers who remained in the government manipulated the conclusions of the Plehve report, but in any event the law marks the first piece of regular legislation which established conditions which any peasant desiring to migrate might reasonably be expected to satisfy.

The provisions of the law of 1889 were as follows. Any peasant might petition for permission to migrate, furnishing "reasons meriting attention" which were not specified in the law. The Ministers of Interior and State Domains—the former discharging responsibility for the homeland, the latter for state lands either west or east of the Urals—were responsible for granting permission. Permission was to be contingent on the availability of free land at the desired destination. In European Russia allotment of state lands was provided for

[25] 3 *P.S.Z.* 6198.
[26] Article, "Krest'iane," in *Entsiklopedicheskii Slovar'* (Brockhaus-Efron), Vol. XVI, p. 724.

on a temporary rental basis for a period of six to twelve years, after which permanent allotment might be made. In Asiatic Russia immediate allotment was provided for. Allotted land could not be alienated or mortgaged. It was to be granted, on the basis of 15 desiatinas per "soul," either to communes or to individual households; however, in settlements which had not less than 40 males, communes were to be organized, in whatever manner the land was held. Exemptions from payment of dues for two years were made for European Russia, for Asiatic Russia three, with the following three years bearing half-exemption, and military service could likewise be postponed for three years.

These provisions set up a "regular" route for migration which was made obligatory for all settlers. It was specifically stated that all irregulars would in the future be returned to their former homes. Nevertheless, persons who had migrated irregularly before publication of the law might be enrolled in their new settlements, provided that they assumed all arrears from their old communes, payment of which could be deferred for three years. In contrast to the rules of 1881, those migrating legally were permitted to transfer to their old communes all arrears in taxes and redemption payments. They could sell their garden plots and livestock, but their allotments were to be abandoned gratis to the old communes two years after departure. The entire law was initially applied to the provinces of European Russia, West Siberia, and the Semirechensk, Akmolinsk, and Semipalatinsk regions of the Steppe. In 1891-1892 it was extended to the Uralsk and Turgaisk regions and to Yeniseisk and Irkutsk provinces. Again, in contrast to the rules of 1881, the law was publicized, with the exception of certain articles mentioning the possibility of loans for the settlers.

By the rules of 1881, state aid was to be extended only in extraordinary cases. In contrast, the 1889 law stated that the government was prepared to advance 30 rubles per family, or 100 more if specially approved, to be repaid without interest over a period of ten years. Very poor settlers might also receive lumber for construction of homes and seed grain.

The effect of the law was somewhat disproportionate to the amount of energy expended in its preparation. In 1887, before its issuance, permission to migrate had been granted to 9,000 families, and in 1888 to 19,000. However, in 1889 the total was only 2,800; in 1890, 7,600. As Kaufman states, "The great mass of migrants even after

79

1889 were irregular."[27] In 1890 and 1891, the Tomsk migrant point registered 70 per cent and 66 per cent irregular migrants respectively, while for the same years the Tobolsk point registered 80 per cent and 70 per cent irregulars. From the time of the promulgation of the law until 1892, a total of 17,289 families received ministerial permissions, while, according to data of migrant registration (which had begun only in 1885), during the same period 28,911 families crossed the Urals. It was manifestly impossible to return all these people to their homes, and the government once again bowed to the inevitable.

Even if the government was going to manage only a small fraction of the actual migration, surveying operations had to keep up with the issuance of official permissions. By 1892, however, the surveyors were swamped, and a circular of 6 March had to stop migration to West Siberia entirely. This prohibition was not lifted until 1895. It is not surprising to learn that irregular migration continued notwithstanding.

In 1892 Prince G. S. Golitsyn was ordered to visit Tobolsk in connection with a study of the consequences of the famine which had swept the whole Empire during that and the previous year.[28] It appears that his recommendations were influential in the Imperial grant, on 22 October 1892, of permission for irregular migrants who had arrived up to that time to be enrolled in their new villages. From its text, one would scarcely have suspected that a law only three years old strictly forbade any such action.

Conclusion

From the Emancipation until the year 1892, migration policy failed to bring resettlement under state control. The government was even compelled to acknowledge its failure by repeatedly legalizing the violation of its own regulations. As Lensky writes, "Already the first legislative acts which permitted migration beyond the Urals in actual fact constituted merely a recognition of the existing phenomenon." Loris-Melikov wanted to go farther, but he was forced out of office before he could establish a policy of encouraging migration, and his successors in the 1880's could not bring themselves either to forbid or to assist the movement effectively. A pattern was established

[27] Kaufman, *loc.cit.*

[28] See D. Golovachev, "Pereselentsy v 1892 godu," *Vestnik Evropy*, August 1893, pp. 803ff., for a horrifying picture of the sufferings of the migrants at the Tobolsk migrant point in consequence of the famine.

whereby migration policy moved slowly and grudgingly, at a disconcertingly safe distance, behind the fact of resettlement. Lensky declares that in general *"the history of migration legislation is the history of the development of irregular migration"* in the Russian Empire (emphasis in the original).[29] Although later legislation did narrow the gap between policy and reality, the extralegal migrants had already had a running start.

When the Trans-Siberian Railway was built, the policy-makers were forced to reopen the whole problem. Peasants clamored to use the new and easy railway route, impatient of legal delays and obstacles. The railway helped to attract both domestic and foreign attention to Siberian migration. In fact, the outside world now heard of the movement for the first time. But the railway was not responsible for the fact that the frontier of Russian settlement, after centuries of slow advance, was just at that historical movement leaving the south behind and crossing the Urals.

[29] Nik. Lensky, "Samovol'nye pereselentsy i pereselencheskoe zakonodatel'stvo," *Voprosy kolonizatsii*, No. 14, 1914, p. 96.

CHAPTER IV

The Migrants Enter Siberia

"Necessity teaches us to eat white bread."*—RUSSIAN PROVERB

An Account of Migrants in the South

The records of migration, as distinguished from migration policy, are of several kinds. Some Russian journalists and scholars wrote accounts of their firsthand observations. The state agencies concerned with migration[1] collected data which give us glimpses of one phase or other of the whole migration process, including the condition of new settlers of several years' standing. But the peasant himself is silent. Not a single manuscript or fragment composed by an actual migrant has come to the attention of this writer. The "mute inglorious Miltons" of the great migration did not write their experiences. Fortunately they talked to visitors, and a few of these have left a record.

One visitor was F. Voroponov, who traveled among the settlers of the Black Sea steppe in the summer of 1886. His report is interesting for purposes of comparison with Siberian resettlement. He traveled at a time when land was becoming hard to find in the south of European Russia. There were still peasants seeking farms north of the Black Sea, and thousands of irregular migrants were pouring into the Kuban in the northern Caucasus. Nevertheless the word about opportunity in the east was spreading fast, and settlers were already turning in sharply increasing numbers toward Siberia.

Voroponov notes that stories of the migrants' misfortunes were plentiful in contemporary newspapers. "There they were hungry, there they wept, here they buried children, here they cursed their own enterprise, and in such and such places they lived off charity, and so forth."[2] The newspapers often left a wholly bleak impression, to which the Siberian writer Iadrintsev contributed by asserting that "the migration of human beings is on a level with zoological migra-

---

* In the migration to the south, wheat bread, hitherto known as a luxury, was eaten; the same was partly true of Siberia.

[1] Such agencies included the Imperial institutions on migrant affairs, the local and provincial authorities of the areas from which emigration occurred, the governmental migrant points, and the local authorities at the migrants' destination.

[2] F. Voroponov, "K pereselentsam. Iz putevykh zametok," *Vestnik Evropy*, June and July 1887.

tions from the animal world."[3] Both in the south and in Siberia migration seemed to be mainly endless suffering. Voroponov evidently suspected that part of the story had been left out, and set out to study the facts for himself.

One of the first things which struck him was his discovery of gentry who were selling out to peasants; east of the Urals virtually no gentry had ever settled at all.[4] He encountered a landlord in Ekaterinoslav province who said: "It is bad for the *muzhik*, but he still gets along better because he works himself; the amount of the wage is no problem to him, because he himself is owner as well as worker, but for the gentry it is very, very hard. So they are willing to sell land. Twenty, thirty years, just wait and see how much estate land is left to us!"[5] This landlord was of course explaining, in terms of his own experience, the economic advantage of what has been called *trudovoe khoziaistvo*.

Later on, in one village Voroponov encountered two brothers. One worked and prospered as a peasant; the other flaunted the papers which proved his gentry origin, alienated his fellows, yet tried somehow to fit into the village. The *dvorianin* (gentry) brother, Iakov, complained long to his visitor about his neighbors, yet concluded: "But my gentry status won't make me fat. My brother came to it long ago . . . I'll ditch it too. . . ."[6] This instance of social mobility may or may not be representative. What is interesting to us is that in this case, movement from gentry into peasantry was undertaken not as a gesture of despair but as a means of self-improvement.

We may examine three of the villages Voroponov visited. In the whole southern area there had been two years of drought, 1885 and 1886. The first settlement, "R———ka," was a new one. The villagers came from a thickly-settled section of Kharkov province. There the family often had tilled only two or three desiatinas. Renting the neighbors' land was unprofitable at a rate of 15-20 rubles per desiatina per year, and such land was in any case difficult to find. Eight of the villagers had wandered south and discovered some landlords who were willing to sell. They returned home and formed an association (*tovarishchestvo*) in order to buy. These "scouts" (the Russian word, *khodoki*, is not used in the account) reported on the land, but some of those interested went south themselves and

[3] N. Iadrintsev, "Polozhenie pereselentsev v Sibir'," *Vestnik Evropy*, August 1881, p. 606.
[4] See p. 37.   [5] Voroponov, *loc.cit.*, Vol. vi, pp. 759-60.
[6] *Ibid.*, Vol. vii, p. 374.

of these some decided for, some against, going ahead. The latter were replaced by others. Word came of the droughts, the beetles, and the gophers which infested the area. At the time of purchase 90 intended migrant families took part in the venture; of these 27 reneged and 7 replacements appeared, making 70. The price of the land was 55 rubles per desiatina; the Peasant Bank furnished up to 500 rubles per householder, and still each household had to dig up about 100 rubles of its own money, for an estate which evidently ran to around 700 desiatinas.

Each household had to travel some 300 versts, bringing cattle and tools. Its members had to construct buildings; a good house cost 200 rubles to erect, even a mud-hut costing 20-30 rubles. In order to till 10 desiatinas of land, purchase of the necessary additional cattle and tools took 60-70 rubles, and therefore many plowed only 5 desiatinas. Of the whole number of migrant families at the settlement, only 6 families had realized 100 rubles or less from selling out; 2 brought 150 rubles; 40 (the majority) had from 200 to 300 rubles; 4 had about 400, one 600, two 700, one even 1,000 rubles. As Voroponov points out, the possession of several hundred rubles did not necessarily prove that the migrant had not been in extreme need at home. Even the muzhik with a miserable 2-desiatina plot might obtain 200-300 rubles; if he had 3 desiatinas, he might get 300-400. The man who had only 5 desiatinas for a whole family, and therefore still suffered from dearth of land, if he had decent farm-buildings might realize 1,000 rubles. The migrant who did not sell, but who left his land at home rented in case he should return, might rent out 4-5 desiatinas for 2 years and obtain over 100 rubles. As a consequence of their removal, the settlers might exchange 3-4 desiatinas for 10. "They go from crowded conditions and the strip system, accompanied by endless quarrels and scandals, to the wide open spaces [*prostor*], to a rounded-off holding, where quarrels with neighbors are almost non-existent."[7]

This did not mean, however, that holdings in R———ka were equal. Some defaulting led to a surplus to be distributed beyond the 10½ desiatina lot, yet many were financially unable to take more. The people of R———ka were not contented, but were complaining bitterly about their last drought and wondering if they should have come. And still there were voices reminding each other that after two bad years the third would probably be better. Since the beetles had come last year, they would not come again, since they were

[7] *Ibid.*, Vol. VI, p. 771.

supposed to show up only every two or three years. As for the gophers, they would hunt them down and pour water in their holes!

The second settlement, Kievka, belonged to a township whose scribe warned Voroponov that the villagers were no good. Out of 50 householders who had planned to leave the homeland (Kiev province), 39 were on the spot; the others had reneged before migrating or had returned after arrival. They had bought an estate worth 30,000 rubles; the Peasant Bank had furnished 500 rubles per family, which left 5,000 to be made up out of their own resources. Of this 5,000 rubles owed, 2,000 had been paid; the remainder of the debt was still to be discharged. Out of the total householders, in the homeland half of them had been landless, the remainder had had tiny plots. Most of them had harvested the grain of others in return for every twelfth sheaf; many had rented small plots, paying 20 rubles per desiatina per year. Only 3 had sold their land; 7 had kept their land in Kiev; others had had nothing to sell beyond a cow or so. Only 3 had built cottages in Kievka, since it cost 80 rubles to build one out of only one tree; others lived in crude straw or board shelters. Families who lived in these shelters wintered at home in Kiev, and in the spring returned again to the settlement. The settlement of Kievka had been established only the previous year. Completion of the purchase had been postponed; the migrants arrived only in the autumn, when the sowing season was already well advanced, and had too few cattle to sow very much. As a result, although they had had a good harvest they were still in bad shape. Everything depended on the next harvest. Their fate hung in the balance. On the one hand they hovered wretchedly together, two or three families per house, thinking sometimes nostalgically of the homeland and thus naming their village Kievka; on the other they thanked God for their good harvest and for the fact that they had escaped the bad harvest which Kiev province had just suffered.

The third settlement was one about whose riches rumors had traveled far, though Voroponov had difficulty in finding it. These villagers, known as the *kiiane* (a Ukrainian word meaning Kievans), likewise came from Kiev province. Voroponov suspected a group of poor gentry. However, with the exception of the Iakov referred to earlier, there were none; these were all peasants. They had purchased no less than 1,500 desiatinas of steppe lands. About 100 householders had obtained 50,000 rubles in loans from the Peasant Bank and to that had added 20,000 rubles of their own. Only 60 had arrived. It appeared that many of those who defaulted had never intended to migrate and willingly allowed their shares to be taken over by relatives. Twenty out of the 60 held three-quarters of the land purchased; one had more than 60 desiatinas, 8 around 50. Only 5 had sold their land at home; the others kept it and rented it, or turned it over to relatives. These people had set up no commune, and stayed away from "peasant" institutions. They said: "We there at home were a commune [*sel'skoe obshchestvo*]. . . . We here are 'private owners'— what do we need a commune for?" They took no cases to the peasant courts: "We are private owners, for us there are the justices of the peace!"[8] They were working hard, prospering, and contented.

So ran the condition of three settlements in the Black Sea steppe. One was composed of people who were working hard to transform previous misery into present adequacy; one of people even worse off, whose fate was not yet clear; one of well-off peasants who were becoming even better off. In these and other villages Voroponov found in some cases leaders of ability who had organized the enterprise, in others a seemingly anonymous sort of collaboration. The State Peasant Bank, founded only four years before, had aided many of them.[9] Sometimes communes had been organized, sometimes not— and of such cases Voroponov asked wonderingly, "How thus can the whole settlement live?" He found literates scattered throughout the migrants and in one moderately well-off village (not one of those described above) found a peasant mother who had taught her daughter how to read out of *Rodnoe Slovo*, a school reader—no doubt not a unique case. Among these migrants, then, there were problems, some of them frightful, but still in general "here they came to the tillage of new lands, to the conversion of miserable wastes into fields of grain and blooming gardens."[10]

The Siberian Peasant on the Eve of the Migration

When the migrants crossed the Urals in the 1880's, they found a scattered and sparse Russian population descended from peasants and exiles who had come into Asiatic Russia at some time or other during the three centuries which had elapsed since the "conquest" by Yermak. These were soon distinguished by name as "old-settlers" (*starozhily*) from the new migrants (*novosely* or *pereselentsy*). There were old-settlers to be found all over Siberia, though they were absent from the newly-acquired Russian Far East, the Steppe region, and Turkestan. Like the Great Russian peasants, they lived

[8] *Ibid.*, Vol. VII, p. 373.   [9] See p. 40.
[10] *Ibid.*, Vol. VI, p. 771.

in villages, often large villages similar to those of the lower Volga. We have various descriptions of them as a type. Kuznetsov refers to them as having darker hair and eyes, a thinner beard, and narrower eyes than their cis-Ural compatriots. "The vast and varied riches of the country have developed in the Siberian a passion for gain." The old-settler was said to be insensitive to the arts—presumably a straight-faced observation—and superstitious. However, he also displayed certain "positive" characteristics: "he is eager to learn, esteems well-informed people and knowledge, he is enterprising, ready to accept every kind of novelty, if it is understandable and useful to him."[11]

Kuznetsov was describing the old-settlers as best he could after they had mixed with the migrants for two generations. One may compare the observations of Alexander Michie, who crossed Siberia a generation before the wave of new settlement in the 1880's. As soon as he had crossed the Urals, which he compared with the Lammermoor range of Scotland, he remarked that houses in Russia were "decidedly inferior to those in Siberia." From then on he was constantly struck by the favorable situation of the old-settlers. They were, he wrote, "well clad, well housed, and at least adequately fed. They have something of independence in their bearing, and the condition of their families, as well as the tasteful decorations often met with in their houses, evince a certain amount of self-respect."[12]

Michie reported the share that exiles had had, and were having, in contributing to the old-settler stock. When a criminal was released, he might cultivate as much land as he chose to clear, use available timber for building or fuel, and was exempt for a time from tax payment and conscription. Many rich miners and merchants of Siberia, according to Michie, were descended from convicts. Criminals sentenced for minor offenses, given good behavior, could after three years' residence marry, settle, clear and cultivate land, were exempt from taxes for twelve years and paid only a trifle after that. They were, however, legally dead, could not hold property in their own name, and could not return to Russia, though even if they could "it is highly improbable that any would avail themselves of the privilege. Siberia is really the land of promise to them. The descendants of these convicts become free agriculturists, and live in independence."[13]

[11] V. K. Kuznetsov, "Russkie starozhily v Sibiri i Srednei Azii," *Aziatskaia Rossiia*, Vol. I, p. 188.
[12] Michie, *op.cit.*, p. 320.   [13] *Ibid.*, p. 322.

After describing the obligations of serfdom in European Russia, Michie wrote, "The peasant in Siberia, on the other hand, is absolutely free in all things to follow the bent of his own will. He has no master to dread and serve, and owes obedience to nothing but the law of the land." The Siberian peasant was treated "with every liberality" by the government, which had as its "ruling purpose" to "colonise it with industrious communities, who will turn its natural wealth to account, and become an arm of support to the state." As far as the Siberian peasant is concerned, "The land he has worked is his own. No other person can disturb his possession, and the government even cannot claim from him any portion of the land so acquired without his formal renunciation. . . . The security of life and property, and the liberation from the arbitrary dictates of a superior will, give the people encouragement to cultivate their talents in the full faith that their labours shall not be in vain. Unlimited wealth is open to all who have the energy to seek it."[14] The great degree of social mobility which Michie observed led him to write, "the amalgamation of classes will consolidate and strengthen the whole body politic, and should that happy consummation ever be realised in Russia, Siberia will have the honour of leading the way." In fact, he implied that this had already occurred on a gigantic scale: "It was probably the growing prosperity of Siberia, and the marked superiority of the condition of the population there, that induced the government to emancipate the serfs of Russia proper."[15]

Michie's intense indignation at serfdom, whose destruction via Emancipation he applauded warmly but whose injustices he had no intention of forgetting, may have led him to speak in unduly sweeping and unqualified language about the non-serf Siberian peasantry. Nevertheless many undoubtedly accurate features of the old-settlers and their life, consequences of the opportunity offered by free land everywhere, were conveyed by this Scotsman who, like most foreigners in decades to come, had been psychologically unprepared for what he encountered in Siberia.[16]

The Siberian Migration: Places of Origin

In the 1880's the wave of migrants, finding less and less room in the European Russian provinces, impelled to leave by the miseries due to agricultural depression yet as a consequence of hard times

[14] *Ibid.*, pp. 323, 326.   [15] *Ibid.*, p. 327.

[16] Michie claimed to be the first in nearly a century and a half to write an account in English of a journey from St. Petersburg to Peking. Whether or not he was the first, quite a number came after him in the next few decades.

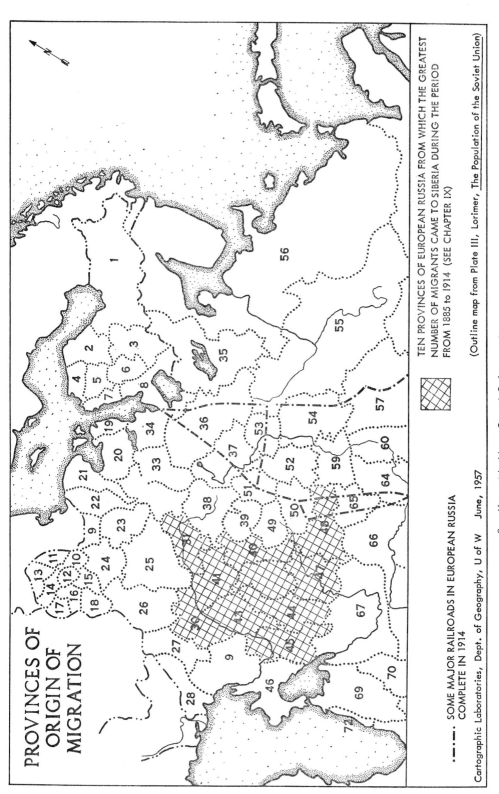

PROVINCES OF
ORIGIN OF
MIGRATION

TEN PROVINCES OF EUROPEAN RUSSIA FROM WHICH THE GREATEST
NUMBER OF MIGRANTS CAME TO SIBERIA DURING THE PERIOD
FROM 1885 to 1914 (SEE CHAPTER IX)

(Outline map from Plate III, Lorimer, The Population of the Soviet Union)

—·—·— SOME MAJOR RAILROADS IN EUROPEAN RUSSIA
COMPLETE IN 1914

Cartographic Laboratories, Dept. of Geography, U of W   June, 1957

See Key with Maps 2 and 3 for province names.

financially least able to leave, pushed into Siberia. Whence did this onrush of people come? What financial resources did they have? What were the conditions of travel? What aid was given them? What was their destination? How many returned? What became of them?

Concerning their point of origin, there are considerable data based on registration of migrants at Cheliabinsk and Tomsk. Doubtless many migrants did not undergo registration. The vast majority probably did, including a large number of the "irregulars," for whom registration apparently entailed no risk of penalties or compulsory return to their homes. The Cheliabinsk registration indicated that the following provinces, in the order given, furnished the largest number of migrants for the period 1887-1893: Kursk, Tambov, Voronezh, Viatka, Samara, Perm, Poltava, Riazan, Saratov, Kazan, Penza, Kharkov, Chernigov. These findings may be compared with the breakdown of the portion of the total Russian population of Asiatic Russia, by the census of 1897, born in European Russia (1,400,000 out of a total of 5,341,745), which gives the European provinces where the largest numbers were born, in order, as: Perm, Poltava, Kursk, Tambov, Voronezh, Chernigov, Samara, Viatka, Penza, Riazan, Orenburg, Orel, Saratov, Kharkov, and Kazan.[17] The order of provinces is somewhat different, suggesting the defects of the registration figures as a complete picture of migration, even though some of the European-born Siberians of 1897 came before 1887 or after 1893. Nevertheless only two provinces do not appear on both lists (Orenburg and Orel, which rank far down the second list), and it is safe to draw certain conclusions.

There were two regions of origin for the early wave of Siberian migrants. First, there was the central agricultural region, chiefly the Kursk-Tambov-Voronezh contiguous arc of provinces, on which the Poltava-Chernigov western fringe gained as the 1890's wore on, and the northern fringe of Orel-Riazan-Penza did the same to a lesser extent. The second was the middle Volga region, chiefly the Perm-Viatka-Samara strip, with the adjoining provinces of Saratov and Kazan playing some part. Note that the two regions constitute one contiguous arc not adjacent to the frontier of settlement of the 1880's and 1890's, but considerably to the rear. Gurvich, apparently referring to the same two regions we have distinguished, imputes migration from the central agricultural belt to a desire to escape from

---

[17] See Appendix 1, Tables 11-13, for the complete figures and their sources. See also Map 1.

"an extremely abnormal economic situation," while he explains migration from the middle Volga as expressing a popular conservatism seeking to "cling to habitual agricultural methods." A report of the Committee on the Siberian Railway asserts that both these reasons represent aspects of "dearth of land" in the broad sense, and tends to emphasize the similarity of both currents of migration.[18] Nevertheless one may well believe that the middle Volga, lying so much closer to the Urals, gave rise to an outward movement at a level of need much less desperate and pressing than that impelling flight from the center.

The center, as has been mentioned earlier, was the area of greatest density of population and of greatest proportion of serfs prior to Emancipation. There allotments were lowest and population grew fastest in the post-Emancipation era; by the late 1870's the population had increased by 20 per cent of the 1858 figure. This led to a diminution of pasture (the underprovision of which to the peasant had been one of the most serious defects of the Emancipation settlement) as the peasants had to plow more land to feed more people—in Kursk, Tula, and Orel the percentage of land plowed rose to 81 and 82 per cent. This in turn meant less stockbreeding, more cutting of forest, and the increased necessity of using manure instead of wood for fuel. The Peasant Bank served to some extent to offset the developing crisis in this central region by financing the purchase by communes of lands for migration, such transactions totalling 24 per cent of all Bank transactions by 1898. Yet, owing to the poverty of this region, out of 388 properties reverting to the Bank on account of defaulted mortgages up to 1 January 1899, 62 per cent were located in this central region, although the percentage of Bank loans taken by the same region was only 27 per cent.[19] Land prices were also rising by 200 and 300 per cent in the two decades following 1861.

It was not surprising that from the central provinces 2,000,000 passports[20] were issued annually for outside work.[21] Most of these workers, it appears, were bound for the Black Sea steppe (New Russia, the Don, and so forth) to perform agricultural labor. How-

[18] *Kolonizatsiia Sibiri*, pp. 131-32; Gurvich quoted here from his *Pereseleniia krest'ian v Sibir'*, p. 59.

[19] *Kolonizatsiia Sibiri*, p. 136.

[20] A certain number of such passports were of dubious authenticity, though they were seldom scrutinized closely, once issued. For a suggestion of the possibilities, see Leskov's story, *The Enchanted Wanderer*, where the hero obtains a passport from a magistrate's clerk in exchange for a silver cross and an earring, though the clerk knows the young man is a runaway serf.

[21] *Kolonizatsiia Sibiri*, p. 139.

ever, as the population in the south increased and the use of machinery spread simultaneously, the demand for transient labor diminished. When the south no longer furnished opportunities for either transient labor or easy settlement, an alternative had to be found. For many people the alternative was Siberia, which was distant enough so that transient labor was largely out of the question, but migration was practicable.

As for the second region, the middle Volga, the pressure for migration was apparently more marginal and less persistent. The Simbirsk-Samara-Saratov-Ufa-Orenburg-Kazan-Nizhny Novgorod group of provinces provided 21.5 per cent of Siberian migrants during the famine period from 1887 to 1894, in 1897 only 5 per cent, in 1898, 16 per cent again.[22] This is not to suggest that the famine of 1891-1892 had no effect in the central region. On the contrary, it seems to have provided the impetus which brought the west-central provinces of Chernigov (1890, 152 emigrants; 1896, 36,198) and Poltava into the migration process to stay. But Kursk and Tambov settlers came before and after 1891, grimly and steadily. If one compares the origin of migrants to the south[23] with that of the early Siberian migrants, it appears that the famine coincided with the widespread realization that the southern steppe was filling up. Thereupon the settlers from Poltava and Kharkov turned from the south to the east. At any rate, we may conclude that the center of gravity of the first decade or two of mass Siberia-bound migration was in the Kursk-Tambov area. The reason for this was not that conditions in the center had become startlingly worse in the 1880's, for settlers had been streaming out of it for many years. The reason was that their usual previous destination, the south, was only then beginning to close, while the east lay open.

The Economic Level of the Migrants

What financial resources did the settlers have? I. I. Popov declares that their cash was in most cases less than meager. In a few cases it was 200-400 rubles, which had been obtained from selling home and furnishings. Most of it was spent en route.[24] V. N. Grigoriev's study of migrants from Riazan indicates that only 21 per cent started with less than 50 rubles per family; 38 per cent had from 50 to 150; 22 per cent, 150 to 300; 16 per cent, 300 to 800; 3 per cent, more than 800.[25] The information which Gurvich gathered in Siberia led him

[22] *Ibid.*, pp. 142-43.
[23] See pp. 90-91. above.
[24] Popov, *loc.cit.*, p. 252.
[25] Cited in Kaufman, "Pereselenie," p. 268.

to conclude that "the peasant of medium means must be regarded as the predominant element in the present migration movement."[26]

Something of the economic status of the migrants may be inferred from the registration of migrants of 1895 and 1896 carried out by the Siberian Railway administration. Their holdings of land at home were:[27]

TABLE 6

Land Held by Migrants of 1895-1896

	PERCENTAGE OF FAMILIES	
	1895 Migrants	*1896 Migrants*
Landless	15.7	18.9
To 1 desiatina	16.5	13.8
To 3 desiatinas	36.5	31.8
To 5 desiatinas	15.0	17.4
To 10 desiatinas	12.8	14.4
Above 10 desiatinas	2.4	3.1
Not indicated	1.1	0.6

Thus around one-third of the migrants had no land, or less than one desiatina, and were for all practical purposes landless; an additional third suffered from shortage of land; one third had a comparatively satisfactory holding. These figures yield an average holding of 2.8 desiatinas per family for the migrants of 1895, 3.0 for those of 1896. Comparing this with an average size of 11 desiatinas per household of an allotment in European Russia,[28] one may see how much these people needed to migrate. Such settlers flew in the face of the central paradox of migration—namely, as Grigoriev puts it, that "the need giving rise to the movement simultaneously limits it."[29] In other words, those who had little land needed to go, but could not afford to go.

The picture is, however, not quite as black as it first appears. There was, in addition to allotments, extensive short-term renting of land among these migrants, though that was a difficult and hazardous method of maintenance. Their livestock holdings were very small: 22-24 per cent had no stock, 35-36 per cent no working stock, 43-46 per cent one horse, only 18-21 per cent two or more. And yet the

[26] Cited *Idem*.   [27] *Kolonizatsiia Sibiri*, p. 151.
[28] According to N. Blagoveshchensky, *Svodnyi sbornik khoziaistvennykh svedenii po zemskim podvornym opisiam*, I, 1893, cited *Idem*.
[29] Quoted by Kaufman, "Pereselenie," p. 267.

conclusion of the Committee on the Siberian Railway was that among these migrants, relatively speaking, "peasants of medium means" predominated. In order to demonstrate this, figures are furnished for the funds realized by selling out at home:[30]

TABLE 7

Cash Realized from Liquidations by 1895-1896 Migrants

SUM RAISED	PERCENT OF FAMILIES REALIZING FROM LIQUIDATION OF THEIR PROPERTIES	
	In 1895	In 1896
Up to 50 rubles	12.8	9.0
50-100 rubles	26.3	23.1
100-200 rubles	30.2	38.6
200-300 rubles	13.8	16.0
Over 300 rubles	16.9	13.3

This table shows that in 1895, 39.1 per cent, in 1896 only 32.1 per cent, of the migrants realized less than 100 rubles. When we add the fact that in 1895 54 per cent of the families registered had no arrears whatsoever, while in 1896 this percentage rose to 73.5 per cent, it becomes clear that the amount of land held was not the full story of the economic condition of the settlers. How could people with so little land keep financially above water? The partial answer lies in the fact of outside employment. Only one-fifth of the families did not need to send some of their number into side earnings, and yet out of the great majority who did so, less than one-tenth had no tillage at all. Out of the migrants who went outside their own land for supplementary earnings, 57 per cent (for both years) went into simple day labor; of these about one-third to industry away from their home districts, from one-fifth to one-third to agricultural labor, and about the same number to non-agricultural labor which was apparently nearby.[31] The Committee report noted simply that such habits had gained for many migrants skills in trade which would be useful to them in Siberia.

It may be concluded that in the early period of Siberian migration the settlers were certainly not rich; on the other hand they were not paupers. Rather, they were people who suffered from lack of land, yet desired to remain farmers and were able to do so by migrating

[30] *Kolonizatsiia Sibiri*, p. 154.   [31] *Ibid.*, pp. 155-56.

across the Urals. It would seem that they were people who, on leaving their homes, commanded considerably less financial resources than the migrants whom Voroponov saw on the Black Sea steppe. The important difference was that in Siberia they went to free state land and could therefore do with a good deal less money.

The Journey

Before the migrants moved permanently, they often sent advance agents to Siberia to locate land and report on conditions at the destination. The practice of scouting (*khodachestvo*) was first given legal sanction in 1822, but had not been mentioned in legislation since 1861. The government, it seems, feared that the encouragement of scouting would precipitate a mass movement.[32] At length, the Ministry of the Interior declared that the sending of scouts by migrants who had received legal approval deserved encouragement. The law of 15 April 1896 finally recognized the right to send scouts and provided exemptions for them. It was subsequently discovered that the resulting increase of scouting helped to reduce irregular migration considerably from 1896 onward.[33] In the early stages, however, scouting was a hazardous operation and often a fruitless one. In 1896, just before the change in policy took effect, only 26 per cent of the scouts who returned from Siberia had chosen places for settlement.

Thus the majority of migrants simply took a deep breath and plunged across the Urals. Near Omsk Iadrintsev met a man who had been summoned back home for military service, He had had to leave his family en route, and when he returned after a few months found that his family had vanished into thin air. There could be an advantageous side to this sort of occurrence, however. Iadrintsev asks, if relatives cannot find them, how can the government?[34] "Getting lost" together might mean a new type of freedom for the migrants.

There were two routes most commonly used by the migrants of the 1870's and 1880's. One was across the Urals via Perm and Tiumen to the Ob River or via the Siberian road (*trakt*) to Ishim, and finally to Tobolsk or Tomsk. The other, farther south, went from Samara or Ufa to Cheliabinsk and through Orenburg by the mail road to Troitsk, Petropavlovsk, and eventually to Omsk. After the Perm-Tiumen railway was completed, the northern route supplanted the previously more popular southern one to a considerable extent. In 1888-1891, 70-80 per cent and in 1892-1894 85 per cent

[32] *Ibid.*, p. 167.   [33] See Chapter VI.   [34] Iadrintsev, *loc.cit.*, p. 606.

of the migrants went through Tiumen.[35] The northern route was then utilized in a way something like the following. Starting at some point on the Volga or Kama, the settlers moved on barges towed by steamboats to Perm; then, after the rail trip to Tiumen, they either went on by cart to Ishim or on boats via the Ob tributaries to Tara, Akmolinsk, Tomsk, and finally Yeniseisk, then by carts again to their destination. This route was not extensively used long, however. With the building of the Trans-Siberian Railway it fell into disuse, and most settlers went via the Samara-Zlatoust Railway to the western terminal of the Trans-Siberian at Cheliabinsk. By the time it was built the Trans-Siberian was badly needed for purposes of migration. When migration increased markedly in the 1880's, the ferries in the Ob system were overtaxed and a bad bottleneck developed at Tiumen, the railway setting down migrants much faster than the boats could carry them on.

Before the Siberian Railway, Popov tells us, the migrant moved with his own horse and cart, often loaded with unnecessary belongings chosen for sentimental value; hundreds of these stretched out in a long line on the Vladimir Road.[36] Usually the night was spent under the open sky. Due to bad food and lack of hygiene and medicines, mortality among the migrants reached 10 per cent among adults, 30 per cent among children. Sometimes whole families died, or sometimes only a child or two might be left, who, if fortunate, might be taken along by other merciful travelers.[37]

To deal with such problems, emergencies, and troubles, the government set up "migrant points" in the 1880's. The staff at these points worked mightily but against odds at their task. The Tomsk migration agent loaned a total of 35,000 rubles in the whole decade from 1884 to 1893, at a rate of 3 rubles per needy family.[38] Since almost all of the migrants had real needs, selection among them must have been an unpleasant and difficult process. The Tiumen agent had only slightly more to loan, about 5,000 rubles annually. In order to fill the breach, some private organizations sprang into action. In 1883, on the initiative of Governor Lysogorsky of Tobolsk province, a committee was formed in Tiumen which set about preparing temporary barracks for 700 families and providing some simple forms of medical

[35] *Kolonizatsiia Sibiri*, p. 178.

[36] The Siberian *trakt*, or road, on the route of which the Trans-Siberian Railway was built, was sometimes called the "Vladimirka'' because the ancient route of exiles to Siberia had proceeded from Moscow eastward through the town of Vladimir.

[37] Popov, *loc.cit.*, Vol. VI, pp. 252ff.   [38] Popov, *loc.cit.*, pp. 253-54.

aid. Similar committees were formed in the late 1880's in St. Petersburg and, in Siberia, in Tomsk and Irkutsk.

The Trans-Siberian Railway led to an improvement in the conditions of the journey, above and beyond the fact that there was now continuous rail transportation available. From 1893 on, distributing points for medicine and food were established at such places as Cheliabinsk and Kurgan. By 1895 mortality en route had as a result fallen to 1 per cent of the migrants registered.[39] In 1894 a general migrant fare was introduced on all roads, at the rate of 0.3 kopeks per verst per person, with those under the age of ten traveling free. By 1898 the special rate was reduced to the equivalent of a regular child's third-class ticket. At the beginning of the 1890's, the cost for a Kursk or Tambov family to travel to Tomsk was about 57 rubles, whereas in 1900 an Orel family of average size (3 adults and 2 children) could travel to Tomsk for 14 r. 70 k. on the special fare, while a family of irregular migrants paid 47 r. 80 k. for a trip by fourth-class.[40]

The conditions of travel for the first three decades between Emancipation and the building of the railway were perilous, full of discomfort and danger. It was much more difficult to do in Siberia what migrants were sometimes doing in the Black Sea region, keeping one foot planted in the homeland until they were sure they could make a go of it in the steppe. A journey into Siberia more nearly required cutting ties with a place the settlers might not expect to see again. "Taking the plunge" in this manner, of course, provided no guarantee of success across the Urals, and some returned. Let us notice, however, that because of the distances involved, the unsuccessful in Siberia were labeled "returners," whereas the same category of people in New Russia were simply "defaulters" or "renegers" who did not go through with the bargain.

The economic consequences for the Siberian "returners" were, of course, much worse than for the Black Sea "renegers." The latter had simply rented the lands at home or sold them on condition that repurchase was possible (even though some such agreements were badly drawn and proved unenforceable). But the Siberian "returners" were presumably worse off than if they had never thought of migrating. We need to keep in mind that migration was never, and

[39] *Kolonizatsiia Sibiri*, p. 188. For a description of the functioning of the Tiumen migrant point, see D. Golovachev, "Pereselentsy v. 1892 godu," *Vestnik Evropy*, August 1893.
[40] *Ibid.*, p. 182.

could not be, given the conditions of the Russian peasantry, a carefree and simple adventure. Many migrants perished, vanished, unwept and unsung. One may admire them for risking everything for the sake of a better life. One may observe that every one of them gave the lie to the presumption that peasants were, above most of God's creatures, slaves of habit who always preferred the repetition of familiar miseries to exchanging them for new ones. In order to tell the whole story, however, one would have to calculate not simply the casualties with which the Siberian road was dotted, but the difference between that total and the miseries which the settlers might have suffered if they had not moved. One should also consider the degree to which resettlement relieved the pressure in the villages of the homeland and enabled the stay-at-homes to attack their own problems more successfully.

The Enrollment

What happened to the migrants when they reached their destination? Iadrintsev, writing in 1881, calculates the usual cost of migration as follows: 50-70 rubles for a wagon, 300 rubles for a pair of oxen, 40-50 for enrollment, and 25-50 for home construction. In addition, there was the cost of extra tools and cattle needed for plowing the fertile virgin soil of Siberia; he declares that at least three horses were needed for that purpose rather than the one horse one might expect. The total comes out at 300 to 500 rubles, and Iadrintsev concludes that only the rich peasant could resettle given the requirement of such an outlay.[41] We have observed, however, that poor peasants were able to migrate successfully into New Russia and pay the purchase price of land besides (though often with the help of the Peasant Bank); and it should be clear from our examination of the economic status of the early Siberian migrants that they were on the whole much less than rich.

Iadrintsev was right, however, in emphasizing the difficulties of enrollment. The law of 1889[42] permitted migrants either to enroll in the communes of the old-settlers of Siberia or to establish themselves in new settlements. This merely recognized established practice. By the mid-1880's the government had experienced misgivings about continuing enrollment in old-settler communes.

The root of the difficulty was that no real plan for actual settlement in Siberia existed prior to the time of the Trans-Siberian Railway.

[41] Iadrintsev, loc.cit., p. 612.
[42] See Chapter III.

In 1871 the Siberian Survey was reorganized as the Surveying Section of the Chief Administrations of Western and Eastern Siberia. This was a title disproportionately long compared to its actual accomplishments—which were apparently negligible. Following the founding in Western Siberia of a local Administration of State Domains, on 22 January 1885 the Imperial Council decreed the organization of a special surveying unit with the purpose of allotting state lands in Western Siberia for migrants. From 1885 to 1893 this unit surveyed 146 "portions" (40 in Tobolsk and 106 in Tomsk) totaling 430,000 desiatinas, on which 14,743 males (therefore roughly double that number of people) were installed.[43] This was grossly insufficient to the need, however. By 1891 this unit was devoting itself solely to a scramble to deal somehow with already-arrived migrants, and was quite unable to prepare for those yet to come. The backlog was an important part of the reason for the circular of 6 March 1892, temporarily halting the granting of permissions to migrate to Siberia, and a similar act of 1891 applying to the governor-generalship of the steppe.

Survey or no survey, many migrants took up state lands outside the old-settler villages. From time to time, the authorities were horrified to discover, as did the steppe governor-general in an investigation of 1884, that new settlements had existed some years even in regions where migration had been prohibited by law.[44] For them no enrollment problem existed, and after they had become firmly settled, their status constituted a problem not for themselves but for the authorities, since it was obviously impracticable to try to move them back home.[45]

In the old-settler villages, however, enrollment was a difficult business. Iadrintsev recounts some of the obstacles.[46] His funds often exhausted by the journey, the settler arrived, fatigued, at some village of his choice, whose name he perhaps had not even heard of a few days earlier, still unsure of whether he really wanted to enroll in that particular commune. In order to be enrolled, he had first to send back to his home commune his taxes for three years. In order to obtain the necessary certificate of admission (*priemnyi prigovor*), he had to pay a sum to the commune and also to the township scribe.

[43] *Kolonizatsiia Sibiri*, p. 198.

[44] *Ibid.*, p. 202.

[45] The squatter was likewise a chronically unsolved problem of American migration legislation. "Legally the settler could not occupy land until it had been surveyed and sold at auction, but thousands of settlers occupied land without the formality of purchase" (Riegel, *op.cit.*, p. 81).

[46] Iadrintsev, *loc.cit.*, pp. 606-08.

At best enrollment thus cost 50 rubles, sometimes 100 rubles or more. The settler then had to send back to his old commune the certificate of admission and request of it his certificate of discharge (*uvol'nitel'nyi prigovor*). If the certificate of discharge was lost, as sometimes happened, he might remain unenrolled, waiting, unsure of his legal status or obligations. He might even become a vagrant. It has already been noted that the cost of the certificate of admission had risen sharply from a nominal figure in the 1870's to 50 to 100 rubles in the 1890's, and furthermore that some old-settler villages had not only ceased enrollment but had begun to expel those not enrolled.

It is not fully clear what general conclusion should be drawn from these data. It is apparent that the peasant, on presenting himself at the new commune, was not at all sure what was required of him, and he might be thrown more or less on the mercy of the scribe and elder. Nevertheless, if he were pushed around too much, he might always take up new lands, surveyed or not, in the vicinity.[47] It is likely that he understood that if he and some of his fellows became established, the government would have to come to terms with the new settlement sooner or later, whatever laws were currently on the books.

Where did the migrants settle? From 1885 to 1893, out of 316,600 migrants surveyed, 75 per cent went to Tomsk province, 8 per cent to Tobolsk province, 8 per cent to Yeniseisk province, 1 per cent to Akmolinsk region. The bulk (80 per cent) of the Tomsk immigrants went into the Cabinet lands of the Altai. In Tobolsk province, the Tarsk and Tiukalinsk counties claimed most; in Yeniseisk, Minusinsk county. In the middle 1890's there was a greater scattering of destinations. From 1894 to 1899, of 800,000 reported on, 51 per cent went to Tomsk, 20 per cent to Akmolinsk, 15 per cent to Tobolsk, 9 per cent to Yeniseisk.[48] At this point the frontier of settlement in Siberia begins to take the shape of a huge wedge whose apex is in

---

[47] Considering the fears, warranted or not, with which many old settlers regarded the migrant invasion, it is a wonder that they did not show more hostility and fleece the newcomers more often than they did. Instead, they often sheltered and aided their new neighbors. The duty of Christian charity was part of the peasant culture of Russia, and Siberia had a special tradition of compassion for the traveler. Note, for example, the Siberian folk tale of the penniless chambermaid who becomes a rich woman keeping an inn on the highroad. On a dark and unhospitable night there comes a knock on her door and her sons advise her that strangers await. She replies, "Ah, my dear children, let them in, if they are wayfarers; I I myself was long a wanderer, I am sorry for them all." (Cited in Y. M. Sokolov, *Russian Folklore*, New York, 1950, p. 462.)

[48] *Kolonizatsiia Sibiri*, p. 197.

the Altai region of Tomsk and whose anchor points are in Akmolinsk and Tobolsk. The Altai was ceasing to be an island of migration in advance of the frontier, and was becoming a peninsula.

Success and Failure

Finally, we may ask what sort of fate befell the settlers in Siberia in the 1890's, and how this was reflected in the movement of returners. An investigation of 93,312 new settlers (*novosely*) in Siberia in 1898 revealed a notable improvement in material conditions over that enjoyed at home:

TABLE 8

Comparative Economic Level of Migrants[49]

	AT HOME		IN SIBERIA	
YEAR OF MIGRATION	% of total having horses	No. of des. of land per family	% of total having horses	No. of des. of land per family
1889	83	2.7	94	7.5
1890	85	3.6	94	5.9
1891	82	3.0	94	6.2
1892	81	2.8	96	5.9
1893	79	2.6	94	5.4
1894	78	2.7	94	5.1
1895	72	2.1	88	4.2
1896	74	2.3	90	3.6
1897	85	2.4	97	5.0
1898	81	3.0	93	3.3

Similarly, there was a sizable increase in horned cattle and other farm animals, as well as in the number of agricultural implements owned. The migrants were proportionately better off the longer they had been in Siberia, this trend being noticeable from the migrants of 1889 through 1896. The migrants of 1897 showed a greater improvement relative to those who came earlier, and, as will be seen later, this fact may be attributed to the more extensive governmental assistance provided beginning with that year. What is noteworthy is that improvement in the well-being of the migrants was steady even before governmental aid was extended.

There was a high correlation between the sums of money the settlers brought with them and the extent of tillage achieved in

[49] *Ibid.*, p. 354.

Siberia. Kaufman, in a survey of Tomsk migrants of the period of the 1880's and early 1890's up to 1894, made this clear.[50]

TABLE 9

Extent of Migrant Tillage in Siberia, by Cash Brought

FOR MIGRANTS WHO	THE AVERAGE HOUSEHOLD HAD TILLAGE OF (DES.)	% OF HOUSEHOLDS		
		Sowing Less than 1 Des.	Sowing More than 10 Des.	Having One or No Horse
Brought no money	2.8	35.5	2.7	43.2
" up to 25 r.	3.7	21.1	3.1	31.6
" 25-50 r.	4.8	13.3	8.5	23.4
" 50-100 r.	6.0	5.6	10.9	11.9
" 100-200 r.	7.2	5.9	19.9	11.9
" over 200 r.	9.1	2.2	38.7	7.4

The amount of cash brought, however, was only one indication of the probable degree of success in Siberia. "The most important factor," according to the Committee on the Siberian Railway, was the amount of labor power available in a given family. Kaufman's survey brings this out:[51]

TABLE 10

Extent of Migrant Tillage in Siberia, by Number of Workers per Family

IN MIGRANT FAMILIES	AVERAGE HOUSE-HOLD TILLED (DES.)	THE % OF HOUSEHOLDS	
		Sowing Up to 1 Des.	With One or No Horse
With none or half a worker	1.9	56.7	64.7
1 worker	2.7	33.1	44.5
1½-2½ workers	5.1	13.2	19.8
3 or more	8.7	5.8	5.6

The same thing was observed in a survey of Tobolsk migrants who had come from the end of the 1870's up to 1893.[52] Evidently many families with ready money also had several workers. More strapping sons meant that more cash could be earned for the trip. Even more important, a large family could till more land sooner. For the prospective or actual Siberian migrant, grown children

---

[50] Cited in *ibid.*, p. 357.   [51] *Ibid.*, p. 359.   [52] *Ibid.*, p. 360.

proved to be an asset rather than the problem they had been in overcrowded European Russia.

Those who stayed for long periods in old-settler villages without enrollment were likely not to do so well. In the late 1880's a survey of Yeniseisk showed that such families possessed from two to two and one-half times fewer horses and from one and a half to three times less sown land than the enrolled migrants. By 1893-1894, there existed in the Altai region alone over 150,000 unenrolled migrants, and a survey of these people indicated that their average tillage ran around 4.1 desiatinas per family as against the comparable figure for the new settlers of 11.6.[53]

The relationship between failure to complete enrollment in the new settlement and failure to receive permission to migrate in the first place is not clear. It is probable, however, that the two groups, unenrolled and irregulars, largely overlapped. In any case it was the irregulars who made up a significant percentage of the returners.[54] According to Gurvich, in 1882-1883, 15 out of every 1,000 migrants returned,[55] while in 1896 the percentage rose to 11 per cent and in 1897 to 18 per cent. As we shall observe, the percentage then fell sharply. Out of those returning in 1897, 69 per cent gave as their reason the lack of permission to migrate. Other reasons included lack of economic viability of the situation they had attained in Siberia, death of the head of the family and consequent homesickness, and so on. The conclusion of the Committee on the Siberian Railway was that the majority of cases of returners could be ascribed to "insufficient consciousness of the step they had undertaken."[56] It is obvious that these reasons overlap. Generally, it seems that the more active the government became in the field of migration, the worse was the competitive position into which the "irregulars" were put vis-à-vis the "regulars." Some could overcome this disadvantage, but more could not.

For those who were attracted by the rumors, reports, and letters about opportunity in Siberia, the early wave of migration provided some of the advantages involved in the principle of "first come, first served." Certainly there were also disadvantages in pioneering in an unknown land, for people many of whose ancestors for centuries had lived much the same sort of life in the same spot. Their adventurous spirit had usually not had much recent exercise, and they were pre-

[53] *Ibid.*, p. 361.
[54] See Table 3, p. 34, for the number of returners.
[55] Gurvich, *Pereselenie krest'ian v Sibir'*, p. 83, cited in *ibid.*, p. 365.
[56] *Ibid.*, p. 366.

pared to unlimber it in varying degrees. The early stage of Siberian migration was so unorganized and amorphous that we should use caution in evaluating the statistics. Many struck out into the unknown and failed, others succeeded. We cannot be sure of knowing the total number of either, let alone their individual stories, which must have had all of the diversity of which human beings are capable. It is probable that many thousands moved and prospered while managing to avoid government statisticians at some or all stages. The data which we do have show that hundreds of thousands moved successfully, despite lack of government aid or even government permission. St. Petersburg was shortly to make the decision that since this was so, more settlers might as well be granted both aid and permission.

PART THREE

THE TRANS-SIBERIAN RAILWAY,

1892-1906

CHAPTER V

Kulomzin and the Committee on the Siberian Railway

A Railway to Siberia

The first proposals for railway building in Siberia were made at the time of Count Muraviev-Amursky's preparations for the annexation of the Russian Far East in 1858-1860, when the realization struck home that Russia was acquiring a Pacific coast with some kind of commercial possibilities. In 1857 Muraviev-Amursky ordered one of his offices to chart a carriage route from the Amur to the Bay of Castries on which there could later be built a short railroad line, but nothing came of the idea immediately.[1] In the same year the Ministry of Ways of Communication began to be approached by a number of engineers and financiers, foreign and Russian, who had vague plans for the construction of a transcontinental line. Two successive governors-general of West Siberia, Duhamel and Khrushchev, complained of the inadequacy of transportation.

It was soon assumed that some railway was going to be built, but there was controversy over what route it should follow. During the 1860's a number of government agencies were considering various alternatives: Perm-Tiumen, Perm-Belozersk, Ekaterinburg-Tiumen.[2] The Ural mining interests stoutly defended a northern approach to Siberia, while certain officials with commerce and migration in mind held out for one farther south. The latter alternative, through Cheliabinsk, was selected by the Committee of Ministers as preferable, owing to its "uniting existing railways with the Ural for further continuation to Siberia, and on account of its coincidence with the general direction adopted by the transport trade for many years past"—that is, with the Vladimir road. The southern route was approved by Alexander II in 1875, but action was postponed because of various complications, including the Russo-Turkish War of 1877-1878.

Meanwhile, new lines approached the Siberian border from several directions. Railways reached Orenburg from the south and Ekaterin-

---

[1] Koulomzine, *Le Transsibérien*, pp. 1-2.

[2] A. I. Dmitriev-Mamonov and A. F. Zdziarski, eds., *Guide to the Great Siberian Railway*, transl. by L. Kukol-Yasnopolsky, St. Petersburg, 1900, p. 53ff.

burg from Perm in the north by 1878, and in 1880 a great Volga railway bridge completed a continuous route in European Russia to Orenburg. Nizhny-Novgorod merchants petitioned the Tsar in 1880 to extend the line from Ekaterinburg to Tiumen, and the decision was taken to do so. A Samara-Zlatoust line was completed in 1888. Count Ignatiev, brother of the well-known diplomat, and governor-general of Eastern Siberia, petitioned Alexander III for the construction of lines from Tomsk to Irkutsk and from Baikal to Sretensk, which would unite the western and eastern Siberian water routes. On Ignatiev's report the Tsar noted in his own handwriting: "I have read many reports of the governors-general of Siberia and must own with grief and shame that until now the Government has done scarcely anything towards satisfying the needs of this rich, but neglected country! It is time, high time!"[3]

As the 1890's opened, St. Petersburg was pondering the problems of Asia anew in the light of the opening of the Canadian Pacific Railway, British economic activity in China, and Chinese military and economic activity in Manchuria. It was decided to extend the railway from Zlatoust to Mias, and the terminus of a trans-Siberian line could now be either Mias, Tiumen, or Orenburg. In 1890 a special conference under A. A. Abaza, former Minister of Finance, considered the alternatives. Estimates showed the Mias-Nizhneudinsk route to be cheapest. In addition, this route "traversed the most populated localities of Western Siberia, following the fertile black-earth zone."[4] Once the location of the railway had been decided, the question arose as to which part should be built first. I. A. Vyshnegradsky, Minister of Finance, opposed beginning it from the east, since the Ussuri line would have no "great economic or strategic importance," but favored building in the west, "traversing a more densely populated country." A. Ia. von Hubbenet, Minister of Ways of Communication, defended the Ussuri line for its "political and strategic significance." The final decision was to recommend to the Committee of Ministers that the western and eastern portions be started simultaneously, and the Emperor gave approval in February 1891. On 19 May, in Vladivostok on the way back from a trip to Japan, the Tsarevich Nicholas laid the first stone of the railway.

The Committee on the Siberian Railway

One last effort was made by the partisans of a northern route, even after the Trans-Siberian Railway had been begun, in the spring

[3] Quoted in *ibid.*, p. 56.   [4] *Ibid.*, p. 60.

of 1892. In the Committee of Ministers during May this battle finally came to an end. The railway was to be extended from Mias to Cheliabinsk, and the Trans-Siberian proper would run from there through a point south of Tomsk. S. Iu. Witte, who as newly-appointed Minister of Ways of Communication had been influential in the decisions of May 1892, became Minister of Finance in September of the same year. He was a strong partisan of the Trans-Siberian, as his predecessor Vyshnegradsky was not. In November he reported to the Tsar on the economic aspects of construction of line. This is how Kulomzin describes the contents of the report:

"C'est en particulier sur la colonisation et sur les échanges commerciaux avec l'Extrême Orient que le ministre insistait avec le plus de détails. Il montrait en effet que le mouvement d'émigration qui se faisait de Russie en Sibérie correspondait à la direction historique suivie par la colonisation de la race grand-russe, direction dont le sens était de l'ouest à l'est. En outre, le chemin de fer, étant relié par Samara au centre de la Russie, recueillerait toute la masse des émigrants, pour les transporter dans les parties de la Sibérie qui avaient besoin d'être peuplées. Ce serait là, en même temps, la solution de l'un des problèmes les plus difficiles qu'eut à envisager l'État: l'établissement durable de la partie de la population rurale qui souffrait du manque de terre, dans la Russie centrale."[5]

Witte doubted that the effect of the railway on trade relations would have any more than secondary importance, though he assumed that Siberian commerce would grow through Russian purchase of Chinese tea and silk and export to China of textiles and metal products. The railway would generally contribute to assuring peaceful relations with the Far Eastern nations and the United States, and serve to supply the Pacific fleet. Thus it was the relationship between the railway and migration which Witte emphasized most strongly of all.

Witte recommended that a special commission be named to consider the economic aspects of the Trans-Siberian. The Tsar promptly appointed Count D. Solsky to head one, and the commission's report, approved by Alexander III on 10 December 1892, resulted in the establishment of a standing Committee on the Siberian Railway. Its functions were to administer a special fund simultaneously set up for "auxiliary enterprises" connected with construction of the line, and to consider other questions relating to such enterprises. In a note which Witte sent to Solsky's commission, the "auxiliary enterprises"

[5] Koulomzine, *op.cit.*, pp. 43-44.

were said to be "such as the colonization of the fertile West-Siberian districts in connection with the progress of peasant emigration, the extension of water communication, and the growth of certain branches of mining industry."[6] The actual construction of the railway was entrusted to the Ministry of Ways of Communication. In other words, the Committee on the Siberian Railway was constituted as a committee on migration, and not properly speaking a committee on railways at all.

The importance attached to the committee by Alexander III was made clear by his appointment of the Tsarevich himself as its chairman, and Nicholas II announced at his first meeting, held following his ascension to the throne, that as Emperor he would retain the post. As Gurko reports, "his chairmanship was purely honorary, and it was common knowledge that he exercised no influence upon the decisions of this committee,"[7] but the symbolic importance of his holding the post was considerable. For the actual direction of business, Actual Privy Councillor State-Secretary Anatoly N. Kulomzin was named Administrator of the Affairs of the Committee and chairman of a special drafting commission in the Committee.

In working out measures to cope with the new conditions which the railway would introduce into migration, Kulomzin was given a clear go-ahead signal by Nicholas II himself. The new Emperor stated in the Committee on 8 March 1895 that one might treat peasant migration "without any particular fears," and that government policy ought to strive to give migration a more "conscious and . . . regular" character.[8] The grounds on which the Committee echoed this pronouncement were somewhat curious. Migration out of the provinces with a land shortage could not, it was said, do any economic damage because the level of migration was insignificant in comparison to the population increase—which amounted to a million and a half per year. One might have added that at the existing level migration could provide little direct economic benefit either. In such declarations it is sometimes difficult to distinguish confusion in economics from the circumspectness of bureaucrats. In any case, the Committee stated clearly that migration was politically and economically advantageous for Siberia.

At the same sitting of the Committee, the Emperor recognized

[6] Paraphrased in Dmitriev-Mamonov, *op.cit.*, p. 64.

[7] V. I. Gurko, *Features and Figures of the Past*, edited by J. E. Wallace Sterling, Xenia Joukoff Eudin, and H. H. Fisher, transl. by Laura Matveev, Stanford, 1939, p. 13

[8] *Kolonizatsiia Sibiri*, p. 121.

"the extreme undesirability of the compulsory return of migrants to the homeland, even though they had left their places of permanent habitation irregularly." The Committee was thus given the highest backing for a policy which would seek to regularize migration, but also to treat irregular migration as a phenomenon which did not necessarily contravene state aims but was even capable of being reconciled with them. In consequence, the Committee put on its docket in 1895 the question of changes in the law of 1889.

Meanwhile, the construction of the railway was proceeding rapidly. The Ekaterinburg-Cheliabinsk branch, connecting the Siberian Railway with the Perm-Tiumen line, was opened for regular traffic almost simultaneously with the first great section of the Siberian Railway proper, the West-Siberian line (1,329 versts, from Cheliabinsk to the Ob bridge near Krivoshchekovo), in October 1896.[9] The mid-Siberian line, 1,715 versts from the Ob to Innokentievskaia (near Irkutsk), was opened in 1898, along with the branch line to Tomsk, and the Irkutsk-Baikal line in 1899. From Mysovaia, on the eastern shore of Lake Baikal, to Sretensk, at the terminus of the Shilka-Amur waterway, for 1,035 versts, ran the Trans-Baikal line, opened in 1900. The Ussuri line from Vladivostok to Khabarovsk was opened by November 1897. Meanwhile the Chinese Eastern Railway, crossing Manchuria from Sretensk via Kaidalovo on the Chinese frontier to Vladivostok, was begun in 1897 and the branch line from Harbin to Dairen (known as the South Manchurian Railway) in 1898. The transport situation in Russian Asia had been revolutionized from one end to the other in less than a decade.

Accordingly the Committee had no time to waste in deciding what ought to be done about the railway's "auxiliary enterprises." A. S. Ermolov, head of the newly-reorganized Ministry of Agriculture and State Domains,[10] visited West Siberia in 1895[11] and again in 1898 on an inspection trip concerned with preparation of land for migrants. Apparently Ermolov's recommendations came to nothing. Gurko reports that Ermolov as minister "left Russian agriculture, about which he had so much information and which was so dear to him, in the same undeveloped condition in which he found

[9] Dmitriev-Mamonov, *op.cit.*, table on p. 79 and *passim*.

[10] This was a rather confusing branch of the government. The Ministry of State Domains, organized under Count Kiselev, existed from 1837-1894; it was reorganized as the Ministry of Agriculture and State Domains, 1894-1905; in May 1905 it was again reorganized as the Chief Administration of Land Settlement and Agriculture.

[11] In 1895 the Director of the Department of State Landed Domains of the same ministry, Tikheev, also made a trip for the same purpose.

it." Gurko could not resist observing: "On a door in the ministry offices was a sign: 'Office of Sand Dunes and Gullies,' which might well have been applied to the whole ministry."[12]

The Inspection Trip of Kulomzin

Kulomzin was a very different sort of man from Ermolov. In him, Pavlovsky remarks, the cause of Siberia found "an enthusiastic and capable protagonist."[13] Born in 1838, scion of an ancient gentry family of Kostroma, Kulomzin had gone from the St. Petersburg law faculty to hold a series of government posts. His record suggests not so much a distinguished and gifted personality as a serious and conscientious bureaucrat, though Legras attributes to him "une des plus belles intelligences que je connaisse dans le grand monde russe." Legras saw him and traveled on his special train with him in Siberia in 1897, at a time when his report on his inspection trip of the previous year had just been published. Of the report Legras declared, "on en parle, depuis un mois, dans toute la Sibérie."[14]

Before Kulomzin set out for Siberia, the drafting commission which he headed had already, on 15 April 1896, rushed into effect a set of rules on the organization of migrant allotments along the Siberian Railway, and on extending the jurisdiction of institutions on peasant affairs to the provinces of West Siberia. The rules of 15 April also dealt with the question of irregular migrants. In 1876, 1881, 1889, and 1892 the government had been compelled to sanction irregular migration, giving the self-starters the same right of settlement as the regulars. Following the law of 1889—despite its provision threatening to return irregulars to the homeland—the proportion of irregulars continued to rise, and in 1894 reached 78 per cent of the whole movement. It then fell considerably; in 1895 it was 24 per cent; 1896, 36 per cent; 1897, 34 per cent; 1898, 44 per cent.[15] In 1894 the question of the irregulars was considered in the Committee on the Siberian Railway and those of the years 1893-1894 were permitted to settle on state lands and to receive state aid. In the rules of 15 April 1896 it was openly announced that irregulars might settle on the designated "migrant plots" (*pereselencheskie uchastki*), though only to the extent that there remained room after regulars had been taken care of. In order to qualify for the migrant plots, the irregulars had to assume all tax arrears, were not exempt from

[12] Gurko, *op.cit.*, p. 70.
[13] Pavlovsky, *op.cit.*, p. 163.
[14] Jules Legras, *En Sibérie*, Paris, 1899, pp. 205-06.
[15] *Kolonizatsiia Sibiri*, p. 162.

recruitment, and were not allowed to use the special migrant fares on the railway.[16] Nevertheless this policy in effect turned them into a sort of second-class regulars despite the fact that they entirely ignored the law.

Kulomzin went to Siberia in the summer of 1896, traveling 2,200 versts by water and 5,000 versts by road, visiting the chief medical and supply points for migrants en route and personally inspecting 135 settlements while sending his aides to an additional 64. His purpose was to study the "causes which gave rise to the departure of migrants from the homeland and the conditions which surrounded departure, to ascertain the needs of these settlers en route, to become acquainted with the several aspects of their initial establishment and their life in the new homeland, with the character of the lands on which at present the new settlers establish their household, and likewise with the localities which might serve as a reserve for future colonization."[17] He accordingly summarized his findings under three headings: the departure and travel of the migrants, their installation, and the ground for future migration.

With respect to departure, he inquired first of all into the reasons behind it. After asking officials and "hundreds" of migrants, he was left in no doubt that lack of land was the "chief cause of resettlement." Noting that both peasants who had nothing but garden plots at home and those who had as many as 8 desiatinas of allotment land gave the same reason, he remarked tartly that land shortage was "purely subjective."[18] However, he conceded that a majority of the migrants doubtless needed more land or even had none at all.

He observed that state aid was not a prerequisite to success in Siberia. He encountered many settlements dating from the 1880's, when no state assistance for home construction was available at all. He even hinted that the introduction of state aid had made matters worse, as a flood of exaggerated rumors of the extent of the assistance available had in recent years evoked an outpouring of "poorer and more ignorant people" into the migrant stream. This element he regarded with an ambivalent mixture of pride and alarm:

"The element migrating at present, that is, its nucleus, appears to me to consist of the direct spiritual descendants of those Russians who in the sixteenth and seventeenth centuries went to the frontiers

---

[16] *Ibid.*, p. 166.

[17] *V sepoddanneishii otchet Stats-Sekretaria Kulomzina po poezdke v Sibir' dlia oznakomleniia s polozheniem pereselencheskago dela*, 2 vols., St. Petersburg, 1896, Vol. I, Foreword, p. I. The report is dated 28 October 1896.

[18] *Ibid.*, p. 2.

of the Moscow State, into the steppe, to the Don, to the Iaik, to Siberia, settled there, created from their own ranks our Cossackry, everywhere consolidated Russian dominion and spread Russian culture. . . . [On the one hand enterprising and fierce in the face of adversity, on the other they were] unable and unwilling to reconcile themselves with a certain lawful order and the constantly growing force of legality in European Russia."[19]

Kulomzin's concern about the character of the newest settlers was reflected in his assertion that the migration of 1896 was exceeding the "actual demand" to move. He believed that rumors had done much of the harm. He was annoyed that the circulars of 1892 and 1894, first halting permissions to migrate, then restoring them while threatening irregulars with legal action, had often been interpreted by the peasants in exactly the opposite sense, or entirely ignored. Such misunderstandings would continue, he feared, "until our villagers learn to understand what they read."[20] It was common knowledge, he said, that the magazines of the intelligentsia usually dwelt on the miseries of migration, but few read them. Popular pamphlets, on the other hand, painted the whole business in much too bright colors, and the villagers were influenced by them.[21] The pamphlets, Kulomzin complained, would warn the migrants to be cautious, then would blurt out that Siberia would hold sixty million people easily! In the guise of simply reporting facts, pamphlets would ignore the law on migration and note that the peasant settlers usually migrated on passports which had to be renewed annually, and were often so poor that they brought little or nothing with them.

Kulomzin lamented that the peasants treated the land captains in the same way as they treated the pamphlets. If those officials advised that it was all right to go on one's passport, the peasant departed straightaway. However, if they advised awaiting permission, the peasant obtained a passport on the sly, sold out, and left, even if less confidently. Such action was natural, since the peasants knew from letters that irregulars did get established in Siberia. Kulomzin wrote bitterly that the peasants behaved toward the land captain "as if he were unsympathetic to their resettlement and was working hand in glove with their landowner neighbors who feared the rise of wages resulting from the departure of migrants."[22] The land

[19] *Ibid.*, p. 6.
[20] *Ibid.*, p. 15.
[21] He cited as his horrible example N. K. Istomina, *Sibir' i pereselentsy*, Izdanie Khar'kovskago obshchestva rasprostraneniia v narode gramotnosti, 1892.
[22] *Vsepoddanneishii otchet Kulomzina*, p. 19.

captain, for his part, was in a very difficult spot. Supposing, wrote Kulomzin, that he refused to send to the Siberian authorities certificates of discharge for irregulars who had already arrived there, and then got from the Siberian authorities a copy of the Imperial order (of 1892) to enroll all such people on free state lands! In such cases the land captain did not know how he should treat passport migration, and he might question whether petitioning for a travel permit was really necessary after all. Some of the concrete difficulties of migration policy emerge very clearly from this part of the report, and such "hypothetical" instances have the ring of truth.

The list of reasons for the "inflated demand" for migration was not yet exhausted. The fact that the Tsar himself was chairman of the Committee on the Siberian Railway gave rise to talk in the villages that the "Tsar-batiushka [Little Father] summons us" to migrate.[23] Reduced railway fares encouraged anyone to get up and go. Local authorities forwarded petitions for permission to migrate without checking the actual need sufficiently. It appeared that migrants from Viatka and Perm, so near the Urals, did not even bother to try to petition; they simply left.

The economic circumstances of departure were reported in some detail. Usually, Kulomzin wrote, the migrant sold out to other peasants of his own village, often to his relatives.[24] Since it was usually a quick transaction, he seldom got full value, and more often than not obtained only a small part of even the agreed-upon price in cash. Thus he might appear in Siberia carrying promissory notes for 1,000 rubles or more, which he could collect only with difficulty, calling on the Siberian authorities for help in doing so. The next step was obtaining the travel permit—or ought to be. When the permit was delivered, "local authorities" (evidently the land captains) might demand that the migrant leave at once, sometimes forcing him to sell out within nine days. Furthermore, once the permit had been received from the provincial authorities, the land captain might inexplicably hold it up, and then the peasant might simply doctor his passport on the sly and leave. Often the permit itself proved in error, directing the migrant to places closed to migration. In some cases one permit was drawn up for several relatives living separately, thus creating a problem of who was entitled to the migrant loan.

The conditions of the actual journey had improved somewhat. Earlier the usual route had been via Nizhny-Novgorod, thence by barges towed by steamboat to Perm, then to Tiumen via rail; then

23 *Ibid.*, p. 22.   24 *Ibid.*, pp. 32-33.

it was either horse-cart to Ishim, steamboat to Tarsk or Akmolinsk, or towed barge to Tomsk. The Trans-Siberian Railway had eliminated most of these transfers, depending on the destination, though of course a journey by cart was still necessary from the railway to the actual plot. Most migrants now reached the Trans-Siberian at Cheliabinsk via the Samara-Zlatoust line. Their only complaint about the railway was the handling of baggage. Kulomzin saw many families waiting for their baggage at Cheliabinsk, Kurgan, and other medical and supply points for a period of two to three weeks.

These points, established in 1893, were operating with success. Hot soup and provisions were sold at subsidized prices and in case of extreme need distributed free. Medical care was provided, and overland travelers were furnished transport. However, Kulomzin noted some malfunctionings. The Cheliabinsk point had been fairly overrun in the spring of 1896. By the middle of May some 15,000 migrants had piled up, and only swift emergency action by the Ministry of Ways of Communication had mobilized rolling stock sufficient to carry them onward. When Kulomzin arrived at the beginning of June, 4,500 were there, all sheltered, the sick all accommodated either in the hospital or in tents. Work on additional new buildings was proceeding rapidly, and when Kulomzin passed through on the return journey in September the migrant point was almost unrecognizable.[25] Up to September 1896, 167,756 migrants had passed through the point.

In Kulomzin's eyes the chief merit of the migrant points was that they kept up the physical strength of the settlers. At the ten points in operation the death rate was only .65 per cent. Certain new points were planned for summer operation only, but Kulomzin declared that in view of the great need then prevailing, year-round maintenance was "most highly desirable."[26] The migrant points cared for more than physical needs. Their managers could furnish up to 50 rubles en-route assistance, acted as a clearinghouse for information from peasant captains[27] as to the location of available free land, and advised settlers how to reach it and what officials to apply to for enrollment. Such a function, one should note, indicated that the

[25] *Ibid.*, p. 42.

[26] *Ibid.*, p. 46. On the copy of the report used by this writer, someone apparently familiar with Siberian conditions of the time has written extensive marginal notations in Russian script (old alphabet). At this point he writes and underlines, "unconditionally necessary."

[27] *Ibid.*, p. 51. "Peasant captain" refers to the *krest'ianskii nachal'nik*, the Siberian analogue of the land captain of European Russia.

travel permits, which were supposed to give the settlers' destination, were very often ignored.

Kulomzin next undertook to describe what happened to the migrants on arrival. He admitted frankly that before the time of the Committee on the Siberian Railway, the actual process of installation took place in very haphazard fashion. Often newly organized migrant villages came as a surprise to the authorities who discovered them. For example, in Minusinsk county of Yeniseisk province, surveyors had only begun to operate, on the instance of the local Chamber of the Treasury, in 1896. Therefore the overwhelming majority of all settlements in the region were irregular.

The process of installation on a plot of land (*vodvorenie*) was important in that from the moment it occurred, the migrant acquired the right to receive aid for housing and food and exemptions of various kinds. Installation was a rather formal ceremony. The peasant captain personally, attended by a priest, was supposed to accompany the settler to the selected plot and there read aloud appropriate passages of legislation and indicate meets and bounds. Probably the captain often did not do so, but merely sent the settler off to the township office equipped with various kinds of documentary baggage; for Kulomzin had to insist sharply that he ought to go to the plot in person, in order to preserve fire regulations in house construction. Forest fires might indeed be a danger, but Kulomzin probably had broader considerations of state in mind as well. It was highly undesirable to pass the migrant along from bureaucratic hand to hand, only at the last to have him ignore the whole business and set up his homestead at will. Nevertheless such final neglect obviously occurred all too frequently.

The final stage of settlement, following installation, was called enrollment (*perechislenie* or *prichislenie*). "Installation" did not end ties with the homeland, and the migrant remained liable for taxes levied there. Only on enrollment in the new village did this tie come to an end. Enrollment fixed the peasant's residence unless he should again obtain a certificate of discharge and a certificate of admission from his newly projected destination. However, Kulomzin indicated that legality was no more secure at this stage than at earlier ones. After enrollment many moved on again illegally. For example, 59 families from Penza in one settlement of Omsk county of Akmolinsk region petitioned for permission to move on to Kokchetav county, and were denied it; yet 53 moved on anyway, abandoning their just-completed houses. Of course this was hard on the remaining villagers, Kulomzin noted, since they were bound by the mutual guarantee for taxation. Still, in most cases other settlers were waiting to take up the abandoned land—although, he hastened to add, this was illegal because the land belonged to those who had moved on.[28] In order to put an end to such horrendous successions of illegal acts, Kulomzin could only recommend swift enrollment. The process had been made easier by the law of 15 April 1896, and Kulomzin rejoiced that the number of unenrolled migrants was then significant only in Tomsk province. This would have been more reassuring if Tomsk had not been in fact the center of gravity of the whole Siberian migration.

Actually the instances of irregular settlement which Kulomzin reported were not in Tomsk at all. On the mining estate on the river Irbi in Minusinsk county, for example, the owner had been first the state, then certain merchants, then an official's widow, then the state again. From somewhere had come peasants inhabiting eight villages who paid no communal levies except for transport, and who had no village elders. Other squatters had come from Tambov, exploiting this rich area "without any kind of legal rights." For twenty-five years the inhabitants had paid no taxes, which Kulomzin thought had a "demoralizing influence" on neighboring settlements and especially on the youth raised under such circumstances.[29] One can picture Kulomzin and the governor-general of Irkutsk, who encountered this phenomenon together on the tour of inspection, shaking their heads over it. At the time of the tour the governor-general named village elders, and it seemed "desirable" to confirm the title of the settlers and to make them pay taxes. Similar conditions were also said to have been found in Akmolinsk, where peasant agents did not yet exist, and elsewhere than Minusinsk in Yeniseisk province.

At the moment, Kulomzin reported that the new settler had to spend something like 160 rubles to get established—40 for his house, 80 for two horses and a cart, 15 for a cow, 5 for a plow, 20 for a sledge, harness, and so forth.[30] The average government loan ran around 60-70 rubles per family. Kulomzin thought this was too much, though he believed the time of granting the loan ought to be speeded up from the usual four-to-six-week delay. The settler was able to wait three years before starting to repay the loan, at the rate of a tenth of the principal per year, the loan being interest-free. Kulomzin felt that three years was too soon for most settlers to begin repayment.

[28] *Ibid.*, p. 56. [29] *Ibid.*, p. 59.
[30] *Ibid.*, p. 65. Compare Iadrintsev's figures for the earlier period, Chapter IV, pp. 98-100.

Recalling that at the same time half of the regular state taxes and the township and village levies had to be paid—making around 13-18 rubles per family—he counselled a longer interval. In view of the need for money occasioned by all these payments, one may be surprised at his statement that in Siberia there apparently were no "kulaks," such as in European Russia, where some had obtained such control over their neighbors' lives.[31]

There were a few miscellaneous remarks which Kulomzin felt appropriate. He found that the old-settlers got along on the whole remarkably well with the migrants who had erupted, often inconveniently, into their midst. He attributed this to the fact that the old-settlers were used to newcomers, whose appearance was the rule rather than the exception in Siberian society, although of course not in such numbers as recently. He regarded the 15-desiatina norm as correct, though he admitted that "some who have not seen" Siberian conditions for themselves had attacked it.[32] The implication seems to be that one needed to see fair-sized peasant farms to be convinced that any good could come of them, and in European Russia one did not see them. He felt that the whole impact of the migrants on Siberia was a good one, since they brought a higher culture. It was they who first sowed buckwheat and millet; churches were more frequent among the migrants than the old-settlers; and so forth.

Kulomzin's third and last point of inquiry related to the extent of the remaining area suitable for colonization, a point which had been mooted in the deliberations of the Committee on the Siberian Railway. Some of his findings sounded quite as breathtaking as the cheap migrant pamphlets to which he had objected.[33] In Tarsk county of Tobolsk province alone, there had been opened for migration, by the rules of 13 June 1893, an area which included over 4,500,000 desiatinas in the Irtysh basin. In Tomsk province there remained great expanses of free land on both sides of the Vladimir Road, including the Baraba steppe, the Mariinsk taiga. In the Baraba steppe 4 million desiatinas could be converted by drainage into cultivable land, in the Mariinsk taiga over 2 million desiatinas were open. In four counties of Yeniseisk province there were 18 million desiatinas of unoccupied land; in four counties of Irkutsk, 22 million. Much of the latter land was not fit for tillage, but a considerable portion appeared cultivable.

---

[31] The word *kulak* is obviously used here to refer to village usurer. On the difficulties of this term, see my article, "Was Stolypin in Favor of Kulaks?" in *American Slavic and East European Review*, Vol. XIV, No. 1, February 1955.

[32] *Ibid.*, p. 109.   [33] *Ibid.*, p. 134ff.

In Akmolinsk when one subtracted, from a total of 47 million desiatinas, some 2 million in the hands of Cossacks, less than 1 million for peasants, 10 million for the so-called Hungry Steppe, and 15 million for desert lakes and salt flats, still 19 million remained. In this vast, partly fertile region almost the size of France, there lived barely over half a million people, of whom the Kirghiz made up 68 per cent.[34] Obviously many more settlers could be accommodated, Kulomzin wrote, though the interests of the Kirghiz ought to be carefully considered. Part of the reason they had stayed nomads was the obligations, including the specially dreaded military service, which they would assume by becoming farmers, and Kulomzin felt some corrective measures could be taken.

While the reserves for future colonization seemed quite inexhaustible to anyone reading the report, Kulomzin fell between two stools in assaying the amount of land actually ready for occupation. "I do not dare to assert positively that in Siberia the places immediately suitable for habitation are many, but likewise I cannot say that such places are few."[35] His estimate was that 1,109,625 desiatinas were ready for immediate settlement.

His overall recommendations were not extensive or startling, and they concentrated on his chief bugbear, irregular migration. Irregulars, he said, should be forbidden to take the newly surveyed migrant plots, although the law of 15 April 1896 sanctioned exactly this practice. In his judgment irregulars might be accepted into old-settler communes on the basis of certificates of admission, even without presenting certificates of discharge from the old communes. If they could obtain the former, Kulomzin thought, they might be granted loans. He justified this recommendation on the grounds that in many places in Siberia old-settlers retained far above the 15-desiatina norm of holding. His last words were in recapitulation of his favorite notion of family scouting, as one of the chief means of reducing irregular migration.[36]

The Results of Kulomzin's Recommendations

Out of the report and out of the experience of Kulomzin's Siberian journey came several significant changes in legislation and administration of migration policy. By a law of 2 December 1896, a special Resettlement Administration (*Pereselencheskoe Upravlenie*) was organized in the Ministry of Interior. The new bureau took over

[34] *Ibid.*, pp. 165-72. The "Kirghiz" of that period are latterly called Kazakhs; "Kara-Kirghiz" was the name given to the people today known as Kirghiz.
[35] *Ibid.*, p. 177.   [36] *Ibid.*, p. 187.

some of the work formerly handled by the Land Section (*Zemskii Otdel*) of the Interior Ministry, which had been organized in 1858.[37] V. I. Gippius became the first chief of the new administration, the rising bureaucratic star A. V. Krivoshein his assistant. Its functions were defined as supervision of the granting of permissions to migrate and in special cases actually granting them, management of the process of installation of the migrants, disposition of the credits allotted for migration affairs, and preliminary work on all legislation dealing with migration—thus relieving the drafting commission of the Committee on the Siberian Railway of the last function. In order to discharge these functions it was to set up a corps of local agents to operate both in Siberia and in the provinces of heavy migration. This was done, and furthermore the number of "officials on peasant affairs" was increased, the latter having been assigned since 1893 the additional task of overseeing the installation of migrants at their destination.

The establishment of the Resettlement Administration was accompanied by a series of other measures designed to encourage migration. The rules of 15 April 1896 had recognized the practice of "scouting" (*khodachestvo*) as a right of prospective migrants.[38] Scouts chosen from the ranks of the migrants themselves and approved by the appropriate administrative organs were permitted to choose places fit for settlement and to hold them for two years. The scouts were granted the same exemptions to which the migrants themselves were entitled. As a result of Kulomzin's recommendations, these rules were extended by a rescript to the Siberian Railway Committee on 7 December 1896. By its provisions "family scouting" (that is, the sending of a scout by a single family rather than by a large group) was permitted as a temporary measure, and those families whose scouts had already been sent and who had chosen lots in Siberia were to be given permission to migrate without delay. As we have already observed, the effect of these measures was to diminish irregular scouting sharply and speedily. Whereas in 1896 the proportion of irregular scouts was 83 per cent, in 1897 it fell to 23 per cent.[39] It seems that the practice of "family scouting" was taken up with especial eagerness in the western provinces; out of the scouts sent from this region in 1897, only 10 per cent were irregulars. From one west-

[37] See Gurko, *op.cit.*, for many observations on the Land Section, especially its work from 1902-1906, when Gurko was chief. The law establishing the Resettlement Administration is 3 *P.S.Z.* 13,464.
[38] *Kolonizatsiia Sibiri*, p. 167.
[39] *Ibid.*, p. 169.

ern province, Vitebsk, the irregulars fell in 1898 to 1.7 per cent, whereas *all* Vitebsk scouts of 1896 were irregulars.

It appears that Kulomzin had by way of the practice of scouting driven close to the roots of the problem which he, and the government for many years previous, had sought to solve. As family scouting was encouraged and aided, the effect was to diminish irregular migration in general. In the provinces of the non-black-earth region, from which irregulars constituted 91 per cent of the 1896 total, the proportion fell to 52 per cent in 1897 as the proportion of scouts for the same area rose from 18 per cent to 49 per cent. In Vitebsk province the changes we have observed in scouting were accompanied by a fall in the proportion of irregular migrants from 100 per cent in 1896 to 17 per cent in 1897 and 1.6 per cent in 1898. On the other hand, the highest percentages of irregular migrants were given by the areas where irregular scouting predominated.[40] In 1898 those provinces were Samara, Ufa, Viatka, Perm, and some others, forming a north-south strip on the edge of Siberia from which without doubt the crossing of the Urals seemed a much simpler matter than from Vitebsk, requiring no government aid. Kulomzin's measures applied to Samara quite as much as to Vitebsk, but no legislation could eliminate the effect of varying distances from the frontier.

Thus in general "family scouting" proved a successful idea. In 1898, 93 per cent of all scouts registered in Cheliabinsk, at the western terminus of the new railway, were "family scouts." However, the government's favorable attitude to scouting in its new form was influenced by the fact that there was a high percentage of failures by scouts to locate suitable lands, which the Siberian Railway Committee cited as "the best proof of the circumspection of the scouts and their conscientious attitude to their complex task."[41] In other words, scouting served to check the unimpeded flow of settlers. The Committee report states plainly that the constant extension of the scope of migration legislation from 1861 to 1900 was "a consequence of the constantly rising number of peasants who had moved to new places irregularly."[42] Since it had proved hopeless to forbid irregular migration by law, it was encouraging to see that some scouts, supported and encouraged by the government, would decide of their own free will against bringing their families to Siberia.

Kulomzin had shown by his own interrogations of migrants entering Siberia in 1896 that irregular migration was usually prompted,

[40] *Ibid.*, pp. 169-70. [41] *Ibid.*, p. 170.
[42] *Ibid.*, p. 127. Compare Lensky's conclusions, in Chapter III, p. 81.

not so much by an irrational desire to avoid contact with authority, as by unsuccessful attempts to obtain the competitive advantages which regular permission provided. Of the irregulars Kulomzin questioned, only 18 per cent had decided from the first to move at their own risk, confident of installation along with the regulars. The majority had tried the legal route and gave up only after various frustrations; 55 per cent of the irregulars gave as their reason delay in obtaining permission. Other reasons were refusal of permission, coming after the peasant had already sold out, which was ignored; or refusal of permission not to the migrant family in question, but to other families which had petitioned jointly with it and with which its own dealings had become entangled. A more efficient system of permissions might clearly serve as a means of reducing irregular migration.

The granting of permissions to migrate to the state lands of cis-Baikalian Siberia was divided between the Ministry of Interior and the Ministry of Agriculture and State Domains, so that the needs of both the homeland and Siberia would be taken into account, but the division of authority had occasioned some delays. Accordingly, in 1896 supervision of permissions was entrusted exclusively to the Interior Ministry, on the grounds that migrant plots already existed in quantity in the area of the Siberian Railway and that in future by existing law such plots would be under this ministry.[43] In case of need, however, the ministry could decentralize action to governors-general and to provincial institutions on peasant affairs. Provincial officials had been entrusted with granting permissions to migrate to the Amur General Government by the law of 18 June 1892.

Permissions for the Altai region crown lands had been given only by the Chief Administration of the region, but by rescript of the Siberian Railway Committee of 27 April 1896 this function too had been transferred to the Ministry of Interior, to be coordinated with the Ministry of the Imperial Court.

Another sort of measure which, if it did not necessarily bring about a lower rate of irregular migration, at least tended to reduce hardship, was the provision of accurate information for settlers. In its circular of 1894, which renewed the suspended issuance of permissions, the Ministry of Interior, while threatening irregulars with legal punishment, still recommended the best time of departure and gave other information quite as useful to irregulars as to regulars—

[43] *Ibid.*, p. 176.

perhaps more so, as the government tried to orient the regulars individually. Altogether, Kulomzin reported, "the peasant population of European Russia had a quite definite, although sometimes distorted, idea of all those measures having in view assistance to Siberian migrants."[44] It seemed that somehow information at the disposal of local authorities or the reading public was seeping down to the peasant class aside from what regular channels reached township or village. The Ministry of Interior accordingly undertook to furnish the land captains and other local officials special handbooks containing migration legislation, a short description of the provinces and regions of Siberia, and also the publication of the Chancellery of the Committee of Ministers called "Travel Routes for Migrants." There were short informational articles inserted in *Village Messenger* (*Sel'skii Vestnik*). All of the necessary data were included in a popular brochure called *Siberian Resettlement*, of which 400,000 copies were distributed to county zemstvo boards, and county and provincial institutions on peasant affairs, for sale to the peasants at the price of 1½ kopeks.[45] In 1897 the Resettlement Administration undertook to publish a series of similar booklets, one type designed for local officials, the other for the use of the migrants themselves or of their scouts.

Additional circulars of the Ministry of Interior aimed at reducing cases of over-hasty liquidation of peasant properties prior to migration, avoiding the choice of autumn or some other unsuitable time to migrate, and coping with difficulties with the travel permit (*prokhodnoe svidetel'stvo*)—a document which certified the bearer's right to migrate during a period of two years and which contained instructions on travel and enrollment at destination. Furthermore, communes departure from which would "assist the raising of the level of prosperity of the remaining members" were authorized to "participate in the expenditures" of the prospective migrants.[46] This provision may seem puzzling until it is learned that in 1896, for example, several provincial officials demanded that prospective migrants produce proof of possession of 300 rubles cash prior to setting out (although these orders were apparently circumvented rather easily).[47]

Aid to the migrants was plainly now governmental policy, and it took many forms. Appropriations for loans were raised from

---

[44] Paraphrased in *ibid.*, p. 174.
[45] *Sibirskoe pereselenie*, St. Petersburg, 1896.
[46] *Kolonizatsiia Sibiri*, p. 177.
[47] *Ibid.*, p. 160.

20,000 to 120,000 rubles from 1890 to 1896.[48] Migrant agents established medical and food points in the regions of new settlement. Churches and schools were built by outlays from the special fund of Alexander III set up for the purpose. A special fund for charity to migrants encountering unforeseen need was established, and so forth.

The problem of allotting land to individual migrant families was tackled at an early stage of the work of the Siberian Railway Committee. By 13 June 1893 there had been issued temporary rules for the organization of migrant plots. By their provisions there was retained the generous norm already established of 15 desiatinas per adult male. Work of setting aside land for migrants was to consider the interests of the Siberian old-settlers, so as not to invade areas where the land was less than 15 desiatinas, or to tamper with their regular tillage, gardens, and so on. Especial care was to be shown in relation to squatters (*zaimshchiki*), whose lands should be included in migrant plots only when unavoidable, and even in that case the squatter should be allowed to remain in place if his former commune would not allow him to return to take up land there.

On the basis of these rules actual work began in 1893 by parties on the ground.[49] The usual way of organizing migrant plots was to form several tens or hundreds of plots of individual size (*dushevye doli*) into one general enclosure (*otrub*). A village would thereby be constituted wherein each family's land would be in one single plot, but the farm buildings remained together in the village.[50] Although, according to the law of 1889, the new settlers might choose either communal or household tenure, even those migrants from areas where the latter prevailed sometimes preferred to take up land under communal tenure in Siberia "since the latter presents certain advantages at the time of initial settlement under conditions which are difficult for the migrants."[51] Whatever the exact meaning of this phrase, it was found in the Tara region of Siberia in 1899 that numerous peasants who had settled on migrant plots wanted to divide their land into household lots. So the Siberian Railway Committee recognized it as desirable to meet the demands of those migrants who, "after being installed under communal tenure, subsequently desired,

---

[48] *Aziatskaia Rossiia*, Vol. I, p. 462.

[49] The rules are 3 *P.S.Z.* 9,804. See *Kolonizatsiia Sibiri*, p. 231, for work done.

[50] An *otrub* was a farm where the buildings remained in the village, though the land was consolidated in one plot; a *khutor* was one wherein the buildings stood on the consolidated plot.

[51] *Kolonizatsiia Sibiri*, p. 232. For further discussion of the Siberian commune, see Chapter x.

after familiarizing themselves with local conditions, to establish special *khutor* plots." It appears that the distinction between "communal" and "household" tenure referred to was not necessarily that between redistributive and non-redistributive practice, but simply between settlements with houses on their land and houses together in a central location. The Committee decided on the basis of the Tara situation to establish special rules on "household and *khutor*" settlement.

The total area of land organized in 1893-1898 either as migrant plots or reserve areas for migration totaled 6,678,000 desiatinas, on which about 730,000 people could be settled. Actually the Committee report of 1900 gives the total number settled as 160,264, or about 64.8 per cent of the total prepared migrant plots (not counting reserve areas).[52] The migrants were right on the heels of the working parties in Akmolinsk and Tobolsk, where the percentage of prepared plots taken up was 80.9 and 75.9 respectively, and the total of settlers occupying them in the two areas was 94,276. In Tomsk and Yeniseisk the proportion of plots taken up was 58.4 and 55.5, the total of settlers about 31,000 each. In Irkutsk only 18.3 per cent were occupied. It seems that the government direction of surveying had not fully grasped the fact that it was the west where work was urgently needed, while the east could wait.

Certain changes in enrollment procedures were forthcoming. By the law of 15 April 1896 the Chamber of the Treasury (*kazennaia palata*)—on receiving passports or other papers of migrants from the hands of the peasant agents, so that their actual presence was proved —without demanding certificates of discharge from the former commune might enroll the migrants immediately. Such action was final unless the peasant was subsequently revealed to have been under court charges or sentence or if it was shown that the members of his family were not provided for. This law applied to migrant plots only. Kulomzin had viewed this provision as harmful, but had nevertheless recommended that the same method of enrollment be used for those entering old-settler villages. This was done by enactment of 27 April 1897. Thus irregular migrants were helped over the previous high hurdle of enrollment with few if any questions asked—one may suspect that a law with such wording was often applied in broad construction.

The irregular migrant, as Kulomzin complained, was able to settle legally on migrant plots by the law of 15 April 1896. He was

---

[52] See table in *ibid.*, p. 235.

entitled to none of the exemptions provided for regulars, but by a law of 27 April 1896 he was extended the right to receive government loans. The reasoning behind this law was that deprivation of credit was of no real use in eliminating irregular migration and could only harm the economic circumstances of new settlers. Irregular migrants were, however, by law of 7 December 1896 forbidden to receive loans for purposes of travel. What interested Kulomzin and the government was aiding the settlement of those who somehow, in spite of the authorities, arrived at their destination, but not financing the act of irregular migration.

Those irregulars who instead of taking up migrant plots entered old-settler villages were likewise extended the right to receive loans, by a regulation of 12 April 1897.[53] This was another direct result of Kulomzin's recommendations.

Free Migration and the New Agriculture Ministry

The legislation of the 1896-1897 period, chiefly implementing the policy of Kulomzin, superseded in many respects the law of 1889, still considered the basic migration law. The continuing flow of settlers, a large proportion of them irregulars, nevertheless soon made plain that something better was required. The signs of a new society were beginning to be visible in Siberia, and the question was raised as to whether Imperial policy ought to consider first the interests of the homeland, as heretofore, or the interests of Siberia. S. Iu. Witte, Minister of Finance, and V. K. von Plehve, Minister of Interior, differed on this issue as they did on several others of importance.

When Witte made a trip through Siberia in 1902, avowedly for the purpose of inspecting the new railway lines in Manchuria, he took the occasion to report on Siberian migration as well. He declared that the work of the Committee on the Siberian Railway had already produced beneficial results, but he made several specific recommendations: 1. that the study under way of the area and location of virgin forest in Siberia be expanded in scope; 2. that more routes and tracks from the railway to inhabited regions near by be laid out; 3. that the agencies charged with allotting lands for migrants be further developed; and 4. that an effort be made to attract to Siberia workers, artisans, and merchants. His overall conclusion was that "the proportions of the migration movement did not suffice either to the internal agrarian needs which made themselves felt at

[53] *Ibid.*, p. 260.

the beginning of the century, nor to those of the colonies with their immense terrain fit for settlement."[54] But while he pointed to inadequacies as regards both the homeland and Siberia, Witte's emphasis in fact was on Siberian needs.

Plehve, on the other hand, was more concerned about the problems of the European Russian peasant. A special memorandum of the Ministry of Interior put it this way: "In the last few years the state in relation to migrant affairs pursued chiefly the task originally indicated by the Siberian Committee—to settle and animate the region of the Siberian Railway" and therefore "in the legislation of the last decade there is almost no attempt to attain other, in any case no less important aims of migration policy, including primarily the improvement through resettlement of the conditions of land use and of the economy of the peasant population of the internal provinces of the Empire. . . . Despite all the importance of the interests of colonization, in accordance with the needs of the current moment, in cases of lack of correspondence of these interests with the interests of improvement of the life of the population of places of departure, preference must be given to the interests of land settlement [*zemleust-roistvo*]"[55]—that is, the interests of the interior. Superficially it seems paradoxical that Plehve, who became identified with a policy of adventurism in the Far East, was less concerned with the needs of Siberian settlement, while Witte, who preferred to refrain from provoking trouble with Japan, placed those needs very high.

There was an issue of fact as well as policy; Plehve believed that the interests of Siberia *had* been placed first during recent years. However, as long as major attention had been given to conditions which departing settlers must meet—which was implied in all the concern about "irregular migration"— and to preserving state control over their movement and installation, it was evident that the government's chief consideration was to preserve "order" in the homeland from damage from the migration movement. True, the legislation of 1896-1897 seemed to treat that consideration less seriously and, despite Kulomzin's ambivalence, was already moving in the direction of free migration.

Although Plehve's conclusions just cited were set at the base of a draft he produced for a new migration law, this draft was shelved by the Siberian Railway Committee. Instead, it approved a draft of its own, which became the law of 6 June 1904. This law, which

[54] Koulomzine, *Le Transsibérien*, p. 188.
[55] *Aziatskaia Rossiia*, Vol. I, p. 463, contains quote from Plehve.

remained in effect until the downfall of the old regime, followed Witte's desires in increasing the emphasis on colonization.

The principles lying at the base of the new law were *"freedom of migration* on the one hand, meaning by this the right of everyone to go to new places without any special permission from the government, and of *stable* settlement in the new places on the other hand."[56] True, absolute freedom to migrate was still to mean for some merely the right to go without any exemptions or assistance from the government. Though the settlers no longer needed to apply for permission, they did have to apply for state aid. In order to receive it, they had to come from regions from which migration was recognized as economically desirable, though wide discretionary powers were provided.

In its particulars the law established compulsory scouting for those whose applications were approved. It further defined the method of liquidating allotments in the homeland and of enrollment of migrants in old-settler communities, allotment to migrants of state lands, organization of settlements and communes, exemptions and favors which approved migrants might obtain, and gave new rules for migrants who voluntarily left the places of new resettlement.[57]

Whether the interests of the homeland or of Siberia were to receive major emphasis, it had become clear by now that the process of migration formed one connected whole, with which existing organs could not adequately deal. The Resettlement Administration of the Ministry of Interior found itself in need of more closely supervising the functions of the whole surveying machinery of the Ministry of Agriculture and State Domains if it was to help the migrants beyond the point of actual installation. Accordingly by imperial ukase of 6 May 1905, the Resettlement Administration passed into the agriculture ministry, which was simultaneously renamed the Chief Administration of Land Settlement and Agriculture (*Glavnoe Upravlenie Zemleustroistva i Zemledeliia*).[58] The Resettlement Administration became its most vigorous subsection.

Ermolov thereupon left his "sand dunes and gullies," and Nikolai N. Kutler took over as chief of the new ministry. Kutler, one of the very few bureaucrats who supported expropriation of gentry lands, became a political casualty of the criticism of his more conservative fellows in April 1906. When the first fright of the Revolution of 1905 was over, he was replaced by A. P. Nikolsky,

[56] *Idem.* [57] 3 *P.S.Z.* 24,701. [58] 3 *P.S.Z.* 26,172.

who soon yielded to Alexander S. Stishinsky. In contrast, Stishinsky was hastened to his fall via clashes with radical deputies in the First Duma, and in the following June he in turn gave way to Prince Boris A. Vasilchikov. Cautious enough to avoid the political troubles which beset both Kutler and Stishinsky was A. V. Krivoshein, who had at first been assistant chief of the Resettlement Administration, then chief in 1904-1905. In 1905 he became assistant chief of the new ministry into which the Administration passed. He was to have an important role to play in relation to migration under Stolypin.

With the establishment of the Chief Administration of Land Settlement and Agriculture, the migration process came under the purview of a single ministry whose functions included all aspects of agriculture. The same process, "land settlement," was being carried out on both the lands of the migrants and of old-settlers in Siberia and on the peasant lands of European Russia. Land settlement and migration were the two chief concerns of the new ministry, and in the later expressed view of both Nicholas II and Stolypin, as we shall see, the chief domestic concerns of the whole Imperial government as well. Only when these two mutually interdependent processes had been carried out much further could the minister afford to examine whether a firm enough economic foundation had been provided the Russian peasantry so that he could sit back to run an orderly, Western-style, caretaker sort of ministry of agriculture. Probably no Western country ever had an agriculture ministry whose functions approached those of Russia's in scope and in their importance to the nation's future.

During the war with Japan, migration had slowed almost to a standstill, and remained so during the Revolution of 1905—which led policymakers to resort to more sweeping and dramatic solutions for the land problem. In 1906 Peter A. Stolypin seemed to have managed to regain control of the political situation and established a stable government. In order to make that stability permanent, Stolypin turned to confront the agrarian problem, including migration, steady and whole, in a manner no individual and no law had adequately done before. Continuing the newly-adopted policy of free migration, he coupled it with a policy of transition to a system of farms. Migration had helped pave the way for a sort of "land settlement" which meant enclosure under all-out government sponsorship.

COUNT P. D. KISELEV

A. N. KULOMZIN

A. V. KRIVOSHEIN

P. A. STOLYPIN

Four officials who made migration policy

Street in old-settler village (Chama, Irkutsk province)

Migrant train between Petropavlovsk and Omsk

Settlers at migrant point en route to Siberia

Migrant group on steppe east of Ob River

New settlers on Velikokemsk portion (Far East), a week after arrival

New settlement near Trans-Siberian Railway, 1,000 miles east of the Urals

CHAPTER VI

The Migrants Move by Rail

"I had to wait for the train, and from want of anything else to do I observed the passengers. What an immeasurable difference from the Siberian *trakt* [road, i.e., before the railway], over which traveled all kinds of solid gentlemen: merchants, Siberian officials, and simply businessmen. The railway carried many people whose social position could not be determined by any kind of chemical analysis. Where were all these anonymous people going, why were they hurrying so, where did they come from?"—D. N. Mamin-Sibiriak's story, *Sibirskie orly*.

From Cart to Railway

The building of the railway, as the Committee on the Siberian Railway noted in a report, was bound to lead—and did—to a new floodtide in migration to Asia. Travel was easier and cheaper for all migrants; many workers came to build the railway and stayed as settlers. Once the railway went into operation, "the serious disadvantages of the extremely abnormal state of migration appeared especially obvious."[1]

In 1896 the first large section of the Siberian railway, from Cheliabinsk to the Ob river, was opened for traffic; the link from the Ob to Irkutsk followed in 1898, and the Irkutsk-Lake Baikal line in 1899. However, the migrants went in greatest numbers to the west, and thus the date 1896 is the significant one for the beginning of migration by rail. The government subsidy permitted for the journey itself, fixed at 50 rubles per family for West Siberia and 100 rubles for East Siberia, the Amur, and the Steppe in 1894, was reduced somewhat in 1898 when a special migrant fare on the railway was established. A special railway fare had first been offered settlers in 1894, when rail could take them to the Urals but not yet beyond, at .3 kopek per verst for each member of the family, children under ten riding free. In 1898 the fare on all migrant rail travel was lowered to the level of a child's third-class ticket. Whereas the cost of a trip from central Russia to Tomsk for an average family had been 57 rubles in 1890, in 1898 it was 15 rubles.[2] A scout paid only one-fourth of the cost of a railway ticket, which still entitled him

[1] *Kolonizatsiia Sibiri*, pp. 118-19.
[2] Koulomzine, *Le Transsibérien*, p. 194.

131

to one pood of baggage. Considering these advantages, it is a wonder that the increase in resettlement was not sharper than it actually was, but it was still considerable.

The Settlements Kulomzin Saw

To understand the impact of the rail-borne colonists, we must first try to gauge the condition of settlement at the time when they began to move. In 1896 Kulomzin visited and described 199 settlements chosen to be as representative as possible. Our chief assurance of the usefulness of the descriptions which he and his staff wrote is their quantity and distribution in a very large number of districts in Siberia east and west. This greatly reinforces the impression made on the reader by the common elements discerned in the story of the development of many settlements. The Siberian village, wherever its location, was characteristically built along a single street, compared by one traveler to "a fleet of dismasted ships riding at anchor in a heavy gale of wind."[3] Kulomzin's report enables us to visualize as well as to analyze the economic and social situation of a large number of individual villages, and thus to break through the wall of statistical averages to a variety of real situations that developed in the course of resettlement.

Let us begin with Tobolsk province. In Ishim county, one settlement contained 64 households with 210 males, 180 females, all from Kherson.[4] They had planned in 1892 to migrate, sent scouts to Siberia, and waited for official permission. Finally one of them visited the Land Section of the Ministry of Interior in St. Petersburg and was informed that permission for their group had already been granted, but on returning home he found that none had arrived. At this point 50 families migrated irregularly, while the other 14 decided to wait for permission. They rented their land, at the rate of 8-15 rubles per year per desiatina, and paid 8 rubles for pasture. In the process of liquidation, they sold their buildings at a rate varying from 35 to 300 rubles per family; their horses at 60 rubles per pair, including cart; their oxen at 100 rubles per pair; their cows for 25

---

[3] Harry de Windt, *Siberia as It Is*, London, 1892, p. 132.

[4] *Prilozheniia k Vsepoddanneishemu Otchetu Stats-Sekretaria Kulomzina po poezdke v Sibir' dlia oznakomleniia s polozheniem pereselencheskago dela*, St. Petersburg, 1896, p. 2. This was poselok Novo-Georgievskii, Teplodubrovskaia volost. Each village here described was listed in Kulomzin's report *second* among those for each *okrug* or *uezd*, except in the case or two where only one village was surveyed within that particular section. The purpose was to avoid taking the village first listed, on the grounds that it might have been so placed by intent, and yet refrain from any possible distortion of Kulomzin's findings by the writer via a random selection.

rubles. They brought with them 29 plows and 8 carts. On arriving too late in 1895 to build, they spent the winter in the homes of old-settlers, for which they paid a rental of from 6 to 10 rubles per family for the whole time. They received government aid totaling 3,805 rubles. They purchased horses on the new place from old-settlers at from 28 to 60 rubles, cows at from 15 to 22 rubles. They built their homes in April 1896, and sowed 102 desiatinas. There was ample forest by the village, and good water in the lake. There was one smith among the migrants. This settlement, reflecting the frequent phenomenon of irregular migration due to delay in granting of official permission, was noteworthy in that state aid had been extended nonetheless, though from the figures given it was not at all clear that such aid was a prerequisite to the success of the settlers.

In the Tiukalinsk county there was a settlement of 45 households (244 males, 227 females), all from Chernigov.[5] Their village had been established in June 1896. At home they had had allotments of from 3 to 4½ desiatinas, renting additional land from a nearby landowner. There was no forest in the vicinity, and the peasants had paid 6 rubles per sazhen (7 feet) for firewood. Every year they had gone to the south for seasonal work in the Taurida and Don regions. Their information about migration had been obtained from their land captain, and they had sent scouts ahead. They petitioned for permission and, failing to receive it, as in the case of the previous village discussed, came anyway, irregularly, on their passports. They arrived in Siberia in the autumn of 1895, then returned home for their families and came back to Siberia for good in the spring of 1896. Their land was sold for 20 to 40 rubles per desiatina, their horses for 10 to 20 rubles, their houses for 10 rubles. With them they brought no tools except their plowshares (*soshniki*). Many of them bought their houses from the old-settlers, at from 30 to 38 rubles, though some built their own. Horses were purchased at from 25 to 40 rubles; cows for 18 to 20 rubles. In the whole village there were 45 horses and 50 cows; none of the households was without a horse. Twenty desiatinas of spring wheat and 19 of spring rye were sowed. They started by hiring old-settlers to plow land for them at 3 or 4 rubles per desiatina. State aid was provided these irregulars at the rate of 40 rubles per family. There was good water available from a nearby lake. This appeared to be a promising settlement of people whose land at home was of the most meager dimensions, though at the moment some kind of "fever" was widespread in the village.

[5] Poselok Durbetskii, Bol'shepeschanskaia volost. *Ibid.*, p. 18.

In Tarsk county, one settlement had been organized in 1890.[6] Unlike the first two mentioned, this one was extremely mixed in origin. There were 20 households; of these 5 were migrants, from Kursk, Viatka, and Kazan. The remainder were Siberians who had migrated from the southern part of Tobolsk province to avoid famine conditions or from areas where they had had to rent land from Tatars. The Kursk migrants had had at home about 3 desiatinas, had rented additional plowland at from 18 to 25 rubles per desiatina, and had no forest or meadow. All came without any cash and had to live as hired laborers with the old-settlers. Ten persons continued to do this, but the others had managed to get set up for themselves. None of these families had received any state aid. Nevertheless, the village appeared to be in good condition. Each household had about 5 horses and there were no families without horses. The sown land so far was, to be sure, only 15 desiatinas for the whole village. This area was so small, it appeared, partly because cutting the nearby forest to expand it was forbidden, partly because the situation of the Siberians in the village was unclear. They had not yet been enrolled, and they feared wasting their effort. The location of the settlement was good, on the river Tuia, a tributary of the Irtysh, and only 15 versts from a school and church.

If we move on to inspect some of the settlements in Tomsk province, we come first in Kainsk county to a village settled in 1894 and 1895 consisting of 82 families.[7] Their origin was also very mixed; they came from Chernigov, Poltava, Saratov, Kiev, Tambov, and Kursk. Some of them had obtained travel permits, some had come irregularly on passports. At home all were short of land and had had to rent additional acreage at high rates—12 to 18 rubles in Poltava, 25 rubles in Kursk. Some had heard about the chance to migrate to Siberia at their township hall, others by way of letters from friends or rumors. The Poltavans understood, by what happened to be a correct rumor, that in Siberia migrant families could receive financial aid up to 100 rubles. Most in fact obtained 60 rubles aid on arrival. There was a total of 100 horses in the village, and only two families had no horses. Most of the horses were purchased from old-settlers at from 25 to 40 rubles. The total sowing was 300 desiatinas, some families up to 7 each. They purchased wheat seed at 34 kopeks per pound cash or the pledge of 50 kopeks against the state aid to be forthcoming. Some brought with them the seeds of

---

[6] Poselok Bichelinskii, Tervizskaia volost. *Ibid.*, p. 79.
[7] Poselok Rozhdestvenskii, Iudinskaia volost. *Ibid.*, p. 93.

apple or other fruit trees. For example, one planted 8 plum seeds and 4 trees came up. In their gardens they raised cucumbers, beets, potatoes, and a little tobacco. During winters they often worked for the old-settlers, at a rate of 2 to 2½ rubles per month. Summers they worked for the railway, at 50 to 60 kopeks per day. Water, though of a bitter-salt taste, was available in a nearby lake, and there was some forest at hand. During the winter and spring 31 children died of measles. It appears that this settlement reflects many of the most frequently observed phenomena of the migration of that period. Balancing misfortunes against achievements, one may suspect that the weight fell on the side of the latter in a way auguring permanent success.

One village in Tomsk county was founded in 1888 and at the time of the survey had 24 families, from Viatka, Kursk, Kazan, Tambov, Perm, and Tobolsk, exhibiting the same sort of mixed origin found in the previous two settlements.[8] With allotments of 5 desiatinas per census soul, the Viatka settlers had at home been unable to feed large families, and had had no forest access nor available fuel, the manure being needed for fertilizer. The Kursk peasants had had too little land and the rental for additional acreage was too high, about 18 rubles per desiatina. (We may note that in this case and others in the area of worst overcrowding—Kursk, Poltava, et cetera—land *was* usually physically available, but the high level of rent reduced the chance of using it.) The Tobolsk settlers had moved, not to escape dearth of land, but land of poor quality. At the time of the survey, the village sowed 40 desiatinas of rye and 40 desiatinas of oats, and each family planted ¼ desiatina of potatoes. There was no family without a horse. The villagers had a total of 64 horses, 80 cows, 144 sheep. Among the Viatkans there were some carpenters who went to nearby villages for work, though not to the city of Tomsk, since they regarded it as too far for them to tend their land regularly and properly. For the same reason the two smiths of the village worked only at home, taking work orders from nearby villages. These migrants gave information as to what proportion of their home villages had left with them. From a Kursk village of 350 families, 17 had come; from another one of 404, 23; from one of 13, only one. From a Viatka settlement of 17 families came 3; from a Perm one of 7 came 1. This village presented a solid, well-built appearance.

In Mariinsk county a settlement of 100 households had 335 males

<hr>

[8] Poselok Viatskii, Semiluzhnaia volost. *Ibid.*, p. 119.

and 262 females.[9] All but one family were from Kursk. At home there had been 18 landless families, the remainder holding from 1 to 5 desiatinas, paying rentals of 25 to 30 rubles for winter-grain land, a little less for spring-grain land. A quarter of them had had no horses. From Kursk many had gone to southern provinces for seasonal labor, others to sugar and other nearby factories. Some had heard of migration prospects at the township hall, though the "authorities" (presumably the land captain) did not advise them to go. They waited two years for official permission, but finally obtained it. Only 4 families came on passports, irregularly. Their first winter in Siberia was spent in old-settler homes, paying a ruble or less per month, though some built mud huts and stayed there. All finally built houses. Their sowing area was 180 desiatinas of winter wheat and 200 desiatinas of spring wheat; some sowed up to 10 desiatinas. There were 3 families without horses, but the total was 240 horses, 170 horned cattle, and 60 sheep for the village. Their harvests had been ample, yielding 80-100 poods of rye and 120 poods of wheat per desiatina. At first many worked on the railway at 75 kopeks per day, but most had ceased this practice. By means of state aid they had constructed a building used for both church and school. This was obviously a flourishing village.

Passing to the next province to the east, that of Yeniseisk, we come to a settlement in Achinsk county, 84 per cent of whose area was forest land.[10] It had 37 households, with 37 other migrant plots reserved by scouts from Orel province. Some migrants had arrived within the year from both Orel and Poltava. Most of the Poltavans had been landless. They had regularly gone for work to Black Sea provinces and thereby earned at first up to 100 rubles a year, later only about 30 rubles. During the last year, with increased numbers of people doing the same thing, work had proved next to impossible to find. Rental prices, 15 to 25 rubles, had been too high, and land for share cropping (otrabotki) was rarely available. The Poltavans had been either Cossacks or peasants; the Cossacks who had land had sold for 80 to 110 rubles per desiatina. But, as Kulomzin's report indicated was often the case, the local officials had told them to liquidate quickly and so this price was below the value of the land. The chief work of these villagers was, so far, cutting and selling firewood in the town of Achinsk. No tillage was yet ready. All lived in

[9] Poselok Novo-Oboianovskii, Baimskaia volost. *Ibid.*, p. 126.
[10] Poselok Malaia Cheremushka, Pokrovskaia volost. *Ibid.*, p. 129.

huts (*shalashi*), though they had now prepared lumber for building their houses.

Moving to Minusinsk county, we encounter a settlement dating from 1888 but including new arrivals of 1894, consisting of 121 families from Nizhny Novgorod, Tambov, Poltava, Perm, Ufa, and Viatka.[11] The land available was short of the 15-desiatina norm per male, coming to approximately 10½ desiatinas instead. The majority were from Nizhny Novgorod, and learned about Siberia from a fellow villager who had worked there in gold mines. As a result of their connection with him, many had earlier gone to Siberia to work as carpenters and stonemasons. One had spent 23 years in the gold mines, sending part of his annual earnings home to his family, and finally returning to bring them to Siberia. Their original allotments of 4 desiatinas per adult male had been squeezed below that level, and rental land was too expensive (12-27 rubles). In the new village, all had their houses and tillage, though many continued to go to nearby villages to work as carpenters for a ruble or slightly less per day. It seems that the village had devoted much effort to establishing its own church, built mainly by the migrants' own money (9,000 out of 14,000 rubles). Almost 500 rubles had been laid aside for the maintenance of the priest to come, and church bells had been ordered and almost paid for.

In Kansk county, a settlement was made up of people from Orel, Tambov, Poltava, and Kharkov.[12] The Orelans, constituting 14 per cent their village, came on the summons of a fellow-villager who had worked as a carpenter on the railway. They and the Tambovans had had one desiatina or less per male soul, distributed in three fields, and often lived as janitors or by other kinds of labor. The Poltavans and Kharkovans had obtained permission to go to the Amur, but, worried about their cash, they had decided en route to remain in Kansk. Most worked on the railway. All three settlements examined in Yeniseisk accordingly showed considerable labor away from the village.

Moving south again to Akmolinsk region we find in Omsk county a village of 45 households, organized in 1894 from Saratov and Samara Germans.[13] At home they had, on the three-field system, ½ desiatina winter grain, 1½ of spring grain and ½ desiatina in fallow, and almost no meadowland. They had sold their homes for about 100

[11] Poselok Berezovskii, Idrinskaia volost. *Ibid.*, p. 136.
[12] Poselok Ol'gino, Rybinskaia volost. *Ibid.*, p. 140.
[13] Poselok Privol'noe, Aleksandrovskaia volost. *Ibid.*, p. 147.

rubles, in one case almost 500, and thereupon went in 1891 to Oren-burg. There they spent two years sharecropping, but encountered a bad harvest and so moved again to Turkestan. There the land proved too poor, and they moved once more to Akmolinsk, where they first worked on the Trans-Siberian. This time some of them inspected the land first and set up the village surveyed. Though they still lived in mud huts, their plowland was 160 desiatinas, mostly wheat, and produced a harvest of 40-45 poods per desiatina. They had 97 horses, 70 cows, and other cattle. Water was a problem. From two wells which they had sunk, they drew good but meager water, from the third ample but bad water. Fortunately a government hydrotechnical party was sinking wells in the vicinity. Twenty-six people had died, chiefly from smallpox, but 14 children had been born. It looked as if these villagers' wanderings would not need to continue; the settle-ment appeared firm.

A village in Kokchetav county, founded in 1890 and fully settled by 1896, included 317 households from Tobolsk, Kazan, Perm, Chernigov, Vologda, Poltava, Voronezh, Penza, Saratov, Orel, Simbirsk, Samara, Viatka, Tambov, Kursk, Orenburg, Ufa, Nizhny Novgorod and Riazan.[14] Among them were many ex-soldiers dis-charged in eastern Siberia and Turkestan who had come to the village directly. They had sowed more than 2,500 desiatinas. Some worked up to 12, the majority 3. All families but the 18 arriving that year possessed tillage. They had taken a harvest of 120 poods per desiatina for three years, then left land fallow for three, of the six the settlement had been in existence. They had their own houses or huts, though the first winter they had spent with Cossacks or had stayed in shelter 80 versts away. The majority had three or four horses each. Water was obtained from wells which they sunk them-selves. Many craftsmen were among their number, and they had almost completed building their own school and church.

In Akmolinsk county, a settlement of 85 households had been settled from 1889 to 1895 of people from Perm, Orel, Saratov, Pol-tava, Orenburg, Taurida, Tambov, Tula, Vladimir, Vologda, and Viatka.[15] Lack of land was as usual the cause of departure; the Permans, after a redistribution in 1879, had had only ¾ desiatina per soul. In Akmolinsk, these settlers had lasted out five years of bad harvest but were now doing better. On the average each plowed 4 desiatinas, while some had 8 and 15. Mostly they worked the land

[14] Poselok Makinskii, Makinskaia volost. *Ibid.*, p. 151.
[15] Poselok Alekseevskii, Alekseevskaia volost. *Ibid.*, p. 168.

themselves, though sometimes they hired Kirghiz, paying them 6 or 7 rubles per desiatina. In the village there were 113 horses (though many settlers still had none), 163 cows, and 40 sheep. Some had received state aid of 50 rubles, which they used to buy cattle.

In Atbasarsk county, a settlement organized in 1879, marked out for 214 families, was overfilled with 240, most of them from Samara.[16] The Samarans had had a 6-desiatina allotment, but could not rent additional land since merchants had taken it up already. Many of them had realized 100 or more rubles on selling out. There were no families without horses, and the total for the village was 400 horses, 600 horned cattle, 800 sheep, and 200 pigs. A church was already built. In 1880 they had gotten 1½ rubles for a pound of flour, at present about ½ a ruble, and with the fall in price they had brought more land under cultivation. It might be pointed out that the rule in these settlements was for the amount of tillage to increase gradually in any case.

The last example is found in Petropavlovsk county, in a village organized in 1895, having 224 families.[17] They came from Chernigov, Poltava, and Tula. State aid had totaled over 16,000 rubles. Too many had failed to build decent houses; most were living in dug-outs (*kopanki*). The consequence was much sickness, especially scurvy, which was combated by opening a free mess hall where all sick persons could get hot food. They had had bad wells—which undoubtedly contributed to their medical problem—but the government hydrotechnical party was now sinking 16 new ones. They tilled 354 desiatinas; 20 families had no horses. The settlement illustrates a fundamental problem throughout much of Akmolinsk region. The land was rich, and needed only water to be productive. But water, especially drinking water, was scarce.

Kulomzin's survey enables us to obtain a remarkable panorama, not of the "average" economic condition or possessions or mode of life of the Siberian migrants, or of the settlers in any given locality, but rather of the sum of the actual tribulations and joys, successes and failures, of several thousand individual families. Some of the nearly infinite number of permutations in the course of the story of the migration of any one peasant family suggest many more to the reflective reader. The head of the family might seek official permission, as the method of obtaining maximum economic benefit and security in his journey and resettlement. If he did seek it, he often

---

[16] Poselok Mariinskii, Mariinskaia volost. *Ibid.*, p. 178.
[17] Poselok Semipolki, Dmitrievskaia volost. *Ibid.*, p. 186.

did not receive it, and went anyway. In that event, he might find that he could obtain state aid notwithstanding, once he got to Siberia. He often joined with families who lived hundreds of miles away from him at home, in a region of Russia he might never have seen. With them he shared the risks and problems of weather, disease, harvest, the immediate availability of shelter, labor opportunities, and all the rest. Neither these risks nor the benefits obtainable were shared equally. Yet there was often a common purpose and a common effort which bound these pioneers together, and might produce not only economic sufficiency but the beginnings of cultural opportunity. The Berezovsky villagers who raised 9,000 rubles for their church cannot have been unmindful of these matters.

A rather quaint, but nonetheless instructive, document which Kulomzin published suggests some of the possibilities and actualities of mutual action.

*Decision of the Novo-Aleksandrovsk Village Assembly No. 9
on support for household and market gardening*[18]

On August 29, 1906, we, the undersigned state peasants of Tobolsk province, Tarsk county, Sedel'nikovsk township, Novo-Aleksandrovsk village community, newly founded in 1893 on the Kuli-Mulinsk portion of migrants from Kharkov and Nizhny Novgorod provinces, containing 47 households, there being from this number assembled in the village assembly by our village elder Tret'iakov the number of 46 persons out of the number of 47 householders who have the right to vote in the village assembly, according to articles 51, 52, and 53 of the General Statute of Peasants, considered whether we, having been accustomed in Russia to carry on market gardening, should find it desirable to pursue this occupation here also. . . . [It is then directed that inquiries and investigations should be made into seeds and products available and suitable.] The present decision we resolve shall be written in the book of commune decisions, and present for the requisite confirmation to our official on peasant affairs. . . .

The signature is by an "illiterate peasant" whose name is given, and the village elder Tret'iakov, and is certified as a true copy of the original by "L. Onore, official on peasant affairs of the second portion of Tarsk county." Very likely it was a shrewd and ambitious minor official who saw that this found its way into the hands of Kulomzin's party. We know that there were many migrants who had no "official on peasant affairs," and undoubtedly all did not keep

---

[18] The text is found in *ibid.*, pp. 211-12. Note that 1896 has evidently been misprinted as 1906 in the first sentence.

their records so neatly. Nevertheless it was true that this sort of decision faced hundreds of thousands of new arrivals. For many of them it was the first time in their lives that it occurred to them, or became apparent, that in some fundamental manner they might order their own existence *de novo*. At home their grandfather might have raised rye in Voronezh, but their grandfather was dead, they were in Siberia, and their neighbors were very possibly from Perm or Taurida. Questions could not be settled either with reference to ancestors or immemorial local custom. It is worth considering these facts concretely, in order to understand why Stolypin might worry about being smothered by Siberian democracy—at the same time that he was assisting its further growth.[19]

Foreigners Discover Migration

We took note of Alexander Michie's claim to have been, in the 1860's, the first in a century and a half to make the complete journey from St. Petersburg to Peking.[20] In the interval from that time to the opening of the Trans-Siberian Railway only a handful of foreigners tried the trip or any large portion of it. Probably the best known of them was George Kennan, who, in his book *Siberia and the Exile System*, helped to give public opinion in the outside world a picture of Asiatic Russia as a bleak land of chains and forced labor, which has never been fully erased[21] Harry de Windt followed Kennan, testily charging that he had mixed up his prisons in Tomsk, attempting to pare the role of Siberian exile down to the size it deserved, and finally, on observing a convict birched, reported, "This birch is now in my possession. It is precisely similar to those used at Eton."[22] George Lynch reported that in 1898 out of 298,574 transported persons living in Siberia—half exiled under the penal code, half banished by Russian communes—by the admission of the director-in-chief of Russian prison administration, "the third of this mass, one hundred thousand men, escape all control."[23] Such reports did not attain wide circulation. Even the law of 25 June 1900 abolishing penal exile in Siberia and restricting political and ecclesiastical

---

[19] See Chapter VII.

[20] See Chapter IV, p. 88.

[21] George Kennan, *Siberia and the Exile System*, 2 vols., New York, 1891. The book had its impact inside Russia as well; for example, the late Mikhail Kalinin told Frank Rounds that it was the "Bible" of early Bolsheviks. Its author was the cousin of the grandfather of the former United States Ambassador to the Soviet Union, who was named after him.

[22] De Windt, *op.cit.*, p. 344.

[23] George Lynch, *The Path of Empire*, p. 210.

offenders to be transported to 100 per year was not widely noticed abroad. No such information could stir the popular imagination sufficiently to compete with prison exposes. As a result, though travelers from the late 1890's onward gave a good deal of attention to the Great Migration, its magnitude and significance simply escaped popular knowledge abroad in its own day, and it is left to the historian to try in some measure to remedy the deficiency.

Though the Trans-Siberian Railway remained unfinished for some years, by the use of lake and river boats it could be and was traversed in both directions. It was probably the travelers from China westward who, meeting the migrants coming from the other direction, were most forcibly struck by the movement. The Rev. Francis Clark, who took his family over the route in 1900, mulled over the obvious fact that the vast domain of Russian Asia had been waiting all the time at Europe's back door, yet "Only now is the door fairly open, and the new settlers are pouring through."[24] George Lynch, who went the same way two years later, wrote: "What strikes the traveller most journeying by the Trans-Siberian Railway from the Pacific to Moscow is the great stream of emigrants flowing eastward along the route. There is nothing to be seen like it at present in any other part of the world. Every day one passes long trains laden with them, which at night are drawn up at the stations."[25] He did not credit peasant initiative for this: "In this great migratory movement which we see in progress along the line which acts as a safety-valve to the revolutionary unrest in Russia proper, while at the same time it is establishing a Greater Russia in Siberia, it is the Government that leads them out, spoon-feeds them on the way, gives them grants of land and tools to till it with, until they are finally established in their new Eastern homes."[26]

Lynch did not object to the government controlling (as he believed) this movement; he declared its "system of arrangements" was "simply admirable."[27] Though paternalism might be justified, he paid tribute to the results the peasants had achieved. If they had been on the spot a year or more, their homes "look a great deal better than the wretched-looking little hovels occupied by the peasants in Russian villages." Lynch queried one group of settlers in Krasnoiarsk who had come from a village one hundred miles south of Moscow. Three years ago they had sent a scout to investigate,

[24] Rev. Francis E. Clark, *A New Way Around an Old World*, New York and London, 1901, p. 182.
[25] Lynch, *op.cit.*, p. 230.   [26] *Ibid.*, p. xvii.   [27] *Ibid.*, p. 233.

then one family went to Siberia and reported to the village. Now six families were taking up adjacent land. "I asked them if they were not sorry to leave their old homes. 'Yes,' one of the women said, but her husband chipped in almost fiercely, 'It was hard to make a living. Out there'—with a sweep of his hand eastward—'the land will be all our own,' and he stamped his foot on the ground expressively. 'The land our own'—is not that the secret of thrifty and industrious husbandry the wide world over?"[28]

While meeting the migrants from the opposite direction might produce the greater surprise, it was also possible to see a good deal of the movement on the eastward journey. R. A. F. Penrose, Jr., reported that "The emigration is now [1901] going on faster than ever; all the trains and boats are crowded, and along the rivers many emigrants are seen on rafts floating down to their new homes, with their families, cattle, horses, hogs, and household possessions."[29]

Then there were the journalist-students, who were neither experts nor novices in Russian affairs, but something between. Pierre Leroy-Beaulieu grudgingly admitted that the Siberian peasants he saw in the late 1890's were better off than the Russian, and had a "much more independent air," but he insisted that the Siberian peasant was lazy. Of course independence and laziness, in the sense he interpreted the latter, were not incompatible: "I have often heard Europeans say that Siberia is the only country where you cannot get work done even for money; and this is perfectly true, for on certain holidays it matters little what you may offer, you will not get a coachman to take you a five-mile drive. The Siberian would rather lose money than earn it against his will."[30]

This man was not a very good reporter. He wrote that "the vast majority of the rural population obstinately refuses to work in the fields" (in an almost wholly peasant region!); that the climate of Siberia was "naturally opposed to the cultivation of cereals," whose production was climbing rapidly; and he declared "everything is done to prevent the crowding together of people who come from divergent provinces, which might give rise to trouble. Thus, the officials always endeavor to avoid mixing the 'Little Russians' with the 'Great Russians,' and never to introduce newcomers into vil-

[28] *Ibid.*, pp. 235-36.
[29] R. A. F. Penrose, Jr., *The Last Stand of the Old Siberia*, Philadelphia, 1922, p. 106
[30] Pierre Leroy-Beaulieu, *The Awakening of the East*, New York, 1900, pp. 19-20.

lages already inhabited by old Siberians . . ."[31]—which assertion was nearly the exact reverse of the truth in all particulars.

Leroy-Beaulieu seemed to swallow the Valuev viewpoint on migration: "It is natural in a country where the peasantry are still so primitive and ignorant as in Russia that the government should closely watch the movements of emigrants, who might, on finding exaggerated promises and illusions dispelled, become troublesome and even dangerous."[32] But like some other journalists he described well enough what he actually saw, which was long lines of carts bearing migrants with their household goods from the railway to their new homes. "The scene is very picturesque, especially toward evening, when the worthy folk encamp on the highroad: the men unsaddling the horses, the women going to the well for water, and the children playing about, whilst some old man, seated on the wayside, reads the Bible out aloud to a group of eager listeners."[33]

Perhaps the best-informed foreign traveler of the 1890's was Jules Legras, who visited Siberia twice in 1896 and 1897. His intention first had been to study the interaction between the Russian and Moslem peoples in Siberia, but soon he realized this was only "un cas particulier d'un grand problème, celui du peuplement de l'Asie russe," and that with the coming of the railway especially, "c'est le flot envahisseur et perturbateur qu'il convient surtout d'étudier."[34] What Leroy-Beaulieu found true of all Siberian migration, Legras found true only east of Lake Baikal: "En deçà du Baikal, les colons travaillent pour eux-mêmes et par eux-mêmes; au delà du rempart de la Transbaikalie, ils sont presque exclusivement dirigés par le Gouvernement."[35]

Legras knew and respected several of the officials in Siberia who were charged with moving the flood of migrants along and were doing their best to do so. Of Peter Arkhipov, the official in charge of both the Cheliabinsk and Tiumen migrant points, he declared "il suffit de l'entendre parler quelques minutes pour comprendre qu'il se donne à ses difficiles fonctions comme à une oeuvre de charité et de dévouement"—and he had done so for fifteen years.[36] With his friend Ivan Kravtsov at Omsk, an engineer whose task it was to construct artesian wells for the new settler villages in the steppe nearby, he passed "des demijournées entières à causer de la Sibérie ou à

[31] Ibid., pp. 21, 25, and 46.
[32] Ibid., p. 44.   [33] Ibid., p. 45.
[34] Jules Legras, En Sibérie, Paris, 1899, p. x.
[35] Ibid., p. xv.   [36] Ibid., p. 6.

étudier des plans de colonisation."[37] Also at Omsk was Arkhipov's disciple and friend, Andrei Stankevich, whose job it was to supervise the installation of migrants who passed through Cheliabinsk, from the Urals to the Yenisei. He was always on the road, inspecting migrant points spread over the vast distance of 2,000 kilometers. He had twice contracted typhus from migrants and recovered—and thus was more fortunate than the migration official whom Legras knew in Tomsk, who had transmitted scarlatina to one of his children, who had died of it. Stankevich's daily routine required him to give instructions to subordinates, plan the furnishing of land, water, wood, and grain, act as architect, agronomist, surveyor, and provisioner to the settlers, get along with the provincial governors, petition his ministry. He was young; born in the 1860's, he had come to Siberia in 1891 at the time of the famine. Legras praised him highly: "une intelligence souple et éclairée, des vues hardies et des connaissances précises, voilà ses armes: c'est un homme du bon coin. . . ."[38] Legras says less about A. V. Durov, the commissioner at Tomsk, though he does not blame him for the grim conditions he inspected with him at the migrant point where miserable people were waiting for the rising river to drive them from the poor buildings in which they huddled.[39]

Though the vast majority of direct settlers were rural dwellers, one of the consequences of the migration movement was the growth of the Siberian cities. Legras describes the boom town of Taiga, where two years previously there had not existed a single building, but now there had grown up a town of 2,000 which had no police and no administrators but ample crime and squalor. Since the town had received official recognition only by virtue of being included in the census of the previous autumn (1897), no order had yet been given by St. Petersburg to organize it.[40] In general the impact of the census was still felt. Tales were current of the anger of the Kirghiz, exempt from military service, because the census-takers had forgotten to omit the question relating thereto; and the wrath of the schismatic Old Believers whose wives had been listed as concubines and children as illegitimate, owing to the insistence of Orthodox priests who could vent their frustrations on them in no other way.

Although his stated objective was to inspect migration, Legras obviously found the cities attractive because in most of even the small ones he encountered his own kind. He found excellent newspapers,

[37] *Ibid.*, p. 30.
[38] *Ibid.*, pp. 31-33.
[39] *Ibid.*, pp. 83-85.
[40] *Ibid.*, pp. 88-89.

especially in Omsk and Tomsk, and museums run by the local intelligentsia. He could always locate a few bright and well-informed people, even when he was stuck in Barnaul during the *rasputitsa* or thaw, with whom he could "talk Siberia" and similar topics. He did not care particularly for the Siberian common people, whom he found generally "plus grossiers, plus brutaux, plus égoïstes, plus indifférents à la morale et à la religion. . ." than most Russian peasants. In other words, they were too rough and individualistic for his taste, and, though he promised to publish soon a book about the migration movement which he set out to study, he wrote little about it directly in *En Sibérie*. Legras suffered no more than other foreign travelers from the psychological effects of the educational and social gulf which lay between the migrants and themselves, but this gulf was almost always broad enough so that the travelers were prevented from seeing matters through the migrants' eyes and stating their problems as the migrants felt them to be. One may be grateful that at least they saw the migrants and reported what they saw.

A Decade of Kulomzinite Migration

In 1896, 200,000 migrants came to Siberia. The next year saw a decline, but in 1898, 1899, and 1900 the figure surpassed 200,000. The three years following the total was lower but still above 100,000. It appears that disturbances connected with the Boxer Rebellion had some effect on the decrease beginning in 1901, and the Russo-Japanese War brought the total very low. Somehow 90,000 did manage to go during the two years 1904 and 1905 despite the burdening of the railway with soldiers, but they had to go on their own means. The proportion of irregulars rose to 82 per cent and 92 per cent respectively during the war years, then dropped sharply again before another rise. By 1906 the Stolypin policy began to take effect, in conjunction with the law of 1904 granting freedom of migration. The stamp Kulomzin had given the process was replaced by another.

During the decade 1896-1906, the railway produced substantial results. The first rail-borne migrants wrote their home folks. In Emil Lengyel's words, "Some of these mujiks had seen only the church steeple of their own hamlet. . . . But now the lure of free soil was in their blood, and so was the lure of distance. The Trans-Siberian took them safely eastward to a new world."[41]

[41] Emil Lengyel, *Siberia*, New York, 1943, p. 133.

In the fourteen years from 1895 to 1908—which includes part of the Stolypin period—3,930,000 migrants and scouts moved across the Urals. Returners included 430,000 migrants and 395,000 scouts —many of whom, as indicated earlier, were only returning for their families. For each 1,000 migrants and scouts, 485 went to West Siberia, 259 to the Steppe region and Turkestan, 134 to East Siberia, 81 to the Russian Far East, 38 to the Ural provinces, and 3 to unspecified places. Not all of the migrants followed prescribed procedures for settlement, though, as already observed, many irregulars obtained the privileges legally restricted to those who did so. It was officially estimated that on 1 January 1909 in Tomsk about 250,000 males (or about 500,000 people) were not yet installed; Popov deduces that there were about 1,000,000 such in all of Siberia.[42] One may doubt that any large proportion of a group that size were still wandering about. The evidence rather points to the existence of a very considerable group which we might call "irregular settlers"—as distinguished from irregular migrants—who had altogether eluded official controls. Kulomzin himself had happened upon many of them, but he treated them as an incredible monstrosity rather than a serious problem whose dimensions the government never seems to have faced.

The source of the migrants of this period confirms the belief that dearth of land was the fundamental reason for movement. For the period 1895-1908 the provinces of origin were:

Poltava	329,000	Kiev	182,000
Chernigov	278,000	Kharkov	167,500
Kursk	234,000	Tambov	158,000
Mogilev	220,000	Vitebsk	153,000
Voronezh	199,000	Orel	152,500

Other provinces yielding above 100,000 migrants were, in order, Samara, Ekaterinoslav, Minsk, Taurida, Saratov, Kherson, Smolensk, Volhynia, and Viatka.[43] Thus 90 per cent came from the black-earth and western provinces, where the need for land was felt most sharply.

Let us compare the provinces with the highest overall totals for the whole period 1885-1914:[44]

---

[42] I. I. Popov, "Pereselenie krest'ian i zemleustroistvo Sibiri," in *Velikaia Reforma*, Vol. VI, p. 256.

[43] *Idem.*

[44] Obolensky, *Mezhdunarodnye i mezhdukontinental'nye migratsii*, p. 91.

Poltava	422,000	Mogilev	215,000
Kursk	309,000	Ekaterinoslav	203,000
Chernigov	295,000	Tambov	198,000
Voronezh	237,000	Kiev	188,000
Kharkov	220,000	Orel	161,000

Except for the substitution of Ekaterinoslav for Vitebsk, the lists are identical. The migrants from the Belorussian provinces (Mogilev, Vitebsk, and Minsk) declined noticeably in the later years.[45] One may speculate that the progress of enclosure, which was noticed by Koefoed and Stolypin in those provinces before the Stolypin laws were passed, had some influence on the reduction of migration. The growth of opportunities for industrial labor may have had an impact as well, but the same occurred in the Ukraine and the Moscow region, so it could not wholly explain the decrease in Belorussia.

The ten provinces from the second list make up a single contiguous region, centered around Kursk in south central Russia (see Map 2). To a notable extent the areas of highest absolute migration were also those of highest relative migration—that is, had the highest percentage of migrants relative to the total rural population. Out of the various regions of Russia, the Ukraine had the highest percentage of migrants for the period 1896-1915, with 12.8 per cent. The individual provinces whose figures are available to us are:[46]

Vitebsk	17.2%
Mogilev	14.4
Chernigov	13.1
Poltava	10.9
Kharkov	10.1

The only province on this list which is not among the ten with the highest numerical totals of migrants is Vitebsk. Vitebsk is contiguous to Mogilev, which is one of the latter ten, at which point one would wish to have figures for counties (into which the provinces were subdivided). In general, then, the provinces which furnished the greatest number of Siberian migrants were the ones most affected by their departure. This fact must be reckoned as of greater importance than overall totals and percentages relating to all of European Russia.

[45] See N. Turchaninov, "Pereselencheskoe dvizhenie v 1909 godu," *Voprosy kolonizatsii*, No. 6, 1910, pp. 1ff.
[46] Pavlovsky, *Agricultural Russia*, p. 181.

If we take the European provinces mentioned as a group, we find that together they form an ellipse at right angles to a diagonal line running northeast and southwest. Many scholars have seen this line as important for the historical geography of European Russia. Sergius Shidlovsky, for example, points out that at the southwestern end of the line one finds that communal tenure was completely absent, while it was most extensive at the northeastern end, its frequency increasing gradually in that direction.[47] In the southwest, one found the best productive methods and the greatest density of population; in the northeast, the worst productive methods and the least density. "Where the population is sparse and the land plentiful, the level of agriculture is not very high, and such a form of tenure as the commune can perhaps be tolerated."

The "congestion" of the rich Kursk-centered region thus presented a picture with two sides. If the prevailing type of land use remained unchanged, the overcrowded area might be in a hopeless economic situation. But if its inhabitants chose to pass from the scattered-strip, three-course system to a system of farms, "congestion" might serve as a spur to the adoption of intensive and diversified agriculture. In order to adopt a new method of land use, as earlier suggested, land tenure also had to be reformed. Such changes did not require that the region be emptied of population or even that the entire annual population increase be drained off—although it was fashionable for critics of migration to charge that since it did not take the whole population increase, migration was quite useless in solving the agrarian problem. It might rather be enough to relieve the sharpest and most immediate population pressures sufficiently to facilitate enclosure and new methods of cultivation. The evidence suggests that migration was beginning to achieve this result in the congested region.

What was needed was the vision of how migration and independent farming might be related. The shrewder officials could see that if the peasant would move to distant Siberia in search of a better life, he might move to a farm in the homeland for the same purpose. The agricultural crisis, viewed in this light, need not have been the certain ground for a future social revolution, as the revolutionaries hoped and the government had begun to fear. The crisis might well serve as the unique opportunity for lifting the peasant to the status of an independent farmer.

[47] Sergius Shidlovsky, "The Imperial Duma and Land Settlement," *Russian Review* (London), Vol. I, No. I, 1912.

PART FOUR

STOLYPIN AND THE DUMA,

1906-1914

CHAPTER VII

Stolypin and Siberia

"It would be empty and stupid democratic phrasemongering to say that the success of the Stolypin agrarian policy in Russia is 'impossible.' It is possible! . . . [If it succeeds,] then the agrarian structure of Russia will become completely bourgeois. . . . Then conscientious Marxists must directly and openly abandon any kind of 'agrarian program' whatsoever and say to the masses, 'The workers have done all that they could . . .' [prior to the final socialist revolution.]"— V. I. Lenin, 1908.

Two Official Travelers

Despite the increasing time and effort which the government devoted to the agrarian problem in general and to migration in particular, a deep gap remained between St. Petersburg theory and Siberian practice right up to the time when St. Petersburg became Petrograd at the beginning of the First World War. Even after 1906, when Peter Stolypin, the most gifted of later Imperial statesmen, launched the most direct possible attack on the whole problem, the gap remained. From 1909-1913 irregular migrants ranged between 31 per cent and 47 per cent of the total, which reached close to a million a year. To the very last, legislation traveled on the heels of the actual population movement. One reason for this was the failure of the best officials to act sooner; another was the migrants' persistent preference for independent action and their dogged resistance to the efforts of lawmakers to regulate their lives.

Totalitarian states have drastically limited the effectiveness of such resistance, but Tsarist Russia was no such state. A striking example of the limits of Tsarist law with respect to the peasantry is to be found in a discussion carried on in the Ministry of Interior shortly after Plehve took it over in 1902. The exchange is reported by Gurko, a participant:

"I happened to mention that the only important difference between communal [i.e., repartitional] and hereditary household land tenure, particularly in those communes which no longer reapportioned the land periodically, was that the members of the commune had no right to sell their allotments while one whose land was held in household tenure had such a right. Yet in localities where both forms of land tenure existed and in communes which had not reapportioned the land for some time, it often happened that even commune members sold their allotments, usually to their fellow-villagers.

"When Plehve heard this, he asked with great surprise: 'Are you sure of that?' and turned for corroboration to Stishinsky, who confined himself to observing that such sales were absolutely illegal and that should a transaction come to the knowledge of the Senate it would no doubt be voided. I admitted that Stishinsky's observation was perfectly correct but maintained that it did not alter the facts of the case."[1]

In other words, years before the Stolypin laws attempted to break down the commune and create private ownership of land, the peasants were often simply acting as if this had already begun. Some officials knew it, others did not. No one could or would try to stop it.

Gurko, like Stolypin, was interested in destruction of the commune, not in enforcing communal laws. He states bluntly: "My experience had formed in me a strong conviction that the most formidable barrier to the development of the peasant masses, *and therefore of the entire empire*, was that anachronism, the land commune" (emphasis added).[2] He once put the argument thus to Plehve, the Interior Minister:

"Village kulaks, I said, were the most stable peasant element, and it was not their fault that they could not apply their entire energy to the problem of land exploitation. Consequently they had turned their activities in other directions and had become small traders and usurers. Seeking a further outlet for their energies, they had begun to use the labor of their neighbors, and in this they had been helped rather than hindered by the commune. A system which is devised to assist the weak and to protect them from the strong only corrupts the activity of the strong and weakens the weak since it does not develop in the latter the ability to oppose the former."[3]

In this statement Gurko attacks the two activities of the "kulak," money-lending and employment of hired labor, which were most repugnant to the defenders of the small peasant. He criticizes the commune for having "helped rather than hindered" the development of both activities. The abolition of the commune would therefore operate in the opposite direction, that is, toward the development of independent peasant enterprise wherein every man could improve his lot without needing to exploit his fellow-villagers. Stolypin ex-

[1] Gurko, *Features and Figures of the Past*, p. 136.
[2] *Ibid.*, p. 132.　　　　　　[3] *Ibid.*, p. 171.

pressed the same thought in very similar words in his report as governor of Saratov for 1904.[4]

Stolypin became Prime Minister in 1906. By the middle of the next year the Revolution of 1905 had been fought to a standstill, the two radical Dumas had been exploded, and a Third Duma had been chosen under the new electoral law of 3 June 1907. By then Stolypin's agrarian program was well underway. In 1908 he appointed Alexander Krivoshein, who had been Assistant Finance Minister from 1906 to 1908 after a career hitherto devoted to agricultural problems, as head of the Chief Administration of Land Settlement and Agriculture. Krivoshein kept this post after Stolypin's assassination, until 1915. He was to become a more important figure than the next Prime Minister, Kokovtsev; in fact, Krivoshein was slated to assume the Prime Ministry in 1913, but a sudden illness resulted in the appointment of Goremykin instead.[5] Who knows what effect it might have had on the fate of Russia had the shrewd Krivoshein had the helm in wartime instead of the senile Goremykin, under whom Rasputin's influence demoralized the government?

Just before Krivoshein was appointed to the agriculture ministry, he announced that he had visited certain districts where the peasant was leaving the commune for individual farms and confessed that he had been in error in previously opposing reform of the commune.[6] Gurko depicts him as a man of ambition rather than of principle, as this anecdote might suggest, yet pays tribute to his effective leadership in the agriculture ministry and his successful diplomacy in dealing with his colleagues and in publicizing the activities of his own ministry. Krivoshein, however, did not confine his interests entirely to agriculture. He seems to have profited by the lesson of Witte, who became identified as an exclusive devotee of industry. Seeking to avoid being labeled, Krivoshein maintained connections with industrialists as well. This was the man Stolypin chose to accompany him to Siberia on an inspection trip in 1910. Fifteen years earlier, St. Petersburg could spare only the bumbling Ermolov and the underling Kulomzin. Now the two ablest men in the government went to see the frontier.

Stolypin's Agrarian Policy

Peter Arkadievich Stolypin did not go to Siberia whimsically, nor only because he was interested in its particular regional problems.

---

[4] "K istorii agrarnoi reformy Stolypina," *Krasnyi Arkhiv*, Vol. 4(17), 1926, p. 85.
[5] Gurko, *op.cit.*, p. 531.   [6] *Ibid.*, p. 194.

He regarded the interests of Siberia as bound up with those of the whole Empire and the Imperial system, and he regarded them as of great importance. More specifically, he realized that the fate of the Siberian peasantry was interrelated with that of the peasantry of European Russia. On a sweeping alteration in the latter's conditions of life, he had staked the social policy through which he sought to save the institution of monarchy in Russia.[7]

The policy of Stolypin's government, in his own words, "had for its one object the establishment of small individual property in land."[8] As his daughter writes in her memoirs, "The abolition of communal land tenure and the resettlement of the peasants on homesteads was the dream of my father from the time of his youth. In this change he saw the principal security of the future happiness of Russia. To make every peasant a proprietor and give him the chance to work quietly on his own land, for himself, this must enrich the peasantry. . . ."[9] In the Duma, Stolypin explained that it was his intention to give land to all "those small-landed peasants who need it and who actually apply their own labor to the land, and also those peasants for whom it is necessary to improve the forms of their present land use." He wished "to see the peasant rich, satisfied, since where there is sufficiency, there, of course, is enlightenment, there also is real freedom."[10]

In order to achieve his objectives, Stolypin coupled a policy of fostering the growth of individualization in land tenure and use with an effort to encourage migration on a broad scale. For several years this policy swept Russia like wildfire.[11] In the words of Pares, "Even the peasant who had merely become the owner of his 'strips' without separating from the village, appreciated the advantages of the change, and, when once he was possessed of individual property, very soon passed on to condemn the whole strip system as quite impracticable." It was often in the most "restless" villages that the new

---

[7] I have dealt with the question of Stolypin's aims in an article entitled, "Was Stolypin in Favor of Kulaks?" in the *American Slavic and East European Review*, February 1955.

[8] Letter of Stolypin to Nicholas II, protesting the appointment of a Slavophile nominee to the Imperial Council, quoted in M. N. Pokrovsky, *A Brief History of Russia*, 2 vols., London, 1933, Vol. II, p. 291.

[9] M. P. Bok, *Vospominaniia o moem otse P. A. Stolypine*, New York, 1953, p. 204.

[10] Speech in Duma, to be found in *Gosudarstvennaia Duma. Vtoroi sozyv. Stenograficheskie otchety. 1906 god. Sessiia vtoraia*, Vol. II, St. Petersburg, 1907, columns 434-46.

[11] See Chapter II, for discussion of the Stolypin agrarian legislation and its effects.

lesson took root, and often the most "restless spirits" in the village led the new movement of land settlement. "To Khrunov, a peasant of Tula, who had earlier been imprisoned for his share in the agrarian riots, his fellow-neighbors said, 'We don't understand where you are leading us to.' But he secured the final redistribution into individual property (*razverstanie*), and set up a two-storied farmhouse which was a great success."

Pares also tells of a particularly troubled district of Saratov province, Balashov, where in the village of Ivanovka a socialist of great ability had gotten himself registered as a peasant, married a peasant wife, and became a peasant clerk. Under the ministry of none other than Plehve, this socialist persuaded the village to build a fine reading room and organized lectures wherein he preached the virtues of the commune and almost succeeded in organizing cooperative trading by the whole commune. This village was widely held up by socialists as a model of what ought to be achieved, and yet the man in question said sadly to Pares in 1910, "Think of it, Ivanovka has gone the way of all the rest."[12] No wonder Stolypin told Pares that same year, concerning the policy of land settlement, "That cannot be stopped now with cannon."[13]

The economic assumption underlying the whole policy was well put by the Octobrist deputy Sergius Shidlovsky: "Capital and labour will be fully applied only by one who owns the land and works for himself, his family, and his descendants; and so the peasant must be put in a position to make his labor as productive as possible."[14] In other words, "peasant enterprise," in the sense Chaianov and other theorists used the phrase,[15] had finally been adopted as a practical objective by the government, despite sneers and outcries from most of the intelligentsia, and was meeting a powerful response from the peasantry itself.

Stolypin believed that the political effects of turning the Russian peasant into a farmer would be the strengthening of the monarchy— that is, constitutional monarchy, rather than the autocracy so long practiced by the Romanovs. So far as is known, the results of land settlement in European Russia did nothing to shake his opinion. However, the results of Siberian migration left him with a certain

[12] Bernard Pares, "The New Land Settlement in Russia," *Russian Review* (London), 1912, Vol. I, No. I, pp. 71-72.

[13] Pares, "Conversations with Mr. Stolypin," *Russian Review* (London), February 1912, Vol. II, No. I, p. 108.

[14] Sergius Shidlovsky, "The Imperial Duma and Land Settlement," *Russian Review* (London), 1912, Vol. I, p. 21.

[15] See Chapter II.

feeling of ambivalence. As we shall observe, his inspection trip thrilled and pleased him, and yet he saw potentialities which troubled him.

A journalist who knew Stolypin well and shared his views reported that he had not traveled much, but "his trip to Western Siberia had produced a deep impression on him." The Prime Minister told Syromatnikov, "The democracy of Siberia will crush us,"[16] and he wrote the same thing to the Tsar. The remarkable fact is that such fears did not lead him to alter his policy. As we shall see, he believed that he might cushion the democratic impact of resettlement by allowing large enterprise to grow in the midst of the Siberian "peasant sea." But he never wavered in his encouragement of independent peasant farming either to the east or west of the Urals.

When Stolypin returned from Siberia in September 1910, Nicholas II welcomed him home in a letter which said, "The stable land settlement of peasants inside Russia and the same such settlement of migrants in Siberia—these are the two fundamental [*kraeugol'nye*] questions on which the government must tirelessly labor. One must not, of course, forget other needs—schools, ways of communication, and so on, but those two must come first."[17]

In reply Stolypin summarized his observations of Siberia briefly:

"My general impression is more than comforting. After a fearful convulsion, Russia undoubtedly is going through a powerful economic and moral upsurge, to which also the harvest of the last two years contributes strongly. Siberia is growing fabulously; in the waterless steppes (*Kulandiska*) which two years ago were regarded as unfit for settlement, during the last few months there have grown up not only villages but almost cities. And the mixed current of rich and poor, strong and weak, registered and irregular migrants bursting through from Russia into Siberia is in general a wonderful and powerful colonizational element. I would add, an element that is firmly monarchist, with a right, pure, Russian outlook. . . . But the comforting present must not blot out the complications of the future. These complications we are preparing for ourselves: lavishly, gratis, we are giving to the peasants, together with the loan lands, also land already worth now up to 100 rubles per desiatina; artificially we are establishing the commune in a land which was accustomed to private property, in the form of squatter's rights; we have not thought yet

[16] Sergius Syromatnikov, "Reminiscences of Stolypin," *Russian Review* (London), Vol. 1, No. 2, p. 86.

[17] "Perepiska N. A. Romanova i P. A. Stolypina," *Krasnyi Arkhiv*, Vol. 5, 1924, pp. 121-22.

of establishing private landed property there where the migrant is perishing without earnings.

"All this and much else—these are urgent and immediate questions. Otherwise, in an unconscious and formless manner will be created an *enormous, rudely democratic country, which soon will throttle European Russia.*"[18]

Speaking of the Volga valley rather than Siberia, Stolypin reported that land settlement was going well there. Much remained to be done:

"But the psychology of the people has changed, among the peasants already there have appeared apostles of land settlement and agricultural improvements. I saw members of the First Duma from the peasant-revolutionaries who are now passionate homesteaders [*khutoriane*] and devotees of order. And how right you are, Your Majesty, how rightly you fathomed what is going on in the soul of the people, when you write that the fundamental questions for the government are land settlement and migration. One must apply enormous forces to these two problems and not let them languish."[19]

1910: a Pause in the Flood

Stolypin and Krivoshein had visited six districts in four provinces and regions of Siberia and the Steppe, including journeys of more than 800 versts on horseback from the railroads and waterways. They listed four regions which they inspected most carefully: the productive northern zone of the Kirghiz steppe and the steppe portion of the Altai, the "Promised Land" of the migrants; the southern zone of the Kirghiz steppe, rich in free land but short on water; the intermediate forest-steppe zone in the vicinity of the railroad; and the Mariinsk taiga on the border of Yeniseisk province, a section difficult for migrants.

The opening sentence of their report reads: "The most important concern of the state in Siberia is the organization of migration."[20] The two men traveled fully conscious of the tremendous acceleration in the movement over the Urals. Stolypin noted that in 300 years a total of 4,500,000 Russians came to Siberia; in the last 15 years,

---

[18] "Iz perepiski P. A. Stolypina s Nikolaem Romanovym," *Krasnyi Arkhiv*, Vol. 5(30), 1928, letter written 26 September 1910 at St. Petersburg; pp. 82-83.

[19] *Ibid.*, p. 83.

[20] *Poezdka v Sibir' i Povolzh'e. Zapiska P. A. Stolypina i A. V. Krivosheina* (St. Petersburg, 1911), p. 1. A German translation exists: *Die Kolonisation Sibiriens. Eine Denkschrift von P. A. Stolypin und A. W. Kriwoschein.* Einzige berechtigte Übersetzung von Carl Erich Gleye, Dr. phil., Berlin, 1912.

3,000,000; in the last three years alone, more than 1,500,000. The figures appear somewhat too low, but the proportions were approximately correct.

Stolypin contrasted "the emptiness of the measureless plains of Siberia and the persistent reports that no more land is available there for settlers."[21] He wryly repeats the official estimates of approaching exhaustion of land. In 1896 the Kulomzin report had given the supply of migrant plots (*dushevye doli*) for the coming years as 130,000. During the fifteen years since then, ten times that number of plots had been allotted and annually a number almost triple that was being taken up. In early 1908 the Resettlement Administration had reported that 3,000,000 migrant plots were available for some 6,000,000 settlers in the future. Many people had found such an estimate fantastic. Yet after three years, more than 1,000,000 plots had been taken up, and the land reserve of Siberia had apparently not diminished but increased in some areas. For example, in Akmolinsk, the Resettlement Administration had calculated in 1908 that 6,500,000 desiatinas for 600,000 plots were available. One fourth of this area had already been settled, but a fuller survey of 1910 now estimated that the number of desiatinas of free land was still 11,877,000.[22]

Without doubt, it was said, the best land reserve in all West Siberia was the lands of His Majesty's Cabinet in the Altai region, opened to colonization by the law of 19 September 1906. Although 18,000,000 desiatinas had already been given the peasants and 3,000,000 more allotted for colonization, not including the forests and the mining areas, there still remained out of the 40,000,000-desiatina Altai district much room in the steppe. Local administrators had shown the travelers certain reports indicating that the empty Narym region, the Chuno-Angara region, the Karabul forest-fire area, were colonizable, though previously they had been regarded as hopeless. "One may take a calm attitude toward all the melancholy prophecies that the land for colonization in Siberia is exhausted, and that migration in two or three years will run up against a stone wall."[23]

Consider that Kaufman and other prominent investigators were on the side of the "melancholy prophets,"[24] and that the Soviet compendium *O zemle* in 1921 affirmed that "the reserves of land, usable as arable without much outlay, in the outlying parts of the country

[21] *Ibid.*, p. 2.
[22] *Ibid.*, p. 22.
[23] *Ibid.*, p. 26.
[24] See Chapters I and VIII.

must be accepted as by and large exhausted."[25] Where does the truth lie? The simplest answer is to point to the fact that the Soviet regime in the 1950's undertook to settle and sow some 30,000,000 hectares of "virgin land" in the fertile strip of West Siberia and what is today called "Kazakhstan." One need hazard no predictions as to the extent of the success of this scheme of forced colonization in order to perceive that Stolypin was right in asserting that much land was still available. No amount of effort could make eastern Siberia more fertile than western Siberia, it is true, nor make the 60th parallel as suitable for grain raising as the 55th. Neither can all American farmers live in Iowa, and fortunately many for various reasons do not desire to do so. The best land is usually taken up first by colonists moving into any relatively empty country, but the next best and the next may still sustain life and prosperity.

Stolypin admitted that an annual allotment of 5,000,000 desiatinas in the best zone of Siberia could not continue indefinitely. One had to go farther east and north, where it was no longer feasible for a surveyor to descend into an empty and fertile valley and drop a few stakes before summoning in a flood of settlers. However, he felt, not enough attention had been paid to the diversity of forms of colonization, not enough study given to the problem, not enough publicity provided for the fact that some suitable regions needed people, and that some qualified people needed places for settlement in Siberia.

He regarded lack of information as the crux of the present difficulties in colonization. On 1 July 1910, for example, there were 344,000 male migrants who had not found land, and yet there were 314,000 migrant plots available in Siberia. Those migrants were mainly concentrated in Tomsk and Akmolinsk, while the lots were in Yeniseisk, Irkutsk, and the Far East.[26] There was free land, a great deal of it, left in Siberia. But the manna was no longer strewn quite so thickly on the open ground; it needed a little patience to find. Stolypin saw that though the government had hung back from giving aid when less was actually needed, it might help mightily at the current stage.

The moment chosen for the journey was one which spurred him to haste. After rising to its highest peak so far (and as it turned out up to 1914), the trans-Ural movement had waned slightly in 1910. From 1 January to 1 September the migrants totaled 323,000 as against 639,000 in the same period the previous year. The decline Stolypin

---

[25] P. Mesyatsev in *O zemle*, Moscow, 1921, quoted by Naum Jasny, *The Socialized Agriculture of the USSR*, Stanford, 1949, p. 119.

[26] *Poezdka v Sibir'*, p. 28.

attributed to the dual effect of a bad harvest in Siberia and two years of good harvest in European Russia.[27] In any case he expected the wave to continue and insisted that the relative respite must be used to good advantage and quickly. Pavlovsky, who was himself an official in the Resettlement Administration, reports that the authorities welcomed the decline since they had "been literally overwhelmed by the human torrent pouring into Asiatic Russia."[28]

Stolypin and Krivoshein undertook to examine all stages of the process of migration and to decide what ought to be done at each stage. The conditions of travel had been vastly improved. The two officials inspected medical stations for migrants at Penza, Cheliabinsk, Omsk, Petropavlovsk, Novo-Nikolaevsk, and Kamna. The quality of their work was shown by the fact that since 1908 when cholera broke out in European Russia, no epidemic had occurred among the migrants. Only three cases had appeared in 1909 and three more in 1910. While in many Siberian cities hospitals had been filled with cholera victims, there had been almost none among the settlers.

It was taken for granted that the Trans-Siberian Railway would continue to be the mode of transportation used by the mass of migrants. In order to build better passenger cars for them, the Duma had appropriated 48,000,000 rubles, but Stolypin did not believe that this was money particularly well spent. Even if the cars were not modern, the trip was short. More important was the level of fares. The railway administration estimated its loss due to the specially reduced migrant fare at 7,500,000 rubles, but this gave Stolypin no qualms. The bulk of migrants needed that reduced fare; those who were somewhat better off usually traveled on ordinary fourth-class cars at regular rates. The government should also subsidize water transport. There were, for example, too few barges on the Ob and Irtysh rivers for the post-railway portion of the journey.

The settlers of 1910 traveled under conditions of less hazard and inconvenience owing to the reduced pressure on transportation facilities. It seems that many of them had a somewhat greater margin of security to start with. More carts passed through Syzran in 1910 loaded with household goods than those carrying people—13,500 as against 9,000.[29] Stolypin explained this in part by the ukase of 9 November 1906, which permitted easier liquidation of home property either through sale to the Peasant Bank or otherwise, but

[27] *Ibid.*, p. 5.
[28] Pavlovsky, *Agricultural Russia*, p. 177.　　　　　[29] *Poezdka v Sibir'*, p. 12.

he also suggested that word might have spread that if some cash could not be realized at once, it was better to delay migration. Not only did the level of migrant affluence rise in 1910, but the percentage of irregulars fell. No longer was it one-half of all migrants, but less than a third. This improvement was offset, however, by a rise in the "returner" movement. By September 1 it had gone above 50,000, or 14,000 more than 1909.[30] The Prime Minister explained this increase, like the decline in the eastward rush, by famine in Siberia coupled with a good harvest at home.

Occupying the Land

Stolypin and Krivoshein examined closely the results of scouting, to which Kulomzin had attached such importance. In 1907 there had been inaugurated a new system of "organized scouting," wherein a certain number of plots in specified areas of Siberia had been allotted to each Russian province. After three years Stolypin pronounced this system a failure. In 1908-1909 only 30 per cent of the scouts returned with their job of finding plots accomplished.[31] This system, which had evoked so much enthusiasm in the Duma and in the press, had in practice hindered free migration to areas reserved in advance. Stolypin thought the system ought to be abolished. Migration, he wrote, "must retain its most valuable quality, that of being a natural phenomenon in the life of the Russian people."[32] He added that this of course did not mean that the Russian government should cease intervention in the process of resettlement. Migration should be facilitated, but external regimentation of the departure and journey was no solution.

The problem seemed to be that certain officials, worried about the heavy influx into West Siberia, were trying to compel the scouts to go east. If the western steppe attracted all the settlers, Stolypin declared, no prohibitions would be successful in forcing them to go elsewhere. All that could and should be done to affect the settlers' destination was to establish, in the less popular regions, conditions which were equally or more advantageous than in the west. Conditions of settlement in the various areas ought to be adequately publicized. Differentials might be set in the reduced migrant fares to favor the areas where free lands were still more plentiful. The extent of government assistance to settlers might be stepped up in such regions. Lands remaining in the best but already crowded areas of Siberia might have a price set on them instead of being granted

[30] Ibid., p. 13. [31] Ibid., pp. 14-15. [32] Ibid., p. 16.

outright. In such ways governmental policy might beneficially affect the choice of destination by the migrant or his scout, but the government ought not to use any direct compulsion or prohibition. Freedom of choice should not be infringed. Therefore Stolypin recommended establishment of freedom of scouting throughout Siberia.

The Prime Minister felt that a false analysis underlay much public discussion of migration—for example, the sort that had suggested or approved the "organized scouting" system. Migration was indeed important from the standpoint of the defense of Russia's borders, the vitality of development in frontier areas, the utilization of suitable land for agricultural production, the mitigation of agrarian difficulties in European Russia, and so forth. But the individual migrant did not have in mind the aim of serving any one of those purposes. 'They are people, living people who are *en masse* taking care of their own migration affairs, are going to Siberia, ending the old life and building a new one . . . their aim is to settle in Siberia better, more advantageously, than they lived in the homeland. . . . To help them reach this, their immediate goal, is perhaps at the same time the best means of guaranteeing the attainment of all state objectives to which migration is related."[33] Were not, Stolypin inquired, all efforts to control the migration movement, to put it exclusively on a single basis which destroyed the economic calculations of the migrant, doomed to failure? "The natural development of the migration process is above all necessary from the standpoint of its state significance as well." Migration, populating the empty frontier, was like bark to the Russian tree; the best way to provide it was freedom of movement.

These remarks embody the most thoroughgoing rejection of paternalism to be found in any official statements regarding migration policy originating with the Imperial government. Starting from an understanding of the effective limits of law, Stolypin pleaded for a liberal approach to the problem of Siberian colonization. He believed it much better, both theoretically and practically, for the government to adjust itself to the economic facts prevailing at a given moment in a given region, to leave people freedom to choose their destination in the light of those facts, and to assist them to accomplish smoothly what they would to a great extent attempt to do anyway.

The Prime Minister next surveyed the availability of land region by region. He believed that an excellent source of land existed in the

[33] *Ibid.*, p. 17.

Kirghiz (Kazakh) regions where those natives were making no use of vast expanses. Many of the Kirghiz were nomads, and so they must remain at least temporarily. Stolypin did not believe the state had any business expropriating Kirghiz holdings, just as he did not believe in seizing gentry estates. He likened the problem of taking settlers into native regions to that of the old-settlers. If the migrants, as well as the old-settlers and natives, were allotted land, not as tenants of the state as at present, but as landowners, with full property rights, then transfer of lands could take place freely by monetary purchase and sale. Perhaps a new Land Bank might be established to furnish credit for such purchases.[34]

It was noted that in Tomsk province in 1909 scouts had in actual fact purchased lands from old-settlers for almost exactly the same number of migrants as those for whom other scouts had received assignment of new plots. In other words, in this province half of the migrant land transactions were already commercial! One wonders if Nicholas II nodded over this section of the report. Stolypin, like Gurko in the incident cited at the beginning of this chapter, hastened to add that of course open sale of land in Siberia did not take place, because "legally" almost all land was the property of the state, the Crown, or the Cossacks.[35] But he did not confuse the law with the facts.

The Cossack officers' lands were being sold legally. They brought about 80-100 rubles per desiatina in the area nearest the railway, and 50-70 rubles in the Irtysh valley. The official travelers visited in Petropavlovsk county a village of migrants from Kursk who had a few years back bought land from a Cossack general at 60 rubles per desiatina.

The question of private property and sale was linked to the existing situation as regards land allotment. From the legally established level of 15 desiatinas per male "soul," in some areas the norm had fallen in recent years to 12 and 10 desiatinas. This still left 35 to 40 desiatinas per family, an area of which only an insignificant proportion was often worked by the peasants themselves. The rest either lay waste or was rented to irregular migrants. Such an abnormal state of affairs was a natural result of inappropriate norms. If the government continued to grant farms of the same size everywhere, certainly no one would take up less fertile land if they could possibly avoid it. Land should be given a price, the Prime Minister felt, a

[34] *Ibid.*, p. 31.
[35] *Ibid.*, p. 30.

price adjusted to geographical accessibility and relative fertility.[36] Since the better land was often the most accessible, the necessary price adjustment ought not to be difficult.

Stolypin did not believe it was desirable to set a price for land throughout Siberia. In the best and most thickly settled areas such a step was timely, in other places it was not.[37] Nevertheless, the law of 27 August 1906 on the sale of state lands to the European Russian peasantry ought to be extended to Asiatic Russia, to be administered by the migration authorities in full consideration of local needs and differences. Such sale would not be a means of obtaining revenue, but rather of directing colonization to new, suitable areas of sparse settlement. For colonists to such regions, government grants of land and monetary aid should continue as heretofore.

The chief necessary conditions for the settlement of the best, south-western zone of the Siberian steppe were summarized by Stolypin as follows:

1. Land settlement of the old-settlers and natives should be expedited, and property rights granted to them.

2. Just determination of migrant portions, considering not merely the 15-desiatina legal norm but also the particular conditions of each region.

3. Sale of portions of state lands to colonists.

4. Facilitation of conditions of migrant tenure of Kirghiz lands.

5. Organization of credit for migrants for purposes of purchase from old-settlers and natives, and extension of the activity of the Peasant Bank (or a new Agricultural Bank) to Siberia. (Under difficult conditions, it would still remain the direct responsibility of

---

[36] Under the American Homestead Act, 160 acres of free land were provided each head of a family. The 15-desiatina norm meant that a family was given an average of a little over 50 desiatinas, or slightly more than 140 acres. Giving Siberian land a price signified commuting the nominal state dues or rental which the migrant had to pay. Note that the legal method of obtaining land in the American West had been by auction, with a stipulated minimum price, from the Ordinance of 1785 until the Homestead Act of 1862, and even the Homestead Act had the provisions that five years' residence and cultivation had to be proved for the land to be given gratis, and that any settler wanting to obtain ownership earlier (but only after six months) had to pay $1.25 per acre. It is not clear whether Stolypin was influenced by American land legislation, but obviously he did not recommend imitating it completely. He believed in freedom of movement and sale of land in full ownership to the settler, but he did not think a uniform norm either of price or size of holding to be wise. The Homestead Act was discussed in Russia. Alexander Kol, in two articles in *Voprosy kolonizatsii* (nos. 10 and 11, 1911-1912), discussed it at length, contending that the American homestead system provided more legal than economic equality among the settlers.

[37] *Ibid.*, p. 32. (My paraphrase.)

the government to prepare land for settlement, involving clearing of woods, drainage, and the construction of roads.)[38]

The government responsibility to prepare land for migrants had so far been unevenly discharged. In the marshy Baraba steppe, 900,000 desiatinas had been drained from 1895 to 1908. In the arid steppe, wells were necessary. It was a fallacy to assume that nature had somehow given these districts to the nomads. In certain of these places the methods of American dry agriculture could be used— piling up the snow and allowing it to remain. In other areas, migrants who came from the Don and similar regions could well pasture sheep and horses. The question of the water supply of both the air and the ground here needed further exploration. There was no less water here than in Argentina. Scientific knowledge and improved technique could make possible much more widespread use of the arid steppe, even though without it thousands had already overcome the obstacles successfully.

As for clearing of forest, this was now left entirely to the settlers themselves. For even some of the colonists Stolypin and Krivoshein saw close to the railway in the Mariinsk taiga, this task had proved too much. The government should take on the job. Roads were a serious problem. During the past three years, 52,000 versts of road had been constructed in the Siberian taiga. The ones observed had been good, but they were far too few. Of the 244,000,000 desiatinas of Siberian forest area, the 92,000,000 of true forest yielded only 3,500,000 rubles of revenue, or less than four kopeks per desiatina. This very low level of productivity was partly explained by inaccessibility, and more roads would serve to raise it markedly.[39] Thus Stolypin's desire to leave full scope for individual initiative did not conceal any wish to reduce government activity or expenditure connected with colonization. On the contrary, he believed much greater efforts were needed.

The Prime Minister next turned his attention to the social conditions of the settlers. The government, the church, and private effort had contributed in a significant way to their cultural needs. In the previous year alone 67 mobile churches had been inaugurated in Siberia, and 48 churches and 98 schools had been built under the aegis of the Chief Administration of Land Settlement and Agriculture. Courses given at the instance of the Metropolitan of Moscow the previous year for prospective clergy for Asiatic Russia had been

---

[38] *Ibid.*, p. 33.
[39] *Ibid.*, p. 37.

of great help. More educational effort was called for, but "the danger of cultural barbarization of the migrants is becoming less threatening."[40]

As had already been noted, medical care was scarce. Often a single hospital tried to manage for a region of 30,000 square versts with a population of 50,000. Appropriations for hospitals had been doubled between 1908 and 1911, however. In Siberia 200 migrant points had now come into existence, one-quarter of them in 1910 alone, but many of them still lacked adequate medical care.[41]

Farm machinery was being made available both by the government and by private enterprise. One-third of this trade was carried on by 90 governmental agricultural stations which served both migrants and old-settlers. Though in 1909 profits from this branch of state enterprise had declined, the previous revenue had been around 330,000 rubles. In part machinery was being provided by "an American company." Stolypin thought it might well build a foreign branch in Moscow in order to reduce costs, but still farm machinery was coming in fast.[42]

Agronomical assistance had been available in Siberia for only three years. Experimental fields had been established and 100 meteorological stations had been founded. So far, so good. However, only the field at Temir in the southern Urals had had any effect on migrant economy, Stolypin felt.[43] He regarded the opening of agricultural schools on several levels as also essential. The logical place for college level instruction in agriculture was Tomsk—to begin with as part of the existing university, the only one in Siberia. Omsk, as the economically most important point in western Siberia, should have the first secondary agricultural school. The establishment of instruction on this level should precede the higher level. All such social institutions could provide real aid to the colonists. Still, in Stolypin's opinion, more direct and easier help could be given them by attention to present methods of land occupation and tenure.

Loans to migrants were a matter of dispute. Some claimed they were too large, some too small. The chief need, thought the Prime Minister, was to make their level dependent upon existing conditions in different regions. That is, to rephrase Stolypin's point, the amount of aid should depend upon the stage of development of the area in question. Aid should not, he declared, be a function of the poverty of this or that migrant, but of the particular economic difficulties of

[40] *Ibid.*, p. 44.   [41] *Ibid.*, p. 45.
[42] *Ibid.*, p. 47.   [43] *Ibid.*, p. 52.

settlement in the region concerned.[44] The law should be altered (presumably by the Duma) in order to fix different norms for loans to different regions, and the government should be empowered to change these norms as conditions changed. The Prime Minister thought that it was time to abolish loans in the best areas. Yet for the northern and eastern taiga, the present ceiling of 165-200 rubles for loans ought to be doubled, and in some cases portions of the loan should be not in money but in kind. Loans for home building should, however, be retained; this was too difficult a matter for the migrant to handle alone. The government should be prepared to provide food in case of bad harvest. The migrant had to face this possibility without reserves. One could scarcely ask him to keep his belief in the land if the crop should fail; in any case he might leave if it did. The temporary rules on alimentation of June 12, 1900, had not been extended to Siberia, and should be.

The tenure of land was at the heart of Stolypin's economic and political policy, and he regarded it as of fundamental importance to Siberia and to the success of colonization. All land in Siberia was legally either state land or belonged to the Cossack army units or to His Majesty's Cabinet. The Siberian commune was the actual mode of tenure (as distinguished from ownership) for the majority of peasants. Stolypin saw that the Siberian commune was significantly different from both the European Russian commune and from individual holding.[45] With a few exceptions in western Siberia, the Siberian commune knew neither periodical redistribution nor any form of "equalization" in which a holder would yield any land to another without payment. He explained the absence of these characteristics by the vast extent of available land, the presence of any sort of commune by the pressure of fiscal demands. In general, he reported, among the old-settlers as well as the migrants, labor in cultivating the land had instilled in the tiller the fervent belief that his land could not be taken from him.[46] So it had been, as Stolypin may or may not have known, as early as the Mongol period of Russian history, when such a belief of the peasant had found recognition even in the courts. Stolypin asserted that from the juridical viewpoint the situation of peasant land in Siberia was identical with the conditions of the lands of the European Russian peasant before 1861, whether serf or state peasant. The Siberian commune differed favorably from the post-1861 situation at home by its lack of redistribution and its greater readiness to adopt new forms.

[44] *Ibid.*, p. 48.   [45] See Chapter x.   [46] *Poezdka v Sibir'*, pp. 55-56.

Stolypin saw a positive good in the fact that the legal notion of state property had been preserved in Siberia so long. The turning of the land over to private ownership could now take place in accordance with the greatly altered values of the land consequent upon migration. The retention by the state of all of this land, even perhaps of reserve lands on the borders, was senseless. Stolypin pointed to what he deemed to be a growing feeling in the general public that the state should be founded "not on the treasury and state property but on a prospering and strong population."[47]

Effort was required in Siberia, as well as in European Russia, to bring private property institutions into legal existence. Laws of 1896 and 1898 had begun the job, and millions of desiatinas had been confirmed in the possession of the peasants. A new draft law, Stolypin declared, would be laid before the Duma in their current session, transforming the whole Siberian population into the proprietors of their land and assuring to each holder definite rights to common lands, free from any dependence on the commune.[48] This was the first step. The second would be to extend to Siberia the provisions for consolidation of holdings on the basis of the law of June 14, 1910. This process would of course take time. The best results in European Russia had been achieved through voluntary means. Allotment by *otrub* (consolidated holding) from existing communes, provision of migrant plots where possible as otrubs, preferential assignment of such plots to those communes which have individual holding—such are some of the methods which might be employed. More survey offices would be needed in Siberia for this purpose. Stolypin saw the problem as one of adjusting governmental action to reality, not vice versa; but he took the need of governmental action seriously.

The proof that "life seems not to notice the juridical deficiency" was shown in the fact that the process of separation of townships into villages, villages into settlements, settlements into households or homesteads, was proceeding in Siberia. Beginning in Tomsk province, the area filled with the most migrants, a pattern of general division was taking gradual shape. Private surveyors appeared and multiplied. In the city of Tomsk alone there were four surveying companies, employing hundreds of surveyors. Many former government surveyors were setting up private businesses. In Tomsk province in 1908, as a result, 21 communes had been divided, 19 into households and 2 into homesteads; in 1909, 69 had divided, 12 of

47 *Ibid.*, p. 58.
48 *Ibid.*, p. 59.

them into homesteads. Comparable developments were reported in other areas. The government had had nothing to do with originating this movement; it was purely spontaneous. The law must follow and assist it, thought the Prime Minister.[49]

New Homes and Old Neighbors

The next area of concern of the official travelers was the economic condition of the colonists in their new homes. A variegated picture was found. The ministers had moved rapidly from poor settlements of Pavlodar county, Semipalatinsk, to flourishing villages in the Kulunda steppe of the Altai region, then, after a three days' journey, to the poorer villages of the taiga. The year's harvest was in general not a good one, but its effect differed a good deal from place to place.

It was on the former Cabinet lands of the Altai region that life was best. In the three years from 1907 through 1909 almost one-half of the migrants had gone there. "One must see the new settlements on the former Cabinet lands to become convinced of the well-being of the migrants."[50] There they had encountered a number of unenrolled colonists who had become temporary tenants while awaiting their independence. Stolypin and Krivoshein themselves had been besieged by petitions from unenrolled colonists, Siberian land officials, and many other local residents, begging to be made independent. From the formal standpoint, Stolypin found the presence of the unenrolled colonists disorderly, but from the economic standpoint "understandable and unavoidable." Economically, in fact, they were not a serious problem since the proportion of enrolled was so high and the economy flourishing.

The "unenrolled" mainly belonged to the category of irregular, voluntary migrants, who for generations had constituted such a thorny problem to the government. From January 1 to July 1, 1910, some 50,000 of them had been settled or sent back, but 49,000 more promptly appeared in their place. Once more Stolypin saw the solution in terms of private ownership and the operation of the market. The portions were plainly too big, and the irregulars gravitated to them as the holders were willing to rent them. There was no right of sale, no regular method of appraisal for those transactions which occurred, outside the law.

Whatever the character of the irregular migrant problem, in general migration was a positive success in western Siberia. Even at first glance one could see that the Siberian migrant had on the

[49] *Ibid.*, pp. 64-65.   [50] *Ibid.*, p. 70.

average more land, more cattle, more grain, and more implements than the average European Russian peasant. Statistics dramatically confirmed these casual impressions. No thoroughgoing statistics were yet available, and the Duma planned this sort of investigation for the following year.[51] Still, in the last fifteen years 765 settlements of some 60,000 families—around 400,000 persons—had been investigated in the steppe and the four Siberian provinces. According to these surveys, the colonist had from 1½ to 2 times the number of cattle he had on arrival; on the average, 5 large livestock, 6 small stock. The number of households in Siberia without livestock was 7 per cent as against 13 per cent in European Russia. As for the average tillage, in west Siberia including the newest plots it included 7.3 desiatinas, in the steppe 9 desiatinas; if we compare the average of 5.11 desiatinas in European Russia, the difference is not discernible. However, out of the Siberian colonists who at present sowed more than 7 desiatinas, 57 per cent had had less than that at home, and 25 per cent had had no land at all.[52]

As regards yield, in west Siberia for 10 to 15 years it had averaged per desiatina 60 poods of rye, 62 poods of wheat, 75 poods of oats, as compared with European Russia's averages of 50 for rye, 40 for wheat, 47 for oats. Whereas in European Russia 31.7 per cent of the tillage was in wheat, in Siberia it was nearly half and according to the Governor General of the Steppe, in his region it was up to 70 percent. From all this Stolypin estimated that the average productivity per desiatina of the Siberian settler was 50 rubles, as against 30 rubles 55 kopeks in European Russia.[53]

The income of the typical family was rising steadily, though faster in the steppe than in the taiga. The income could be broken down as including 57 per cent from land, 18 per cent from cattle, 15 per cent from crafts, the other 10 per cent scattered. After eight to ten years on the new dwelling place, the land gave 60 per cent, the cattle 20 per cent. The craft income was largely from drayage (*izvoz*), this making up two-thirds of the total. The remainder came from wood and leather work chiefly intended for household use, and sold locally. As Stolypin noted, this was the picture of a natural economy, but a positive picture. On the average, the wealth of the settler household was rising by 15 rubles per year, while in the already consolidated household, the rate was 30 rubles.

[51] This survey was in fact carried out, and its results are discussed in Chapter IX.
[52] *Poezdka v Sibir'*, p. 73.
[53] *Ibid.*, p. 74.

In order to complete this picture, it must be asked; how many migrants returned? In the fifteen years from 1896 to 1909, about 3,000,000 migrated, and 301,046 or about 10 per cent returned. In every realm of human life, thought Stolypin, "one always will find 10 per cent unlucky people," and some would simply chalk up this figure as failures without asking why. Although the returner movement was still, to be sure, "a black shadow over migration," nevertheless the overwhelming majority of returners just paused in Siberia and never set up a household at all.[54] Almost two-thirds of all returners were irregulars who had tried their luck and found none. Those who fought fruitlessly with the new conditions and returned constituted only 3.8 per cent, not 10 per cent, of the inflow. These figures, Stolypin reported, tallied with what he had seen for himself. There had been rumors that in the current year there were many returners, but the official travelers reported meeting almost no migrants who wished to go home, and few who even wished to change their location. Half of the returner movement, furthermore, did not go back to European Russia but to other and better parts of Siberia. For example, in 1909 out of 16,500 returners, 7,828 went home, while 8,754 went to other parts of Siberia,[55] especially into the Semireche area. Stolypin, however, did not brush aside the returner movement as insignificant. Although some such movement was a natural concomitant of any large-scale migration, involving a complete alteration of normal environment, he still believed that the inflexible and blanket migration policy, taking the same form for all regions, was the cause of some of it. Under such conditions, leaving the place of first settlement was not always a sign of economic failure, and these conditions should be changed—this was the entire burden of Stolypin's report.

Evaluation of the significance of migration for the economy of European Russia was next attempted. Of course in general it was found to be much less than for Siberia itself. In toto, migration had not yet encompassed half of the annual natural increase of population, and only in a few provinces and districts did it overtake and surpass the increase. However, it was concentrated with respect to point of origin in the southern, western, and black-earth provinces. In the last four years, according to computations by the communes, up to 1,500,000 desiatinas in the black-earth and steppe country of European Russia had been left vacant by migrants. In the year 1909 alone,

[54] *Ibid.*, p. 76.
[55] *Ibid.*, p. 78.

30,000 desiatinas were vacated in Ekaterinoslav, 25,000 in Kursk; and these figures were closely parallel to those of Peasant Bank sales, indicating transfer into the hands of other peasants on the spot.[56] Such results were noteworthy; however, Stolypin considered them of secondary importance.

Migration, he concluded, was not a solution to the agrarian problem in European Russia. It could powerfully influence the homeland economy only if the rate rose to several millions per year. A German scholar, Professor Auhagen, evaluated the Great Siberian Migration as likely to be of greater importance to Germany than the future role of Siberia in the world market. In other words, the mass exodus of Russians eastward would be advantageous to Russia's neighbors, rather than to European Russia.[57]

In contrast, the effect of migration on Siberia was tremendous. In the Akmolinsk region in 1893 settled farmers had made up 5 per cent of the total population; now they constituted 45 per cent. In Tomsk province, during the last three or four years, three-quarters of a million farmers had been settled. Migrants were plowing 4,000,000 new desiatinas. If one figured a gross return of 50 rubles per desiatina, this represented an increment to the gross national product of 200,000,000 rubles per year. The example of the Kulunda steppe (in the southern part of Barnaul county of Tomsk province) was illustrative. It had 913,000 desiatinas, and had netted the Emperor's Cabinet only 3,000 rubles annually from Kirghiz farms and Pavlodar townsmen. In 1907, 1,089 Kirghiz farms were there. The Resettlement Administration had left them 167,000 desiatinas (more than 150 desiatinas per farm) and had turned 746,000 desiatinas into migrant lots. Within three years, 200 villages were settled with some 55,000 peasants (Ukrainian and in part Mennonite). There arose a trade center, Slavgorod. In place of one earth hut, in a year there sprang up a church, administrative building, two mills, bazaars, hospital, and pharmacy; there were preparations for opening a church school for girls and a school for boys; land was set aside for an experimental field.[58]

Against instances like that of the Kulunda steppe, one had to put the fact that such development had taken place at the expense of natives and (in other cases) old-settlers. The old-settlers had lost about one-quarter of their lands to migrants. Productivity had gone

---

[56] *Ibid.*, p. 80.

[57] *Ibid.*, p. 81. For discussion of German reactions to migration, see Chapter VIII.

[58] *Poezdka v Sibir'*, p. 83.

up significantly in regions where part of old-settler lands had passed into migrant hands. The figures of tilled area and productivity of land were about 20-30 per cent higher among migrants than among old settlers in general. Nevertheless, since the latter retained 40-50 desiatinas per household, and were still considerably more affluent than the peasants of European Russia, one could believe that "they had successfully survived unavoidable changes in their economic life."[59] Stolypin warned, however, that more intensive cultivation which continued to employ fallowing methods presented its dangers, and he insisted on the necessity of widespread aid from agronomists.

The old-settlers had held 33,500,000 desiatinas. After a decade, a total of 6,000,000 of these (1,500,000 in 1909 alone) had been turned into migrant lots. The new law which had already been approved by the Council of Ministers had in view to accelerate this process, and likewise to give the old-settlers their land as property. This, Stolypin declared, was the surest means of improving the economy of the old-settlers and speeding the transfer of surplus lands from their hands into the hands of migrants. The extension of the law of 14 June 1910 (Stolypin's most important land law) to Siberia was needed. Previously, this law had only aided migrants to sell their holdings in European Russia, while in the future it ought to help them buy their own land in Siberia.

The plight of the natives also received some attention in this connection. Their holdings had been considerably restricted, but the loss of millions of desiatinas had not been without its compensations. For one thing, the land the natives retained had acquired a market price for the first time.[60] In general, the influx of Russian migration had been accompanied by the raising of the level of Kirghiz economy, according to two surveys conducted in the Akmolinsk region in 1898 and 1908. When the two sets of results were compared it was found that the number of poorer households in the three northern counties declined by half; the percentage fell from 83 to 50 per cent in Petropavlovsk, from 75 to 49 per cent in Kokchetav, 67 to 55 per cent in Omsk. At the same time the land belonging to the Kirghiz doubled. The number of tiller-owners in the three districts increased from 5,500 to 11,000, the tillage from 11,000 to 25,000 desiatinas. The increase in Omsk was tenfold, and in some areas therein the percentage of tiller-owners reached 95-100 per cent. Kirghiz cattle-raising likewise had benefited, owing to the higher prices obtainable.

[59] *Ibid.*, p. 85.
[60] *Ibid.*, p. 86.

The number of horses and horned cattle in Petropavlovsk rose 120 per cent, in Omsk 52 per cent, in Kokchetav 68 per cent. A comparable development was seen in the adjoining Kustanai county of Turgai region. The Kirghiz population was increasing 2.3 per cent annually, whereas in all Russia the rate was below 2 per cent. Prices obtainable for cattle in the steppe rose 50 per cent in the previous five years. In the Cossack-held regions, where sale was legally possible, land in the same localities had brought 40 to 60 rubles three years before, and was now bringing 80 to 100 rubles. The Kirghiz in the steppe over the past three years, Stolypin reported, had bought more than 100,000 rubles' worth of agricultural machinery annually. If these people were at all susceptible to civilization, they could not forever remain nomads.[61] Experience had shown that they could and had become tillers; that up to the present the migration process had worked for and not against the interests of the nomads. The Russian Prime Minister quoted with approval John Stuart Mill: "The transfer of workers and capital from old lands into new ones, from a country where they have little into a country where they have a greater productivity, increases the sum of riches in the old as well as in the new country."[62]

Siberia's Future

For evidence that the Siberian migrants were establishing themselves with success, it was necessary to look to conditions of the market for the grain which they were producing. The tilled area in 1909 was about 6,000,000 desiatinas, and was increasing rapidly. The chief grain of Siberia was wheat. In Tomsk during the past twelve years the wheat tillage had risen from 588,000 to 1,157,000 desiatinas, in Akmolinsk from 98,000 to 279,000. In that province, during the previous four years, the tilled area had increased even faster than the swift rise in population.[63]

A bad harvest in 1909 had checked the rise to some extent. But nevertheless on 6,000,000 desiatinas an average harvest yielded, at the rate of 50 poods per desiatina, an annual 300,000,000 poods. For the 10,000,000 people in Siberia, at a rate of 15 poods per person per year, only 150,000,000 or half the harvest was needed for food. Even if the need was placed higher and additional grain was used for fodder, a great surplus remained. The Far East and part of eastern Siberia lived on imported grain from the steppe and western Siberia.

[61] *Ibid.*, p. 89.   [62] Quoted *ibid.*, p. 92.   [63] *Ibid.*, p. 93.

In the latter regions, during years of good harvest almost three-quarters of the grain represented marketable surplus. Stolypin discounted the importance of the China market. The route to central Asia lacked a direct railway. In the north lay the Arctic Ocean. In the east, competition of Manchurian and American grain blocked the way. In the west there existed an internal customs barrier, the tariff at Cheliabinsk on the Trans-Siberian Railway.

Stolypin emphasized the potentialities of the northern sea route.[64] He thought the simplest way would be to float cargoes up the Ob and Yenisei and then transport them to London by ocean. He recalled that in 1905 the Ministry of Ways of Communication had stated that ships could reach the mouths of the Siberian rivers for two months during the summer. During the period of the Second Duma, the government had declared the mouths of the Ob and Yenisei to be free ports, in order to attract foreign ships. Other improvements in communication were urged. Some of them were an Ob-Arkhangelsk railway, a seven-verst canal between the upper Chusovaia (a Kama tributary) and the Irtysh system, and a Turkestan-Siberia rail line designed to exchange Siberian grain for Turkestan cotton. The building of two segments of the latter—from Novo-Nikolaevsk to Semipalatinsk and from Arys to Verny—was already planned.

The problem of supplying the Far East was difficult. In 1896, when the Siberian railway had been opened to freight, tariffs had been established at both Cheliabinsk and Irkutsk. In 1900 the Irkutsk tariff had been abolished, but this had had little effect in bringing Siberian grain into the Far East. Only about 3,500,000 poods went through Irkutsk eastbound, and most of it did not go beyond Transbaikalia. It was for the most part on Manchuria that the Amur and Ussuri regions depended for grain. Distance and higher transport costs were against west Siberian grain, for its local price and that of Manchurian wheat were about the same. Even though it would mean a loss for the Chinese Eastern Railway, Stolypin suggested the tariff should be restored. The alternative was to depend almost entirely on the "good will of China" for the supply of the Russian Far East.[65]

[64] See Constantine Krypton, *The Northern Sea Route: Its Place in Russian Economic History before 1917*, New York, 1953. There were also more ambitious proposals for linking this route to the Far East. See "K voprosu ob ustanovlenii morskago soobshcheniia Dal'niago Vostoka s Evropoi cherez vody Severnago okeana," in *Sibirskii Torgovo-Promyshlennyi Ezhegodnik, 1914-1915*, Petrograd, n.d., Pt. II, pp. 410ff.

[65] *Poezdka v Sibir'*, p. 100.

On the west, however, he advocated abolition of the Cheliabinsk tariff. The fear of "cheap Siberian wheat" could be allayed. While the price of work cattle and fodder was 30 per cent lower in west Siberia, the price of labor was 20-25 per cent higher than in European Russia. Freight rates could be adjusted a few kopeks to cover the differential. Stolypin's optimism had a shadow cast on it by his own footnote, however, giving average 1903-1909 prices:[66]

	Wheat	Rye	Oats
Central Agricultural provinces	97	78	62
West Siberian provinces	72	54	40

Nearby European Russian provinces might in any case benefit from Siberian prices. Stolypin's major point was that ending the Cheliabinsk tariff would aid export of grain abroad, and the current figure of 100,000,000 poods would rise tremendously. He based this hope on somewhat doubtful predictions. He concluded that world reserves of grain were diminishing. The American market was taking more and more of its own production, so that it appeared that American grain export must come to a halt within a decade. He felt little concern about Argentina. Canada was a stronger competitor, but here he thought "raw nature" would hold back agricultural development. While urging caution in evaluating future world prospects, he thought present conditions were favorable to the expansion of Russian agriculture, especially as Europe and America became more industrialized. He did note that Russia likewise had been consuming more of her grain production, which accounted for some of the decline in export by 45 per cent from 1904 to 1908. Stolypin concluded that the Cheliabinsk tariff should be lifted, even though it might take a few years to do it successfully.[67]

The Siberian economy, however, ought not to be considered purely in terms of grain production. For example, out of 27,000,000 desiatinas of land reserves in Akmolinsk and Semipalatinsk regions, only 7,000,-000 were entirely suited for agriculture; on the remaining 20,000,000 more cattle raising was possible. The raising of sheep assumed new importance with the decline of the breeding of fine-wool sheep in European Russia, and the wormwood section of the Kirghiz steppe was well suited to sheep-raising. Kirghiz horned cattle were being successfully used as draft animals and were also marketable for meat.

[66] *Ibid.*, p. 102.
[67] *Ibid.*, p. 106.

Butter production was one of the most hopeful trends. In 1894 it had begun with a production of 400 poods. In ten years the total had risen to 2,000,000 poods worth almost 25,000,000 rubles. By 1907 butter exports from Siberia reached 3,500,000 poods. This constituted very nearly the entire butter export from the Russian Empire (3,600,000 poods in 1907, valued at 47,500,000 rubles).[68] The government had given support to this industry, consisting of loans and the establishment of dairying laboratories, a training center for workers, and the like.

The by-products of dairying, sour milk and buttermilk, were capable of being used as food for pigs, and pig-raising had been successfully introduced into the Kurgan county of Tobolsk province, the center of butter manufacturing. In 1909 the peasants of Kurgan had realized 400,000 rubles from the sale of pigs. These were some of the ways in which grain production could and should be supplemented in the development of the Siberian economy.

In order to prepare for the future, Stolypin contended, the government could not limit itself to the individual problems of the migrants, but must seek to introduce new economic elements which would have a broadly beneficial effect. Such necessary new elements were three: the establishment of the right to property in land, the construction of new railway lines, and the diversification of agriculture.

"The right of property in land," said the report, "must serve as the chief security for the raising of the productivity of the peasant households and the reorganization of the pattern of migration. But Siberia needs not only small peasant property. One must secure for the migrants the proximity of privately owned enterprises of a higher cultural level. Purely agricultural, purely peasant Siberia will not develop all of its productive capacity."[69] Stolypin suggested that amidst the small holdings there should be established farms of a larger industrial type, improving crop rotation and productivity and providing work for those peasants needing money. Still more needful were some comparatively large holdings for developing other branches of agriculture like sheep-raising. Finally, private property in land would permit industrial and trading centers to develop. The law of 8 June 1901, on the establishment in Siberia of private property in land, ought to be brought into effect as quickly as possible.

Plainly Stolypin's recommendations for the diversification of agriculture were bound up closely with his expectations regarding

[68] *Ibid.*, pp. 107-08.
[69] *Ibid.*, p. 117.

the results of the introduction of private property. The recommendations for new railways were for swift completion of the Amur line and the construction of the proposed South Siberian line. The latter should begin not at Orenburg but Uralsk, pouring Siberian grain directly into the Volga mills and linking up with Semipalatinsk, the natural terminus for the projected Turkestan-Siberian Railway, via Barnaul to Novo-Nikolaevsk.

Administrative organization needed revision to conform to changes in trade and population patterns. Akmolinsk had formerly been Kirghiz country, but now it had a Russian population in its three northern districts. However, it did not include the similar and adjoining Kurgan and Ishim counties which belonged to Tobolsk province with its distant capital. Tobolsk now included Tiukalinsk county, whose interests were so closely linked with Omsk that the migration organization must make its headquarters there. As to Tomsk province, a part of Zmeinogorsk county was under the jurisdiction of the governor of Semipalatinsk, but in all other respects it was subordinated to Tomsk province. Barnaul county was ready to become a separate province.[70] Many towns required city status to obtain adequate police and judicial protection; such were Kamen, Tatarka, Taiga, Bogotol, and many others.

Siberia lacked the zemstvo. It lacked proprietors of land who could bear its burden. But when the old and new settlers possessed their own land and the feverish migration process had slowed, the population, "linked by common interests, will so to speak crystallize and cease to be a mechanical mixture of migrants strange to each other from Perm, Poltava, and Mogilev."[71] And then—a time not long distant—the time for the Siberian zemstvo would come.

Summary

Finally the ministers came to summarize their overall conclusions:

"1. It is necessary to make allotments to old-settlers and migrants in Siberia not for indefinite use, as at present, but as property. . . .

"2. It is necessary to achieve gradual unification of governmental land policy on both the hither and farther sides of the Urals . . . [to pursue the objective of support of] small personal property in land. . . .

"3. In the best regions of Siberia, simultaneously proceed to the sale of land to the migrants. . . .

"4. It is desirable to establish freedom of scouting. . . .

[70] *Ibid.*, p. 119. [71] *Ibid.*, p. 122.

"5. Apportion cash loans to migrants for home construction not on the basis of the greater or lesser poverty of the individual migrants, which is beyond calculation, but on the basis of the greater or lesser difficulty of settlement of the given region. . . .

"6. It is necessary to create and develop agronomist aid to the migrants. . . .

"7. Beside the small peasant holdings, secure the formation beyond the Urals also of private landed property. . . .

"8. One must continue the constant settlement of the Kirghiz steppe by Russian migrants. . . .

"9. It is necessary to be concerned about the security of the sale of Siberian grain and other products of the Siberian economy. . . .

"10. It is necessary in general to broaden and deepen the organization of migration. . . ."[72]

These recommendations ranged over the entire panorama of problems which confronted the Siberian economy. They did not take as their starting point, however, the "economy," but rather the people who lived and were coming to live in Siberia. The great majority of them were peasants. They were developing into smallholders whose actual economic status had advanced beyond that recognized by the law. The natural tendency of the frontier was to develop private landholding. The government's task was to further this tendency and to remove the fetters from it by means of legal and financial policy. Such was the central conclusion of Stolypin's report.

"Private property in land" was a phrase which Stolypin used ambiguously. Sometimes it referred chiefly to peasant tenure, sometimes chiefly or solely to possible future capitalist farming, sometimes to both. He saw a place for both peasant enterprise and capitalist farming in Siberia's future. So far there was all peasant farming in Siberia, no capitalist farming, and, as has been observed, this fact gave Stolypin pause. He wished to see peasant farming grow and prosper, but he believed the economic consequences of the presence of a few larger capitalist enterprises in the midst of the millions of smallholdings would be beneficial. Furthermore, he thought the political consequences would be favorable, in the sense of helping to prevent Siberian democracy from "crushing" the homeland.

In European Russia Stolypin's policy excited the opposition of the Right, much of it based on landlord interests.[73] There he en-

[72] *Ibid.*, pp. 127-30.
[73] As V. A. Maklakov says in his *Vtoraia Gosudarstvennaia Duma*, Paris, n.d.

couraged the peasant, while taking a passive, laissez-faire position in regard to the gentry. In Asiatic Russia he saw the logical conclusion of his own peasant policy taking shape before his eyes, and it frightened him a little. Here, as west of the Urals, he strongly believed it necessary to encourage and assist the peasant, but he felt it incumbent upon him to do something about fostering capitalist farming as well. One may well believe that some capitalist farms could have been started in Siberia without exciting the degree of fear or opposition which might have manifested itself if Siberia had ever known serfdom. At least it seems clear that peasant enterprise and capitalist agriculture might have been able to coexist in Siberia under the same financial and market conditions. We have already pointed out the ability of the former to compete with the latter successfully under the market conditions of European Russia.[74] In actual fact, Siberia was never invaded by capitalist farming. It remained peasant until the Communists established large agricultural enterprise there, using compulsion rather than the wage system, and exterminated peasant enterprise.

It is noteworthy that Stolypin, being as Pares said "no theorist," never seems to have decided exactly what it was that pleased him and what frightened him about Siberia. He remarked with pride on the emergence of a society which would have new regional interests but at the same time would, he believed, cherish its ties with the rest of the Russian Empire. In Asia as in Europe, he pointed with satisfaction to the development of a "sturdy individual proprietor" which would serve as a barrier to revolution. But he spoke of the threat that a "rude democracy" in Siberia might "crush" the homeland.

What did Stolypin mean, exactly, by "democracy" in this context? He did not seem to refer to the possibility of universal suffrage. In politics he was more concerned about the danger to the regime he served from the revolutionary intellectuals than from the peasants. He said to Pares in June 1906, just after the stormy sessions of the First Duma, "The peasants simply do not care about politics."[75] Their concerns centered in the realm of economics. If the peasants of Siberia, and the whole Empire, were monarchist in the sense that they became more satisfied with the rights and opportunities they

---

pp. 36-37, "It was no accident that the reform of peasant life so dear to Stolypin was almost wrecked precisely in the Imperial Council, that last support of 'reaction.'"

[74] See Chapter II.

[75] Pares, "Conversations with Mr. Stolypin," *Russian Review* (London), February 1913, Vol. II, No. 1, p. 105.

enjoyed under the old regime, then whether their support of the Tsar was expressed in terms of attitude or in terms of franchise might not have made much difference. Bismarck had managed to combine monarchy with universal suffrage, and Stolypin might not have been unwilling to do the same eventually. What appeared to concern Stolypin in regard to Siberia was not whether the affluent *sibiriak* would demand the vote, but whether an equalitarian type of society was developing which would serve to revolutionize the value system of Imperial Russia. He relied heavily on the independence and initiative of the European Russian peasant to destroy the commune and to create homesteads. However, when he found the psychology of the free man as fully developed as he did in western Siberia, he was vaguely troubled, even though he did nothing to restrict it and much to enable it to grow. It was a democratic state of mind which impressed and perplexed Stolypin in the Russian East.

CHAPTER VIII

Migration, the Intelligentsia, and the Duma

The Intelligentsia and Migration

There is no doubt that the problem of resettlement rose during the interrevolutionary period to become a focus of the attention of a sizeable section of Russian "society," as well as of a considerable number of foreign scholars. The inspection trip of Stolypin and Krivoshein to Siberia attracted the attention of many of the latter. In France such men as Paul Leroy-Beaulieu and Pierre Chasles studied Russian colonization,[1] and in Germany a particularly active interest was aroused. In May 1912 an expedition of observers was organized by the Vereinigung für Staatswissenschaftliche Fortbildung of Berlin, led by Professor Max Sering of the University of Berlin and including Otto Auhagen and K. Ballod. In consequence a volume of essays on the subject appeared in 1913. Auhagen wrote, "The results achieved by the Russian land-settlement authorities within so short a period are extremely impressive," but noted that the achievements were conducted in the face of steadfast opposition from the entire Russian Left.[2] W. Preyer published a book in 1914 emphasizing that "the reform met the real needs of the population," and in 1917 he rejoiced that the war and Revolution had brought the operation of the reform to an end, since he feared that the Russian state would otherwise have been dangerously strengthened.[3] The attention of foreign observers was further caught by the journeys of Krivoshein to Turkestan in 1912 and to the Caucasus in 1913, also for the purpose of inspecting the results of migration.[4] The foreign reaction might be summed up in the words of Max Sering, writing in 1911: "in the domain of internal colonization, by far the greatest activity among all countries is being displayed by Russia."[5]

---

[1] See Leroy-Beaulieu, *De la colonisation chez les peuples modernes*, 6th ed., 1908, ch. 13; and Chasles, "Les réformes agraires et l'évolution des classes rurales en Russie," *Revue économique internationale*, October 1913.

[2] Quoted in Bilimovich, *loc.cit.*, p. 346, from *Russland: Kultur und Volkswirtschaft*, Berlin and Leipzig, 1913.

[3] Quoted *Idem.* from W. Preyer, *Die russische Agrarreform*, 1914.

[4] See "Zapiska Glavnoupravliaiushchago Zemleustroistvom i Zemledeliem o poezdke v Muganskuiu step' v 1913 godu," *Voprosy kolonizatsii*, No. 14, 1914, pp. 134ff.

[5] Quoted in Pavlovsky, *op.cit.*, p. 160.

The domestic reaction was no less pronounced, but it took a somewhat different form. An anonymous reviewer of an essay on migration to the United States wrote plaintively that although Russian migration to America had attained the same height as that to Asiatic Russia,[6] all the excitement centered around the latter.[7] The "excitement," however, was often of a critical sort. The chief effort of the foremost scholars—or at least those who, like A. A. Kaufman, had the ear of the opposition parties—was devoted to minimizing the effect of migration and to attempting to show that it could neither justify the hopes being placed in it nor serve as any kind of viable solution to the agrarian problem. One of the minority, I. Iamzin, recalling in 1914 how bitterly he had been criticized "in scientific societies" for his alleged "faith" in official statistics and his generally "optimistic" views, triumphantly cited the recently published survey of Kuznetsov as confirming those views fully.[8] He might have saved his breath. The view of Kaufman rather than Iamzin (and the Germans for that matter) continued to prevail, and it was passed on so successfully to many Western scholars that little interest has been shown in the problems of Russian colonization since that time.

The view of Kaufman was expressed in the foreword to his well-known volume, *Resettlement and Colonization*. He wrote that "the author, after fifteen years of literary and scientific and in part practical work in the realm of resettlement, considers himself morally obliged to come out with the present book, in order with his unfortunately too weak voice to warn against that enthusiasm for the 'broad tasks' of resettlement which apparently again has replaced the cooler and more cautious view, which was beginning to predominate, of its future and possible significance." Although, said Kaufman, he was not one of the extreme pessimists, the available land was ex-

[6] Although migration to America had in fact exceeded that to Asiatic Russia in 1903 (136,902 as compared with 125,500) the former total was made up of Poles, Jews, Finns, and other minority peoples, with only a small proportion of Russians. A few years later the ratio had changed substantially. In 1909, 707,463 crossed the Urals, while only 120,460 immigrants from the Russian Empire entered the United States; in 1910, the figures were 353,000 and 186,792 respectively. Of the latter total, 151,062 were Poles and Lithuanians. Thus immigration from Russia to America included few Russians and Ukrainians, and its total was far smaller than that of Siberian migration. (See N. Turchaninov, "Emigratsiia v Sev. Amerikanskie Soedinennye Shtaty i novyi immigratsionnyi zakon Shtatov," *Voprosy kolonizatsii*, No. 9, 1911, pp. 34-57.)

[7] Unsigned review of "Pereselenie v Soedinennye Shtaty v prezhnee i v nastoiashchee vremia," by D. A., in *Zemlevladenie*, 1906, No. 1, in *Voprosy kolonizatsii*, No. 1, 1907, pp. 312-13.

[8] I. Iamzin, "Pereselencheskaia statistika i khoziaistvennoe polozhenie pereselentsev po izsledovaniiu Pereselencheskago Upravleniia," *Voprosy kolonizatsii*, No. 14, 1914, pp. 73-95.

tremely insignificant in quantity compared with the existing need, and migration was coupled with "colossal risks."[9] Paradoxically, Kaufman, representative of the anti-governmental intelligentsia, here sounded some of the pessimistic tones which we have discovered in the official attitude and government propaganda of an earlier date.

Whether the source of Kaufman's pessimism was entirely academic or partly political, many of his readers drew political comfort from his writings. The Left of course feared that successful reform would make revolution impossible and contribute to the preservation of the power of the Tsar in some way or shape. Particularly did this fear center in the area of agrarian reform, and many sought and found reassurance on the subject in Kaufman's books.

Among such people was Lenin. In 1907 he wrote: "In this connection A. A. Kaufman is entirely right, who ridicules the search for free lands for resettlement on the basis of data on the number of square versts. He is entirely right also, undoubtedly, when he indicates how little land suitable for resettlement there is at the present time on the frontiers of Russia, how incorrect is the opinion that the lack of land of the Russian peasantry can be remedied by means of resettlement." Naturally, the Kadet Kaufman did not fully win the approval of the Bolshevik leader. Kaufman implied, wrote Lenin, that if there were sufficient land for migration, there would be no need to expropriate the landlords, and this premise Lenin attacked as a false deduction. "The reasoning of Mr. Kaufman and his innumerable adherents among the Russian intelligentsia must be altered, in order for it to become accurate."[10]

It must be noted that Lenin did not discount the importance of resettlement. On the contrary, in a passage not fully consistent with the above quotation, he compared Russia with America in this respect: "To speculate exactly how much land could be converted in Russia from 'unsuitable' into suitable, is useless. But it is necessary carefully to recognize a fact which is proved by the whole economic history of Russia and which constitutes the great peculiarity of the Russian bourgeois overturn. Russia possesses a gigantic colonizational fund, which will become accessible to the population and accessible to culture not only with each step forward of agricultural technique in general, but with each step forward in the act of liberation of the Russian peasantry from the serf yoke. This circumstance

[9] A. A. Kaufman, *Pereselenie i kolonizatsiia*, St. Petersburg, 1905, p. iv.
[10] V. I. Lenin, "Agrarnaia programma S.-D. v. pervoi russkoi revoliutsii," *Sochineniia*, Vol. XIII, 1947, p. 225.

constitutes the economic basis for a bourgeois evolution of Russian agriculture on the American model."[11] In Western Europe, he added, the available land was already taken up at the time of the bourgeois revolution.

However, when there was any question of drawing political conclusions from the progress of migration, Lenin's pessimism was sharply expressed. In 1913 he undertook to evaluate the whole Stolypin agrarian program: "In order to understand the causes of this *collapse* of the so-called 'Stolypin' land policy of the government, which it is proposed that the State Duma again approve by means of confirmation of the budget (and which, of course, the landlord parties in the Duma do approve), I dwell a little more in detail on the *two* chief, so to speak, *trump cards* of our 'new' land policy: first, resettlement, second, the celebrated *khutors*" (emphasis in the original).[12] Lenin thus recognized the interdependence of migration and land settlement.

"Did the government achieve success?" Lenin inquired. "Did it achieve any kind of *pacification* of the peasantry and improvement of its condition in Russian and in Siberia? Just the reverse. The government achieved only a new sharpening and worsening of the condition of the peasants *both in Russia and in Siberia*."

He then undertook to prove that Stolypin had encountered double failure. Turning first to resettlement, he referred to the data in the Minister of Finance's explanatory memorandum to the budget of 1913. "The migrants, we are told, convert waste regions into 'cultured places,' the migrants are becoming richer, improving their economy and so on and so forth. Typical bureaucratic doxology! . . . It is only a pity that in the explanatory memorandum there is *completely left* in silence the data on returning migrants!! A strange and noteworthy silence!" The data showed that in 1911 the returners numbered 60 per cent.[13] "This great wave of finally ruined returner-migrants with incontrovertible obviousness tells us of the complete collapse of the government's policy." But the evidence which Lenin used to clinch his point was not drawn from the statistics on returners, but from a brochure written by a bureaucrat named A. I. Komarov, who had served in Siberia "27 years, *twenty-seven* years, Messieurs!" Komarov declared that the trip of Stolypin and

[11] *Ibid.*, p. 229.
[12] Lenin, "K voprosu ob agrarnoi politike sovremennogo pravitel'stva," *Soch.,* Vol. XIX, 1948, p. 158.
[13] On the returners, see Chapter IV.

Krivoshein was a "buffoons' journey," and made other critical comments. Komarov had not been directly concerned with migration at all, but had served in the forest administration. It seems that his chief objection to the migration policy was that it meant the wreck of "rational forestry."[14] For all one knows, this might well have been partly true, though the assertion seemed a feeble reed for Lenin to rest his argument on.

Having disposed of resettlement, Lenin turned to the farms. He declared that it was known that the farmers were of two types. The first, a negligible minority, was made up of kulaks who lived well anyway; the second was composed of ruined peasants who went to the farms out of need. "They beat themselves against the khutors, like fish against the ice; they sell all their grain in order to obtain a loan at the bank; they are eternally in debt; they become desperately poor; they live like beggars; they are *driven out* of the khutors for *arrears in payments*, and they finally are transformed into homeless vagrants."[15] One might suggest that if it were actually true that any considerable number of the new farmers were being thus quickly transformed into landless proletarians, Lenin need not have worried so much about the possible success of the Stolypin policy.

In these remarks Lenin stated a good deal more sharply than others, and perhaps less convincingly, an attitude which was widely shared among the Russian intelligentsia. Few scholars believed that migration was going to make any considerable difference in the fate of the Russian peasant. It was accordingly left to the practical workers in the field of colonization to attempt to bring to public notice, not a rose-tinted sketch of the whole matter, but rather a locus of serious discussion of the problem.

A group of local workers in resettlement affairs, assembled in St. Petersburg in February 1906, conceived the idea of publishing a journal through which all such workers, scattered far and wide in Asia, could obtain a general picture of the progress of colonization and in which they could find a center of moral support. It was felt likewise that Russian "society" also could profit by such an organ, since it was so "badly informed"—though certainly not uninformed— on questions of migration.[16] Thereupon a journal entitled *Problems of Colonization* was founded. It began to appear in 1907, edited first by O. A. Shkapsky and later by G. F. Chirkin and N. A. Gavrilov,

[14] *Ibid.*, p. 161.
[15] *Ibid.*, p. 164.
[16] See "Ot redaktsii," *Voprosy kolonizatsii*, No. 1, 1907.

and was published right up to World War I. Another organ of local people practically concerned with the matter was the *News of the South Russian Regional Zemstvo Resettlement Organization.*[17] It was published in Poltava by an association of nine provincial zemstvos from the most congested region, where most of the movement originated. This organization had been formed in October 1907 at a congress in Kharkov, which had elected as president Prince A. D. Golitsyn, future chairman of the migration commission of the Third Duma. Such publications of the "practicals" had their effect, but did not materially alter the view which continued to be accepted in many circles of public opinion.

Stolypin did not concern himself unduly with hopes that a successful migration policy would convert the intelligentsia. He hoped to bring social stability to the mass of the people, the peasantry, by way of land settlement and migration together. Unlimited movement, unaccompanied by measures intended to secure solid settlement, would entail risks. If the safety-valve of migration operated smoothly, economic pressures in the homeland might be gently and gradually relieved, and the monarchy would be easier to preserve. If migration should entirely escape the confines of governmental assistance and direction, the result might be the "rude democracy" about which Stolypin mused. Some kind of upheaval from below might upset the regime, even though a doctrinaire revolution of the intellectuals were successfully averted. Stolypin and the officials of the Resettlement Administration supported migration steadily and firmly, but they thought it neither economically warranted nor politically prudent to stake everything on it.

However, that was precisely what many voices of the Right demanded. Its spokesman Markov II declared, "The government must resolve the agrarian problem chiefly by means of migration, and this must be underlined, it should not at all be said that in this there is something shameful."[18] The position of the Right was that at least the entire annual increase in population of European Russia, or approximately 2,000,000 people, should be aided to migrate.[19] On the Left, both inside and outside the Duma, there were many who denied that migration could have any serious effect on the agrarian problem. Even liberals charged that the great wave of migration

[17] *Izvestiia iuzhno-russkoi oblastnoi zemskoi pereselencheskoi organizatsii.*

[18] Speech of Markov II, *Gosudarstvennaia Duma. Tretii sozyv. 1908 g. Stenograficheskie otchety. Sessiia* I, *Chast'* II, col. 1307.

[19] V. P. Voshchinin, *Pereselencheskii vopros v Gosudarstvennoi Dume III sozyva*, St. Petersburg, 1912, pp. 28-29.

had been "artificially inflated" by the government.[20] The Left contended that "migration had been chosen by the government as the chief means of resolution of the land question, and from this standpoint were inclined to regard any kind of concern about migration as interfering with the development of various political plans which were in this connection one-sided."[21] So a government report put it —quite accurately. The Left thus accused the government of having adopted the policy which the Right vainly demanded that it adopt. For the Left, almost any level of migration was too much; for the Right, almost any level was too little. The Left thought resettlement could solve nothing; the Right believed it could put the whole agrarian problem to rights. The Right's attachment to migration was the greater as its hostility toward land settlement mounted. The gentry was having difficulties enough already; why simply strengthen the peasantry, and forget the gentry? The Left's hostility to migration was partly based on fear that the agrarian programs of the opposition parties would lose their appeal if migration (as well as land settlement) should be successful.

The Socialist Revolutionaries demanded that all private lands should pass to control of the communes; the Mensheviks, that landlord lands should pass to peasant (communal) organs of self-government; the Bolsheviks, that the land should pass to the state; the Kadets, that private lands should pass into a state fund.[22] None of the opposition parties aimed at strengthening individual proprietorship, which both migration and land settlement tended to do. These parties opposed the policy of Stolypin because he was the chief officer of the government they wished to overthrow, but also because he favored private ownership, which they either opposed in principle or did not wish to support.

The Government and the Duma

In the First Duma, summoned while the urban Revolution of 1905 was still a fresh memory and the rural revolt was not yet at an end, there was in general little attempt to legislate seriously. The Kadet plurality (often leading a working majority) was intent on making a revolutionary demonstration rather than on passing laws.

[20] Speech of N. K. Volkov II (Kadet), cited by Voshchinin, *op.cit.*, pp. 52-53.
[21] "Krest'ianskoe pereselenie i russkaia kolonizatsiia za Uralom," *Aziatskaia Rossiia*, Vol. I, p. 465.
[22] See V. Maklakov, "The Agrarian Problem in Russia before the Revolution," *Russian Review*, January 1950. My own *Lenin and His Rivals*, New York, 1955, treats the various party agrarian programs at greater length.

There was no discussion at all of the problem of resettlement. Not a single piece of proposed legislation on it was introduced, and there was only one interpellation concerning migration presented. It concerned "the illegal organization of migrant portions on the Kirghiz steppe," and did not even receive examination before the Duma was dismissed in June 1906.[23] However, the minister of agriculture, Stishinsky, indicated to the Duma that the government would support migration. Voshchinin, the chief student of migration affairs in the Duma, declares that thereby "migration was fully openly recognized already as a means for resolution of the 'agrarian' problem," although no deputy even commented on "such a sharp reversal of front."

The Second Duma, hopelessly split between intransigents on both Left and Right, was also short-lived. Nevertheless it left behind two documents relating to migration. One was a "formula of passage to the next business" on the proposal of the minister of agriculture concerning measures to accelerate the organization of migrants plots, and the other was a draft report of the budget committee on the migration budget for 1907, drawn up by deputy N. L. Skalozubov (Kadet, Tobolsk). The conclusions of this report centered the charge that the government treated migration in too centralized a manner and the recommendation that the Duma elect a migration committee.[24] Three draft laws had been introduced by the Chief Administrator of Land Settlement and Agriculture, but had not been acted upon.

There was some discussion of the course of migration on the floor of the Second Duma. Despite the promulgation of the law of 1904, which left to the land captains discretion in issuing travel permits (although proclaiming complete "freedom" of migration), the settlers had in accustomed fashion ignored the law. Despite the Japanese war, 79,000 had crossed the Urals (apparently through its duration), and of those 71,000 had done so irregularly.[25] As a result, in March 1906 the Council of Ministers had ordered the land captains to issue permits to all applying for them. The only restriction retained was the discretionary power of the Minister of Agriculture to issue permits to scouts intending to reach localities where free lands were insufficient in quantity. The consequent rise in the level of migration was sharp; in 1905 migrants and scouts totaled 44,029; in 1906, 213,886. It is striking that the only requirement remaining for the

[23] Voshchinin, *op.cit.*, p. 13.
[24] Report summarized in *ibid.*, pp. 14-15.   [25] *Ibid.*, p. 16.

191

ordinary migrant to satisfy in order to become "regular"—that of previous dispatch of a scout, on the reduced fare—was evidently repugnant to many. More than half of the migrants of 1906 still went without permission, and most curious of all was the fact that as many as one-tenth of the scouts were irregular, "as if in principle unwilling to use the right of cheaper travel."[26]

This was the situation when the Third Duma convened. Neither the First nor the Second Duma had gotten around to approving the migration budget, which had risen from 2,500,000 rubles before the Revolution to 5,000,000 in 1906 and 11,000,000 in 1907. The government asked almost 19,000,000 for 1908, and the Duma approved a figure only 6,000 rubles smaller.[27] Thenceforth the annual occasion of a discussion of migration in the Third and Fourth Dumas was the time of consideration of the migration budget in the late winter or early spring. A number of questions were always raised, but the sums voted continued to rise though the level of migration fell off slightly after the peak year 1908. In 1909 the appropriation was 23,209,000 rubles; in 1910, 25,208,000; in 1911, 27,103,000; in 1912, 27,120,000; in 1913, 28,068,000; in the draft budget for 1914 it was 30,229,000. The increase since 1906 was over six times.

During the entire period of the Third and Fourth Dumas—that is, from 1907 to the outbreak of the war, when attention to migration gave way to more pressing matters—both Duma and Imperial Council took an active role in the consideration of resettlement problems. By and large, the last two Dumas were neither radical, as the Emperor and especially the Empress often felt them to be, nor reactionary, as the revolutionaries steadfastly asserted. They were rather moderate and Centrist. The largest single party in both the Third and Fourth Dumas was the Octobrists, who with the Nationalists fought on two fronts against smaller competing fractions on Left and Right.[28]

The Third Duma

The Third Duma, in contrast to the first two, considered migration a matter which deserved serious attention as well as large appropriations. In its fourth sitting it approved an Octobrist pro-

[26] *Ibid.*, p. 18.

[27] See Appendix 1, "Razvitie assignovanii po smetam Pereselencheskago Upravleniia 1908-1912 gg.," *ibid.*, 144-45, and article on migration budget in "Khronika," *Voprosy kolonizatsii*, No. 14, 1914, p. 183.

[28] See Warren B. Walsh, "Political Parties in the Russian Dumas," *Journal of Modern History*, June 1950, p. 148.

posal to establish a special Duma committee on migration, which deputy M. V. Rodzianko introduced. On 15 November a committee was elected consisting of 66 members, and it chose as its chairman Prince Alexander Dmitrievich Golitsyn (Octobrist, Kharkov), who had been elected president of the First Zemstvo Regional Congress on Resettlement. V. A. Karaulov (Kadet, Yeniseisk) proposed that 5 members be added, one for each Siberian province and region, since they were the areas most affected. With 71 members the migration committee was the largest one of the Duma.[29] On 7 December the Chief Administrator of Land Settlement and Agriculture, Prince Vasilchikov, made a statement to the deputies by which he said he hoped "to make a beginning at establishing the necessary solidarity of views on the significance of migration affairs between the executive power and the legislative institution."[30] Karaulov immediately welcomed the declaration in the name of the Siberian deputies. In general the Siberians were rather active in the Duma's deliberations on migration. The Kadet party was at best lukewarm to migration, but it would appear that Karaulov and Skalozubov were at times more Siberian than Kadet.

In 1907 the number of migrants and scouts who passed over the Urals had gone well above the half-million mark, and on 13 March 1908 the Council of Ministers again restored restrictions on free movement. The Chief Administrator could now halt the granting of permits not only where free lands were insufficient but on the grounds of any "necessity recognized by him for a given region." The ministry utilized this act at once to prohibit scouting to practically all regions. It undertook a system of allotting the prepared plots of Siberia and the steppe region to individual provinces of European Russia, the migrants to be selected by the land-settlement commissions. This measure was a resounding failure. The number of scouts did fall during 1908, but the majority of them were irregulars, and the total number of migrants and scouts surpassed three-quarters of a million, the highest level ever reached by Siberian migration. The Resettlement Administration telegraphed frantically on 7 October 1908, but without success, begging for authority to reduce the norm of allotment below 15 desiatinas per male soul so that it could handle the flood of settlers.[31]

The Resettlement Administration, through its head (*nachal'nik*), Actual State Councillor (promoted during the Third Duma to Privy Councillor) Glinka, made clear to the Duma from the first that it

[29] Voshchinin, *op.cit.*, p. 19.   [30] Quoted in *ibid.*, p. 21.   [31] *Ibid.*, p. 34.

stood ready to apply any policy which would be clearly and consciously adopted. During the budget discussion of 1908, Glinka declared that if some ends of resettlement had not been attained, the cause was in part insufficient funds, but also "in fact not sufficient definiteness of governmental views on the matter of resettlement."[32] In the discussion of 1909, Glinka spoke even more bluntly. He asserted that the Resettlement Administration could not be properly held responsible for some of the shortcomings referred to by orators in the Duma, and contended that the government must either assign almost unlimited funds, or "perhaps" adopt a new system of selling migrant plots to the settlers, though he warned that many of the migrants presently moving might not have the ability to pay for them.[33]

The following year, 1910, Glinka listened to something of a melee. Prince Golitsyn spoke of the need to introduce private property institutions into Siberia; the Kadet Vinogradov denied the existence of any such need, and so on. Glinka once again pleaded to be told what it was that the Duma desired to be done, since several orators believed radical changes were necessary.[34] Actually the Duma attached several "desires" to its approval of the 1910 budget, including the introduction of the zemstvo into Siberia, reduction of the tariff on grain for sale in White Sea ports, and specifically demanded an accurate report of "irregulars" up to 1 January 1911. (It is not clear that the last-named was ever received, but the self-contradictory nature of the phrase, "accuracy about irregulars," was called to the attention of the Duma.)[35] The Duma did not need to express itself again on the question of granting the migrants land as private property for Siberia. It had already in March 1908, at the instance of the Octobrists, done so favorably, despite the protests of the Kadets.[36]

During the discussion of the migration budget in 1910, the Chief Administrator of Land Settlement and Agriculture, Krivoshein, criticizing the two-year-old system of bureaucratically organized scouting, declared, "In affairs which involve the life of the people so deeply, one ought to beware of such methods,"[37] and announced that for the summer of that year scouting had already been made free again for eastern Siberia. He thought the government was taking

[32] *Stenograficheskie otchety. Sessiia* I, *Chast'* II, col. 1280.
[33] *Ibid. 1909 g. Sessiia* II, *Chast'* III, col. 538.
[34] *Ibid. 1910 g. Sessiia* III, *Chast'* III, col. 862.
[35] Voshchinin, *op.cit.*, p. 44.
[36] *Ibid.*, p. 33.
[37] *Stenograficheskie otchety. Sessiia* III, *Chast'* III, col. 814.

too much responsibility trying to plan the movement in detail, and said insufficient information was available anyway. The alternative system toward which he contemplated moving was sale of migrant plots, and it was this statement which Vinogradov had denounced.

It was the failure of bureaucratic methods to organize scouting which thus prompted Stolypin's and Krivoshein's journey to Siberia in 1910. The recommendations contained in their report, which was made available to the Duma, "as a whole undoubtedly constituted a prepared and considered resettlement program,"[38] as Voshchinin declared. As noted above, Stolypin and Krivoshein recommended that both old-settlers and migrants should receive their land in consolidated holdings as private property, that freedom of migration should be restored, that the sale of plots to newly arriving settlers should begin in the best and most thickly settled regions, and a number of other measures.

Action on certain of these recommendations was soon forthcoming. On 4 March 1911 the Council of Ministers ordered land captains to resume the unrestricted granting of permits, and freedom of scouting was restored as previously established by the rules of 10 March 1906. The Ministry of Agriculture undertook to put into effect the recommendation that "larger and more complex" farms than the usual migrant ones should be established among the latter. It set aside 135,000 desiatinas in the Amur general governorship and Semipalatinsk region for this purpose, and introduced into the Council of Ministers a draft law to be presented to the Duma.[39] A law was enacted on 27 January 1911 to provide city government for Tatarka, Taiga, and Bogotol, as Stolypin had recommended, while deferring action on other cities until more data were obtained. In February 1911 Krivoshein delivered a report to the Council of Ministers in which he contended that "the aspirations which are developing among the Siberian peasantry in connection with migration from European Russia for individual enterprise and liberation from the commune, so burdensome for agriculture, require us to put on the first order of business the task of setting Siberia, like European Russia, on the road to the foundation and strengthening of private property." A first step would be allotting all land to migrants in consolidated plots. Krivoshein thought this should begin at once. How-

[38] Voshchinin, *op.cit.*, p. 46.
[39] "Proekt obrazovaniia v zaselennykh raionakh za Uralom krupnikh chastno-vladel'cheskikh khoziaistv," *Voprosy kolonizatsii*, No. 9, 1911, p. 459.

ever, inaugurating the new system would require alterations in the Resettlement Administration budget before the Duma and a good deal of preparatory work, and thus it could not be applied everywhere instantly. Krivoshein proposed that allotment by consolidated plot begin at once on a portion of the migrant land, and the Council of Ministers decided that not less than one-third of the land within each migrant region should be so allotted during the current year.[40] Finally, a kind of Siberian "homestead act," granting the settlers firm title of ownership in place of the hitherto existing right of perpetual use to the state property of Siberia, was prepared and submitted to the Duma.

Neither the measures taken by the government and Duma in 1911 nor the actual state of resettlement diminished the hostility of the Left toward the whole process. In 1911 the representative of the Social Democratic fraction, Voiloshnikov, declared that the increase of the returner movement—which reached its peak in 1910, henceforth to decline—proved the failure of the government's policy, and he ended by demanding "complete cessation of the migrant wave."[41] The Social Democrats had proposed the rejection of the entire migration budget in 1908 on the grounds that the government migration policy since 1861 had been framed in the interests of the landlords rather than of the peasants.[42] By demanding that migration be halted, Voiloshnikov was only carrying the position to its logical conclusion, or, if one likes, reducing it to absurdity.

However, the migration policy of Stolypin did not excite such reaction from the rest of the Duma. As Voshchinin says tartly, "In general, the program of the government was received sympathetically by the Duma, in the absence of one of its own."[43]

The relative slackening in trans-Ural movement which was noticeable by 1910 did not at all prove that the government's policy had failed. Stolypin did not expect that all unhappy or poverty-stricken people in European Russia would go to Siberia, there to become happy and rich. He linked his Siberian policy to the overall adjustment he sought in Russian agriculture through fostering individualization and property rights on both sides of the Urals. According to the explanatory memorandum of the Resettlement Administration which accompanied the migration budget of 1912, it was proposed to make the

[40] "Novyi poriadok obrazovaniia pereselencheskikh uchastkov za Uralom v 1911 godu—preimushchestvenno khutorami, otrubami i melkimi uchastkami," *Voprosy kolonizatsii*, No. 9, 1911, pp. 342ff.

[41] *Stenograficheskie otchety. Sessiia* iv, *Chast'* iii, cols. 312-17.

[42] *Ibid., Sessiia* i, *Chast'* ii, col. 1247.   [43] Voshchinin, *op.cit.*, p. 49.

chief objective "not outsettlement of the toiling masses of the homeland, but settlement of the frontiers by Russian people, and to transfer the center of gravity of resettlement affairs to its qualitative side—the stability of settlement of the migrants.[44]

Despite the fact that the Resettlement Administration had been subjected in the Duma to the sharpest attacks delivered on any agency of the government, a majority of the deputies had given the thoughts and labors of the migration committee serious attention and action. The Third Duma followed neither the extreme optimism of the Right nor the extreme pessimism of the Left in regard to resettlement. Its results, to be sure, were somewhat untidy. Twenty-six draft laws on the subject had been introduced, but none passed.[45] Chairman Golitsyn of the migration committee informed the Duma that its report could not be completed due to "special physical conditions."[46] And yet a foundation had been laid which was used to some extent, and could have been used to a much greater degree, to carry through significant legislation and provide intelligent consideration and criticism of government policy and practice during the period to follow.

The Fourth Duma

In the Third Duma, the Siberian delegation had been made up of 3 Social Democrats, 3 Trudoviks, 6 Kadets, 1 Progressist, and 1 "non-party Leftist."[47] The 14 deputies which made up the delegation in the Fourth Duma were of approximately the same political coloration: there was 1 Social Democrat, 5 Trudoviks, 7 Kadets, and 1 non-party man. The chairman of the "Siberian parliamentary group" was N. K. Volkov II (Kadet, Transbaikalia). It is noteworthy that Siberia yielded not a single deputy from a party to the Right of the Kadets, which may serve to justify Stolypin's fear of Siberian democracy. In any case the lengthy interviews with all of the Siberian deputies which may be found in the *Siberian Yearbook of Commerce and Industry* for 1914-1915 suggest that their interests were more urgently political than economic.[48] The Tomsk deputy A. A. Durov summed up his view of Siberia's immediate needs as "zemstvo, zemstvo, and

[44] Quoted in *ibid.*, p. 50.
[45] See Appendix II, listing draft laws on migration introduced into the Third Duma, *ibid.*, pp. 146-48.
[46] V. Mugansky, "Voprosy kolonizatsii v chetvertoi Gosudarstvennoi Dume," *Voprosy kolonizatsii*, No. 13-14, 1913-1914, No. 13, 1913, p. 4.
[47] See "Sibirskaia parlamentskaia gruppa," in *Sibirskii Torgovo-Promyshlennyi Ezhegodnik, 1914-1915*, Pt. II, pp. 445-49. Article is followed by short biographies of all deputies from Siberia in the fourth Duma.
[48] The interviews are given in *ibid.*, Pt. II, pp. 257-339.

zemstvo"; the Irkutsk deputy I. N. Mankov declared, "the basic need, the fundamental cultural and economic demand of our region, is the zemstvo"; and the zemstvo issue was the most persistent theme of all the fourteen interviews.

As noted previously, the proposal to extend the zemstvo to Siberia aroused some apprehension based on the fact that the gentry, whose role in the European Russian zemstvo had been from the start so vital, was absent from Siberia. In his Siberian report Stolypin had expressed the feeling that the solution of the problem might be postponed. Nevertheless as long ago as 2 April 1905 there had been an Imperial rescript to the governor-general of Irkutsk, Count Kutaisov, to encourage discussion among local Siberian groups of the problem of introducing the zemstvo in the governor-generalship of Irkutsk and in Tobolsk and Tomsk provinces.[49] The upshot was that in the Third Duma in May 1908, 101 deputies had introduced a draft for the extension of provincial and district zemstvos into these areas. The draft was approved by the Duma but rejected by the Imperial Council, and there the matter rested at the coming of the war. Local self-government for Siberia had thus become a more burning issue than ever in the minds of its deputies. There was also dissatisfaction with the extent of Asiatic Russian suffrage. Deputy Volkov, during the Fourth Duma debate on the Kadet draft on universal suffrage, criticized sharply the situation in which the steppe, Central Asia, and Yakutsk region were deprived of the vote (under the Stolypin law of 3 June 1907). One looks in vain, however, for any evidence of profound concern on the part of the Siberian deputies regarding migration or land settlement.

Of the parties with large Duma representation, the Octobrists showed the most interest in migration, and none of them came from Siberia. In a speech during the early months of the Fourth Duma,[50] M. I. Simonov (Octobrist, Voronezh) discussed the principles which he felt ought to be fundamental to migration policy and toward which it seemed to him that the government was moving, judging by the explanatory memorandum to the migration budget of 1913 and by the draft legislation introduced into the Duma. First he discussed "freedom of migration" in connection with the successive limitations and extensions of it by the government from 1906 to

[49] See interview with deputy N. V. Nekrasov (Tomsk), *ibid.*, Pt. II, pp. 330-31.
[50] Text complete as "Ocherednyia zadachi kolonizatsii. Rech' chlena Gosudarstvennoi Dumy M. I. Simonova, proiznesennaia v obshchem sobranii Gos. Dumy 10-11 iiunia 1913 pri razsmotrenii smety Pereselencheskago Upravleniia na 1913 god," *Voprosy kolonizatsii*, No. 14, 1914.

1910 which have been noted. The second principle, he noted, was that of stability of migrant settlement. Four types of activity were involved in this respect: allotment of land, actual movement, installation on the plots, and land settlement. Here Simonov expressed support for the pending draft Siberian "homestead act." Another draft dealt with the sale in certain places of migrant portions as personal property, which appeared to Simonov as an attempt to attract "economically more substantial peasant holders." Up until then the economically weak element had predominated among the migrants, so he regarded it as necessary to watch any change carefully. Yet if one examined the data of migration, he noticed that despite the existence of much free land, "the most energetic element for colonization leaves for other countries." The government thought it should strive for "the creation of strong [*krepkii*], small [*melkii*], founded on personal labor, peasant, but I should add, nonclass, entrepreneurial economy."[51] There had, however, been introduced by the agriculture ministry another law on the organization of "cultured privately owned enterprises," granting free land in rental with the stipulated right of later purchase, with the aim of developing the raising of cattle, sheep, and horses beyond the Urals. This would be a first step to attract capital, brought by a more substantial element than the migrants, to the great empty spaces of Siberia, Turkestan, and the northern provinces of European Russia.[52] Simonov, while approving the main ideas of the government, declared again, "I consider that precisely *peasant settlement must be put at the center of things*" (emphasis in the original).

Here Simonov, one of the chief spokesmen of the strong Duma center, posed a difficult problem. In order to attract industrial capital for Siberian cities, or large amounts of agricultural capital for the Siberian countryside, it would be necessary to admit the legal institutions of private property. At the same time the development of peasant farming was moving in the direction of private property, and the process needed only legal sanction to be completed. Would such legal enactments create problems for the stable settlement of the migrants, or could the two objectives be harmoniously reconciled? Was Russia ready for the end of the system of protective legislation for the peasantry?[53] In such a new order, could the peasant hold his own?

[51] *Ibid.*, p. 5.   [52] See p. 195, above.

[53] Maklakov notes (*loc.cit.*) that the Kadet "equal rights" bill presented to the Duma was equivocal about the special legislation protecting the peasantry (such as the prohibition of sale of peasant land to non-peasants, etc.).

From the time of the enactment of 1842 on the resettlement of state peasants,[54] migration legislation had dealt only with the peasantry. The rules of 1900 had permitted hereditary gentry who worked by their own labor to obtain inalienable allotments. The law of 6 June 1904 provided exemptions only for peasants and burghers (*meshchane*) who were personally engaged in agriculture. The principle of exclusive *trudovoe khoziaistvo* in the field of resettlement was thus preserved. The first breach in this principle was made on 14 March 1909, when the agriculture minister was granted the power to extend permissions for trans-Ural migration to other than these three groups under certain conditions. By enactment of the Committee of Ministers on 12 July 1912, peasants and burgher-cultivators were no longer required to obtain permission to migrate; hereditary gentry-cultivators could migrate with the permission of provincial governors; all others, including noncultivating gentry, could migrate only with the permission of the agriculture ministry. Migration was becoming a prerogative of all citizens, instead of the peasantry alone. Probably capitalism would soon have come to exist alongside peasant enterprise in Russian Asia. If the experience of European Russia was any indication, such competition would not have endangered the self-employed farmer.

According to Mugansky, student of the migration question in the Fourth Duma, that body was rather indifferent toward migration, an attitude which had begun to be evident in the last year of the Third Duma.[55] Not until the end of the third week of its sittings did the Fourth Duma establish a migration committee of 33 members. Unfortunately, of the deputies who had belonged to the committee in the Third Duma, 25 had for one reason or another failed to be re-elected. Father A. L. Tregubov (Nationalist, Kiev), who had been secretary of the previous committee, declared that there should be a committee to deal not merely with migration but with colonization in the broadest sense, including the economic development of the free lands and the cultural growth of both old and new settlers. His argument for establishing a committee of broader competence restated the view of the Resettlement Administration expressed in the explanatory memorandum of 1912, but the Duma ignored it.

The new migration committee was faced with draft laws still

---

[54] See "Zakonoproekt GUZIZ po Pereselencheskomu Upravleniiu, o predostavlenii litsam vsekh soslovii prava pereseleniia na kazennyia zemli Aziatskoi Rossii na obshchikh s sel'skimi obyvateliami osnovaniiakh," in "Khronika," *Voprosy kolonizatsii*, No. 14, 1914, p. 287ff.

[55] Mugansky, *loc.cit.*

pending on "land settlement of peasants and natives in Siberia" (the Siberian "homestead act"), on the sale of migrant portions, on another reorganization of the Chief Administration of Land Settlement and Agriculture (especially the Resettlement Administration), and so on. A draft law on "the attraction of private enterprise to the cultivation of lands lying idle in sparsely settled localities" and other new projects were introduced into the Fourth Duma.

Mugansky asserted that the committee would need to consider a long list of matters, including transportation problems, the introduction of the institution of private property into Siberia, reconsideration of outmoded local statutes (such as the Steppe Statute, promulgated in 1891, which had in view only nomads), the tariffs of Asiatic Russia, the founding of urban settlements, and the legal establishment of real "classlessness," permitting ownership by all persons, and not only peasants. For whatever reason, the committee was not even assigned several drafts dealing with migration problems. The draft on land settlement of peasants and natives in Siberia went to the land committee, that on reorganization of the Chief Administration to the agricultural committee, the migration budget went solely to the budget committee.

Nevertheless, the migration committee did have some important business, the consideration of the draft law already mentioned on lands "lying idle." By its terms, private individuals and institutions were to be granted the opportunity to rent for the purposes of agriculture, trade, and industrial enterprises, state lands which were lying idle, with the right of subsequent purchase as property. A law with the same end in view had actually been issued earlier on 8 June 1901, as Stolypin had pointed out, but had never been put into operation. It appears that that law had envisaged a method of implementation which was simply too centralized to be effective.

The draft on lands "lying idle" raised important economic and legal questions. The fact was that Russia imported much wool and cotton although Russian Central Asia was suitable for their production, and the Russian Far East brought in grain and dairy products though land was available there for their supply. Mugansky regarded it as incontrovertible that migration "of the usual type" was unable fully to exploit the economic potentialities of Russian Asia.

The concept of lands "lying idle" was unknown to existing law. The draft defined such to be all free state lands except for (1) those necessary for the land settlement of the local peasant population or migration, (2) needful to the state for purposes of forestry, (3) petroleum-bearing lands, and (4) border territories necessary for defense. The central question, as many of the committee members saw it, was how to protect the migration land fund as against the needs of private enterprise to be satisfied by this law—that is, how to protect the peasant settlers. Governmental representatives declared in the hearings that the draft put this very consideration "at the center of things"—as Simonov had insisted—and that only land "unfit for agriculture" would be assigned under the law. The discussions were inconclusive.

Two months later the government introduced a revision of this law in the form of new rules "on the granting to private entrepreneurs of free state lands for the purpose of their productive utilization." Among other changes, it was specified that purchase would depend on actual productive employment of the given portion for a period of at least three years. Apparently this provision was designed to reduce the chance of land speculation. The committee insisted on changing the phrase "free state lands" to "state lands free and lying idle," though G. V. Glinka, head of the Resettlement Administration, cautioned that these adjectives ought not to be regarded as separate or different. In the steppe region, for example, there were no actually idle lands since all were in the use of the local population, but Glinka implied that there was nevertheless free land available.

The committee then debated the new rules. One deputy proposed that they be limited to the gentry class, and it was apparent that his only purpose was to reduce the whole draft to absurdity. There was no action taken.

In June 1913 the migration budget was debated in the full Duma. Father Tregubov lamented the "noticeable indifference of the majority of the State Duma to the general problems of colonization—the cherished offspring of the Third Duma." Simonov was the only other speaker on the general questions involved. The Kadet leader of the Siberian deputies, N. K. Volkov, II, noted that since there was an obvious impatience to end the session, he would deal only with the neglect of the interests of the Buriats, Kirghiz, Tungus, and other natives by local land settlement officials. Glinka replied for the Resettlement Administration with data intended to disprove his charges. A number of deputies announced certain subjects they would like to talk about, but would not. Deputy Bishop Anatoly, after speaking ten minutes, was cut off by the President of the Duma and the debate was declared ended to "applause from the Left."

Mugansky concluded that the first session of the Fourth Duma apparently found "the attempt at serious work of a general character useless." He did not attempt an explanation. There may be several. The influence of Rasputin in the government, the renewed rise of the revolutionary movement, and international tensions created an atmosphere of emergency in which parliamentary labors for peaceful purposes seemed less relevant than earlier. The obvious development of Siberia and the progress made by colonization there made the whole matter appear less urgent than in 1907 and 1908, when the broad lines of policy were being laid out. Some of this development excited the envy of certain deputies from European Russian provinces. For example, during the discussion of the draft law on the "consistent colonization of forest expanses," some deputies from the central provinces objected that the draft projected roads and telephones for parts of Siberia settled a mere ten years, while "we gentry have neither roads nor telephones!"[56] The majority of the migration committee ignored these protests, but spokesmen for regions with ancient and profound problems could scarcely be expected to contemplate the rapid development of the frontier with selfless enthusiasm.

Despite various degrees of ambivalence on the part of public opinion and various groups in the Duma, government work in assisting migration went forward on a large scale during the whole period of the last two Dumas. Over a quarter of a million migrants continued to cross the Urals annually, aside from some 80,000 laborers. These last were not sufficient to meet the demand. Glinka noted that in many cases, as on the big holdings of the Cossacks, it was difficult to prohibit the importation of workers of the yellow race, since "migrants did not want to become workers."[57]

The work which went forward was in the main on behalf of migrants who stayed farmers. A million and a quarter desiatinas of land were being prepared, and for this purpose 4,000,000 rubles were being spent. New roads and communications necessitated 5,000,000; hydrotechnical works, 2,000,000. Thus, over 10,000,000 rubles annually were being devoted to the whole task of preparing and organizing migrant portions. An additional 16,000,000 went for aid to the migrants en route and at their destination, of which 10,000,000 went for loans to new settlers, the remainder for medical, food, and veterinary assistance. So-called "general purpose" loans were furnished the migrants to enable them to care for various cul-

---

[56] *Ibid.*, No. 13, 1914, p. 34.
[57] Quoted in *ibid.*, p. 20.

tural and social needs; they built 150 new churches and 500 new schools during the five-year period from 1906 to 1910. A law of 1909 broadened the scope of needs for which such loans were granted, and by 1914 they totaled around 2,500,000 annually, which could be compared with a total of 25,000 rubles yearly allotted for all types of loans to migrants as of 1900.[58] Loans for home construction were one of the most important types. A law of 1912 distinguished for the first time between various areas according to the difficulty of construction and instituted a loan differential in favor of the migrants who had the hardest job in building. For the entire functioning of the Resettlement Administration, including its whole army of employees from the high officials to local agents, only 1,300,000 rubles was spent.[59]

Besides the Resettlement Administration, some new institutions came into existence, such as the Committee for the Settlement of the Far East, under the chairmanship of Stolypin himself, with Krivoshein as his deputy (after Stolypin's assassination Kokovtsev became chairman).[60] In 1911 there was founded a special council for working out a general plan of railway construction and waterways in Siberia which were connected with colonization, and it was this body which made the decision to construct the South Siberian Magistral. These bodies and others did useful work, but it was the Resettlement Administration, as the Octobrist M. I. Simonov declared, which had accomplished more in regard to its responsibilities than the government had achieved in any other realm.[61]

In 1913 the budget committee of the Fourth Duma reported that "to establish with complete accuracy at the present time the whole significance to the state of the gradual settlement of broad empty land spaces is impossible, but in any case the results of it are apparent and demonstrate the paramount role of colonization affairs in the life of Russia."[62] For the results alluded to by this statement, the government deserved more credit than the Duma. Nevertheless if the officials concerned with the Siberian frontier had not been able to draw on the support and labors of the Duma Center to counterbalance the critical attitude of both Left and Right and of most of the intelligentsia outside the Duma, their task would have been much more difficult.

[58] Aziatskaia Rossiia, Vol. I, pp. 471-72.
[59] Ibid., pp. 488-89.
[60] Ibid., p. 468.
[61] Simonov, loc.cit.
[62] Aziatskaia Rosssii, Vol. I, p. 494.

CHAPTER IX

Migration at Flood Tide

Less Room, More People

In the record of his journey into Siberia and Mongolia during the summer of 1910, Philips Price declares: "It is only by living among the people, as far removed as possible from officialdom, and by learning from their own lips the simple story of their lives, that the foreigner can ever hope to appreciate the true character of the Russian people, and to understand the real forces that are at work in the social structure of the Russian Empire—forces which will some day mould its policy and action."[1]

Price could not know that the lips of the Siberians would soon be sealed to the foreign investigator, or indeed that foreign investigators would consider many things more important than learning their simple story even during the early years of the Soviet period when it was possible. Fortunately the statistical material, supplemented by the reports of travelers, enables us to reconstruct a reasonably satisfactory picture of Siberia in the last decade before the First World War.

This picture is one of the continuation and acceleration of most of the same processes observable in the 1890's. As Price writes, "undoubtedly the chief element in the evolution of Siberian society, especially during the last fifty years, is to be found in the peasant immigrants from European Russia, who have voluntarily settled under Government supervision on the fertile lands of Western and Central Siberia."[2] Before 1900 the beginning of widespread pressure from the growing stream of migrants was being felt on the existing landholding arrangements and mode of life of the old-settlers. The Committee on the Siberian Railway reported that scarcity of land in any form was unknown to the Siberian old-settlers until the last two decades of the nineteenth century,[3] and this problem was seldom deeply felt before the twentieth century. Scarcity, as we have previously insisted, in any case must be related to the means of exploitation which is employed. The Committee noted that the means of exploitation was in fact changing: the entrance of the migrants into old-settler villages was hastening the transition from the *perelog* or

[1] M. P. Price, *Siberia*, London, 1912, p. x.
[2] *Ibid.*, p. 187.
[3] *Kolonizatsiia Sibiri*, p. 372.

simple clearing to the three-field system. What might be too little land for the system of indiscriminately plowing virgin land might be ample for three-field cultivation, and even surplus for the intensive and diversified farming which might develop later.

In the period from 1906 to 1910 alone, almost 30,000,000 desiatinas of free land were occupied by Siberian migrants. During the same years the number of cattle and the total tillage across the Urals rose more than twice as fast as the total of population. From the peak year of 1908 onward the rate of migration declined slightly. Pavlovsky noted that the authorities "who have been literally overwhelmed by the human torrent pouring into Asiatic Russia" welcomed this decline. It enabled them to take stock, to catch up, to prepare for the next flood crest. Though the rate of movement still remained high, the migrants themselves enjoyed something of a breathing spell in settling and in some cases resettling. The migrants of some years earlier meanwhile plowed, sowed, and harvested. The results of all this were recorded by the most careful survey ever conducted of migrant settlements in Siberia.

The Survey of Kuznetsov

This survey was conducted mostly during the summer of 1911, though a small portion of it was done in June 1912. It was performed under the supervision of V. K. Kuznetsov, who also edited the report.[4] It was undertaken by the Chief Administration of Land Settlement and Agriculture, to satisfy the desire of the budget commission of the Third Duma for a statistical overview of the economic situation of the migrants in Siberia. In accordance with a plan approved by the Resettlement Administration, it selected districts and settlements in Akmolinsk region and Tobolsk, Tomsk, Yeniseisk and Irkutsk provinces. The settlements were chosen on the basis of differing environments, nearness to railways, water, or road routes, distance from industrial and cultural centers (cities), length of time the settlements had existed, differing numbers of households, and greater or lesser development of industry (craft or otherwise) in addition to agriculture. The survey employed for its inquiries two units, household and settlement.

The conclusion of the survey was that in the main the migrants were solidly established in Siberia. Only a negligible number of those

---

[4] Pereselencheskoe Upravlenie GUZIZ, *Sbornik statisticheskikh svedenii ob ekonomicheskom polozhenii pereselentsev v Sibiri.* Materialy po obsledovaniiu tipichnykh pereselencheskikh poselkov, sobrannye i razrabotannye pod rukovodstvom i redaktsieiu V. K. Kuznetsova, 2 vols., St. Petersburg, 1912.

persons who had been actually settled on migrant portions had gone elsewhere, and such cases were almost always due to reasons unrelated to the suitability of the allotments. More important, the economic condition of the migrants was in general superior to that which they had known in the homeland. The extent of their landholding had increased almost nine times. The average migrant household had 38.3 desiatinas of allotment land, as against 4.5 desiatinas in the homeland, working 5.4 desiatinas of tillage and 6.1 desiatinas of pasture in Siberia as against 2.4 of tillage and 0.6 of pasture at home. The respective totals were thus 11.5 as against 3.0. On leaving the homeland the average migrant household had cash and other personal property to the value of 239 rubles, as against 466 rubles in Siberia at the time of the survey. The increase in capital was thus almost double, but the actual rise in welfare was said to be even greater. On actual installation on the allotments, the migrant family had only 161 rubles capital, and during the period of existence on the portions (averaging 11 years) the increase was thus almost treble. The level of physical well-being was shown by a growth of population at the rate 33 per 1,000 as compared with the figure of 22 per 1,000 for the Empire as a whole.[5]

The survey first dealt with general conditions of the migrant economy. It was found that no very clear pattern was followed by all migrants. Some came on their own resources, some received a good deal of government aid. Some brought money, tools, and livestock; others, only money. Of these, some brought a few rubles, others hundreds. Of those who did receive government loans, some got 50, others 150. Some got settled immediately, others only after a year or two, during which time they often worked for others. The regulars' course was clear enough in getting enrolled on their new lands. The irregulars sometimes lived on passports in the new settlements, tilling rented land or working in nearby industry, but more and more often they too were receiving allotments, in the shape of special cut-off portions or otherwise. According to the report of Kuznetsov, difficulties between the older and more recent migrants were more and more frequently being resolved by the establishment of farms (either *otrubs* or *khutors*). In Tomsk province, for example, *otrubs* already accounted for more than 6,000,000 desiatinas of land.

The survey encompassed 31,984 families in 447 settlements in the following regions (commas separate counties from regions or provinces).[6]

[5] *Ibid.*, Vypusk I, p. x.   [6] *Ibid.*, p. 7.

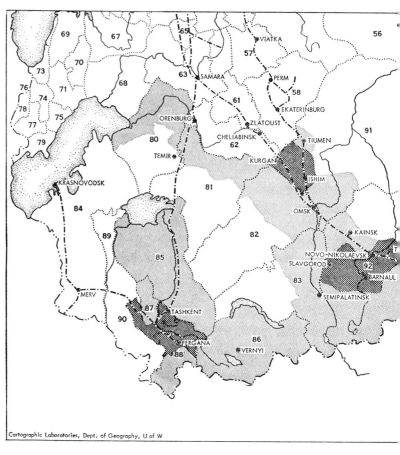

Cartographic Laboratories, Dept. of Geography, U of W

Key to Administrative Divisions for map on p. 89 and these pages

(G—guberniia   Ob—oblast   Ok—okrug   U—uezd)

GRAND DUCHY		20. Lifland	G	44. Kharkov	G	67. Don	Ob
OF FINLAND		21. Kurland	G	45. Ekaterinoslav	G	68. Astrakhan	G
1. Uleaborg	G	22. Kovno	G	46. Taurida	G		
2. Vasa	G	23. Vilna	G	47. Voronezh	G	**CAUCASUS**	
3. Kuopio	G	24. Grodno	G	48. Tambov	G	69. Kuban	Ob
4. Abo-Bjorneborg	G	25. Minsk	G	49. Tula	G	70. Stavropol	G
5. Tavastehus	G	26. Volhynia	G	50. Riazan	G	71. Terek	Ob
6. St. Michel	G	27. Podolia	G	51. Moscow	G	72. Black Sea	Ob
7. Nyland	G	28. Bessarabia	G	52. Vladimir	G	73. Kutais	G
8. Viborg	G	29. Kherson	G	53. Yaroslavl	G	74. Tiflis	G
		30. Kiev	G	54. Kostroma	G	75. Daghestan	Ob
VISTULA PROVINCES		31. Mogilev	G	55. Vologda	G	76. Kars	Ob
9. Suwalki	G	32. Vitebsk	G	56. Arkhangelsk	G	77. Elizavetpol	G
10. Lomza	G	33. Pskov	G	57. Viatka	G	78. Erivan	G
11. Plock	G	34. St. Petersburg	G	58. Perm	G	79. Baku	G
12. Warsaw	G	35. Olonets	G	59. Nizhny			
13. Kalisz	G	36. Novgorod	G	Novgorod	G	**CENTRAL ASIA**	
14. Piotrkow	G	37. Tver	G	60. Kazan	G	80. Uralsk	Ob
15. Siedlce	G	38. Smolensk	G	61. Ufa	G	80a. Uralsk	U
16. Radom	G	39. Kaluga	G	62. Orenburg	G	80b. Lbishchensk	U
17. Kielce	G	40. Orel	G	63. Samara	G	80c. Guriev	U
18. Lublin	G	41. Chernigov	G	64. Simbirsk	G	80d. Temir	U
		42. Kursk	G	65. Penza	G	81. Turgai	Ob
EUROPEAN RUSSIA		43. Poltava	G	66. Saratov	G	81a. Kustanai	U
19. Estland	G						

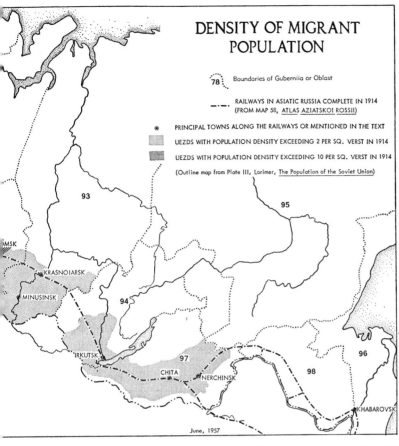

DENSITY OF MIGRANT POPULATION

78 ⋯ Boundaries of Guberniia or Oblast

━ ▪ ━ RAILWAYS IN ASIATIC RUSSIA COMPLETE IN 1914
(FROM MAP 58, ATLAS AZIATSKOI ROSSII)

⊛ PRINCIPAL TOWNS ALONG THE RAILWAYS OR MENTIONED IN THE TEXT

▨ UEZDS WITH POPULATION DENSITY EXCEEDING 2 PER SQ. VERST IN 1914

▓ UEZDS WITH POPULATION DENSITY EXCEEDING 10 PER SQ. VERST IN 1914

(Outline map from Plate III, Lorimer, The Population of the Soviet Union)

June, 1957

81b. Irgiz	U	86. Semirechensk Ob	91g. Kurgan U
81c. Turgai	U	86a. Lepsinsk U	91h. Ishim U
81d. Aktiubinsk	U	86b. Kopal U	91j. Tara U

81b. Irgiz U
81c. Turgai U
81d. Aktiubinsk U
82. Akmolinsk Ob
82a. Petropavlovsk U
82b. Kokchetav U
82c. Omsk U
82d. Atbasar U
82e. Akmolinsk U
83. Semipalatinsk Ob
83a. Pavlodar U
83b. Semipalatinsk U
83c. Karkaralinsk U
83d. Ust-Kameno-
    gorsk U
83e. Zaisan U
84. Transcaspian Ob
84a. Mangyshlaksk U
84b. Krasnovodsk U
84c. Ashkhabad U
84d. Tedzhen U
84e. Merv U
85. Syr Daria Ob
85a. Kazalinsk U
85b. Perovsk U
85c. Chimkent U
85d. Aulieatinsk U
85e. Tashkent U
85f. Amu Daria otdel

86. Semirechensk Ob
86a. Lepsinsk U
86b. Kopal U
86c. Vernyi U
86d. Pishpek U
86e. Dzharkent U
86f. Przhevalsk U
87. Samarkand Ob
87a. Katta-Kurgan U
87b. Samarkand U
87c. Dzhizak U
87d. Khodzhent U
88. Fergana Ob
88a. Namagan U
88b. Kokand U
88c. Andizhan U
88d. Skobelev U
88e. Osh U
89. Khiva
90. Bukhara

SIBERIA
91. Tobolsk G
91a. Berezov U
91b. Turinsk U
91c. Tobolsk U
91d. Surgut U
91e. Ialutorovsk U
91f. Tiumen U

91g. Kurgan U
91h. Ishim U
91j. Tara U
91k. Tiukalinsk U
92. Tomsk G
92a. Tomsk U
92b. Kainsk U
92c. Barnaul U
92d. Kuznetsk U
92e. Zmeinogorsk U
92f. Biisk U
92g. Mariinsk U
93. Yeniseisk G
93a. Yeniseisk U
93b. Achinsk U
93c. Krasnoiarsk U
93d. Minusinsk U
93e. Kansk U
93f. Usinsk
    frontier region
94. Irkutsk G
94a. Kirensk U
94b. Nizhneudinsk U
94c. Balagansk U
94d. Verkholensk U
94e. Irkutsk U
95. Yakutsk Ob
95a. Verkhoiansk Ok
95b. Kolymsk Ok

95c. Viliuisk Ok
95d. Yakutsk Ok
95e. Olekminsk Ok
96. Maritime Ob
96a. Nikolaevsk U
96b. Khabarovsk U
96c. Olginsk U
96d. Imansk U
96e. Nikolsk-
    Ussuriisky U
97. Transbaikalia Ob
97a. Barguzin U
97b. Selenginsk U
97c. Verkhneu-
    dinsk U
97d. Chita U
97e. Nerchinsk U
97f. Nerchinsko-
    zavod U
97g. Troitskosavsk U
97h. Aksha U
98. Amur Ob
99. Kamchatka Ob
99a. Chukotsk U
99b. Anadyrsk U
99c. Gizhiginsk U
99d. Petropavlovsk U
99e. Okhotsk U
100. Sakhalin Island

I. steppe: Akmolinsk, Akmolinsk; southern Achinsk, Yeniseisk.
II. *lesostep* (intermediate between forest and steppe) of West Siberia: Omsk, Akmolinsk; Tiukalinsk, Tobolsk.
III. *lesostep* of East Siberia: northern Achinsk, Krasnoiarsk, and Kansk, Yeniseisk; Nizhneudinsk and Balagansk, Irkutsk.
IV. forest: Tarsk and Turinsk, Tobolsk; Verkholensk, Irkutsk.

Of these 31,984 families, 30,012 were enrolled, 1,972 (or 6 per cent) unenrolled. When these same people settled, there were 25,616 families; the additional 6,368 were accounted for by family divisions made possible by the new situation. There were on the average 6.1 persons per family as a result of the division, which may be compared with the figure of 6 given for the average Russian peasant family. The actual increase of population among them had been 33,959, with an average annual growth of 4,717 or 3.3 per cent, compared with the figure for the whole empire of 2.2 per cent for the period 1897 to 1911. The largest increase was in the steppe region, 4.7 per cent. Of 178,504 people in these families actually surveyed, there were 92,857 men and 85,647 women, a ratio of 100 to 92. The proportion of persons of working age (given as 18 to 60 for men and 16 to 55 for women) was 45.3 per cent. The proportion of working-age women was higher everywhere than that for the men.

The enrolled families held 1,268,689 desiatinas of "suitable" land and 277,218 "unsuitable," totaling 1,545,907. Allotment was to 85,362 males, so the "suitable" land averaged 14.9 desiatinas per male, 38.3 desiatinas per household.[7] One may thus see that a household averaged slightly more than two "census souls," or mature males. Allotment was by "census soul" at the rate of 15 desiatinas each. The survey found this norm had been adhered to generally. In rare cases, in exceptionally productive areas, the norm had been reduced slightly. In the homeland 22 per cent of the households had been landless, while none were so in Siberia. The overall landholding had increased almost nine times. On the average, out of the 38.3 desiatina allotment, only 14.4 or 35.1 per cent of the area was actually being worked; this proportion rose to 55.2 per cent in the steppe Region I.

More revealing is the relationship of land actually worked to the time the settler had been established on his holding. Of the 27,192 enrolled households surveyed, only 3.8 per cent had been *in situ* more than 18 years. Thus, most families (96.2 per cent) had come since

[7] *Ibid.*, p. 18. See Table 15, Appendix I.

1893: 31.1 per cent from 1893 to 1903, 30.1 per cent from 1904 to 1907, and 35 per cent from 1908 to 1911. The amount of land actually worked increased steadily the longer the settler had established himself. The average migrant whose period of residence was less than three years worked only 9.2 desiatinas; when the period exceeded 18 years, the average migrant worked 20.6 desiatinas.[8] The average amount of land worked by all migrants studied was 14.4 desiatinas. This figure (rather than the average total allotment of 38.3 desiatinas) may be compared with an average of 3.9 desiatinas held at home.

Beyond the obvious gain in total land held and used, there was even a greater proportionate improvement in the ratio of hayland to plowland. At home the average migrant had had 3.3 desiatinas of plowland to only 0.6 of hayland, for the total holding of 3.9 desiatinas. In Siberia, he had 8.3 desiatinas of plowland to 6.1 of hayland for the total worked of 14.4. Thus he was much better provided for from the standpoint of keeping cattle. It should be noted that the migrants settled in the steppe region of Siberia (Kuznetsov's Region I), though much better off than their fellows in Siberia (average area worked of 21.1 desiatinas to the 14.4 overall average for migrants), had been slightly worse off than the others at home (landholding of 3.7 to the 3.9 overall average).

Industry brought in an average of 43 rubles income per household.[9] The least return came from Region II (West Siberian *lesostep*), 29 rubles, where agriculture and cattle-raising provided abundance without needing to resort to industry. Region I (steppe) was high, with 51 rubles, but much of that (13 rubles) came from dairying. Region IV was highest, with 52 rubles, 21 of that coming from forest industry. Work for wages provided 18, 10, 12, and 8 rubles in Regions I-IV respectively, a very minor portion of the total "industrial" income.

The rise in economic well-being of the migrant household obviously could not continue indefinitely. The end of the increase in the area cultivated, the survey estimated, would come when the full labor power of the migrant family had come into play. Kuznetsov estimated that although this time had not yet come for even the longest-settled group after 19 years, it might come in around 25. The Siberian migrant economy would then begin gradually to reach its maximum development.

[8] *Ibid.*, pp. 21-23. See Table 16, Appendix 1.
[9] *Ibid.*, p. 36.

The next question investigated was what buildings, cattle, and machinery the migrants possessed. Building was the first concern of the newly arrived migrant. Generally it was found that he threw up a hut and if he brought livestock, also fences and sheds. Often he waited until the second year to build a permanent dwelling. For this purpose he used turf and clay, if he built in the steppe, elsewhere lumber or logs, which he often drew from government forest stores. Almost all enrolled migrants had permanent houses. Only 2.8 per cent had none, though 15.4 per cent had had no houses of their own in the homeland. Of the small unenrolled group, 71 per cent had no houses, though 19.5 per cent had lacked them even at home.[10] The average enrolled migrant household had 2.2 farm buildings (barns, sheds, etc.) in addition to its dwelling.

Of cattle, the migrant had on the average, excluding the newest arrivals and unenrolled, 13 head. These included 4.2 "big" (grown horses, oxen, bulls, and cows) and 8.8 "small" cattle (two-yearling horses, calves, sheep, goats, and pigs). As to machinery, the household had 1.4 pieces of the "most valuable" agricultural machines (apparently excluding hand tools, though it is impossible to determine exactly what this category included) and 4.0 carts and other transport and agricultural machines. Of the 4.2 "big" cattle, 2.3 head were "working cattle" and 1.9 cows; when to this was added 1 harvesting machine on the average to every two to three households, this provided an impressive set of aids to the Siberian farmer. The unenrolled migrant had on the average only 1 agricultural and 1 transport machine, however.[11]

It was striking that the three-year household in the case of both buildings and livestock was almost as well off as the 4-7 year category and only slightly below the average enrolled level. Kuznetsov concluded that "the migrants after three years of homesteading on their portions succeed in reaching such results as indicate a propitious foundation for the further development of their economy."

To complete the picture of the migrant economy there was given an economic breakdown of the households concerned. Of the total ⅐ "consists of rich households" with more than 28 desiatinas of plowland and hayland, more than 30 head of cattle and more than 11 pieces of machinery.[12] Next came the more than twice as large group of middle status, fully established in a favorable and improving situation, who had at least 12 desiatinas, 15 head of cattle, and more than 6 pieces of machinery. Then came two groups constituting ¾ of all

[10] *Ibid.*, p. 59.   [11] *Ibid.*, p. 68.   [12] *Ibid.*, p. 72.

households, mainly in the recently arrived group, which had respectively 3.4 and 6.5 desiatinas, 4 and 8 head of livestock and 2 and 4 pieces of machinery. For them the road was open and their foundation laid.

The Legal and Economic Situation

As has been stated earlier, the migrants settled on free state lands allotted them for perpetual use. The village assembly had the legal right to establish whether tenure would be communal, household, or farm in type. In actual fact, the surveyors found that many migrant villages did not so choose, and squatting was admittedly widespread, though Kuznetsov seemed evasive about its exact extent. Out of 447 settlements, 413 had communal tenure, 8 hereditary household (*podvornoe*) tenure, 26 farm (*khutor*) tenure. Of the 413 communal tenure settlements, only 65 had immediately on arrival employed equal division or repartition (the same process when performed the first time is called equal division, all subsequent times repartition). After several years of squatting, 143 had gone over to division. Forty had partial division, with squatting being used in some portions of the village. The largest number, 159, used squatting exclusively. There were 6 others outside all these categories, making the total of 413.

"Squatting" here seems to mean simply staking one's own claim, and in what sense the abovementioned 159 villages could be called communes would be difficult to say clearly. Thus, as Kuznetsov noted, only about one-half of the communes were actually repartitional (208 out of 413), and therefore, if one likes, not actually communal.[13] He then examined the 143 which had gone over to division and found the communal tendency not solidly established there either, due to the considerable amount of dissatisfaction among the migrants with arrangements which deprived them of land they had worked. In 11 of these there had occurred agreement for division into *otrubs*, which was in part already carried out. Even the group of 65 "complete communes" was not counted as solidly communal because of the short time many had been established. The only type of land universally held in common was pasture, which was never found divided among households. Kuznetsov declared that "communal methods of land use in those settlements in which there exists communal tenure of allotted land, are weakly developed and receive very

[13] *Ibid.*, p. 78.

limited application." The conclusion as to tenure thus turns out to be nearly the reverse of that indicated by the figures first given.

Communal tenure was formally predominant; but in fact it had few if any solid roots at all in Siberia. Why then did it exist so widely, legally or otherwise? Kuznetsov suggests the answer when he reports that there was a great deal of pulling and hauling between settlers all over the area investigated. The old-settlers strove to retain their surplus land, the new settlers to obtain it through *equal division*. Given the absence of the legal institution of private property, the most obvious means of gaining control over the free land which was already nominally under the control of Siberian peasants (whether or not they had been in place long enough to be called old-settlers) was to demand equal division. Just as the division after the Emancipation had been preserved more often than not in European Russia except under the governmental pressure exerted under Alexander III, so division was widely regarded in Siberia as a means of obtaining land permanently. One may compare the so-called "revival of the commune" in late 1917; it was a device for obtaining the land of others, not for "restoring" communal principles.

Kuznetsov noted that in 1910-1911, the last year before the survey, 17 villages had passed to farm tenure, 11 of them from squatting, 6 from communal holding. This showed that the migrants themselves were coming to recognize that the "surest, swiftest, and solidest way" to avoid disputes was to fix permanent boundaries, "wherein each householder has in his own possession and use a definite area of land, with the disposition of which no one else interferes, where the initiative and the economic activity of the holder is restricted by no one and finds free application."[14]

But this was not the whole story. A total of 34 settlements now had what we might call fixed tenure—Kuznetsov gave it no name, but by lumping the 26 *khutor* and the 8 hereditary-tenure villages together indicated that a name was needed. Of these 34, organized from 1884 to 1911, 22 had accepted fixed tenure at once, and 12 had passed over from communal or squatter holding. Only 8 had done so in the period 1884-1900; 26 had acted in the shorter period 1902-1911. There was apparent a tendency toward fixed tenure, and Kuznetsov in effect recommended that the government assign its own funds to assist the development of that tendency.

In respect to the actual manner in which the land was used, a picture of extensive agriculture and unused land was drawn. Settlements totaling 1,112,318 desiatinas in area were surveyed. Of this

14 *Ibid.*, p. 89.

37.6 per cent was in the actual use of separate households, while the remaining 62.4 per cent was in reserve in both steppe and forest.[15] Of the 37.6 per cent belonging to households, 80.1 per cent was under cultivation, the remaining 19.9 per cent not yet so. Adding the latter area to the reserve area, it was seen that 69.9 per cent of the land had not yet been tilled. Much of it was used only as pasture, some of it was not used at all. On an average, 30 per cent of the holding was used as garden, plowland, and hayland, or a mere 4.5 desiatinas out of the 15 desiatina-per-soul portion. Out of the plowland, only 57 per cent was actually sown, the remainder being in fallow. This percentage was 60 in Region IV, the least fertile; it was only 53 in the most fertile Region II. In brief, where the land was most fertile and plentiful the type of agriculture was the most wasteful, and it was rather wasteful throughout migrant Siberia. Simple fallowing was most common, though already beginning to yield here and there to three-field or even many-field cultivation.

In Akmolinsk, said to be typical of the steppe region, the cropping took place as follows. The land was sown continuously for four or five years, then allowed to rest fallow for two to three years, then sown again two, three, or four years. Wheat was the prevailing crop, sometimes replaced by other crops, though for the fourth year of sowing the chief crop was oats, next barley, and wheat third. Rye, so common in the homeland, was almost absent from Akmolinsk county. In Irkutsk, however, no such lavishness could be afforded. There the three-field system was already widespread, being used in 29 out of 56 settlements. Kuznetsov reported that the use of manure for fertilizer was much more prevalent in the forest region than in the steppe. Thus it is indicated that the transition to improved agricultural methods was beginning on the farthest frontier of settlement. The change depended, as in European Russia, on two factors, fertility of land and density of settlement. The poorer land of the Irkutsk forest region seemed to be the cause of the beginning transformation, since congestion of population could not be said to apply as yet to any region of Siberia.

The crop yield of Siberia was obviously going to be abundant. Wheat was the chief grain of the whole area, constituting 50 per cent of all sowing, and rising to 65 per cent in the steppe region.[16] Oats was next with 17 per cent; rye was third, and was the chief grain of the wooded regions though accounting for less than 45 per cent there. Food grains gave 70 per cent of all sowing, feed grains 24 per cent, and remaining 6 per cent certain other crops. During the

[15] *Ibid.*, p. 93.   [16] *Ibid.*, p. 113.

past 10 years, the average yield in poods per desiatina of all grains for the four regions respectively had been: rye, 42, 49, 54, 50; wheat, 45, 44, 46, 42; oats, 49, 47, 56, 46. During bad harvests yields fell to 15-25 poods; in good years it rose to 70 to 100 for all three chief grains.

The rental of land proved to be a minor quantity. Only the unenrolled migrants appeared to need to rent plowland, and the total of plowland rented was only about one-third of the total land rental of 98,318 desiatinas for the households studied. The great majority of enrolled peasants (23,005 small and middle households) rented no plowland, and only a little hayland. If the enrolled peasants were divided into five groups according to affluence, the fifth group, consisting of the 4,187 richest households, did most of the renting.[17] The form of rental was chiefly annual, paid in money, and personal rather than communal or some other collective type.

The Financial Condition of the Migrants

The obligations of the migrants were threefold. They had to pay the state *obrok* or perpetual rent for their allotments of land granted for their indefinite use; they had to pay a land (*zemskii*) tax; and they had to pay township and village taxes, as well as insurance payments on their buildings. For the state rent and land tax, migrants were exempt entirely for the first five years after settlement; for the next five they were half exempt, and then were fully obligated. The village taxes had to be paid from the time of the organization of the *sel'skoe obshchestvo* or commune, whose establishment required by law the presence in the settlement of not less than ten households.

The total sum of all the enumerated payments for the year 1911 (for Turinsk county, 1912) was 264,477 rubles for all households studied. The distribution was as follows:[18]

State rent	50,892 r.	19.2%
Land tax	23,793 r.	9.0
Local taxes:		
Township	88,589 r.	33.5
Village	78,044 r.	29.5
Insurance	23,159 r.	8.8
	264,477 r.	100.0

[17] *Ibid.*, p. 126. See Table 17, Appendix I.
[18] *Ibid.*, p. 133.

Accordingly local levies made up a full 63 per cent of the total, although the first two items would rise as the full ten-year exemption period ended for more households. The average payment per household came to 12 r. for Region I; 10 r. 42 k. for Region II; 8 r. 45 k. for Region III; and 7 r. 27 k. for Region IV.

Of the local levies, the larger part went for administrative purposes. Of the township taxes, 75 per cent went to salaries and maintenance of the elders, scribes, and so forth; 5 per cent to economic needs (roads, etc.); and 20 per cent to general rather than local administrative expenses (post buildings, etc.). The village levies went 40 per cent to village administration (elders, scribes, and other village officials), 15 per cent to economic needs, 15 per cent for churches, 10 per cent for schools, and 20 per cent for general administrative purposes.

To the total of 264,477 rubles of money levies was to be added "natural" levies (apparently labor of various kinds) valued at 106,822 rubles, yielding a grand total of 371,299 rubles. This total averaged 2 rubles 21 kopeks per person. Given an average family of 6.2 persons, money and natural levies of 13 rubles 65 kopeks were required.

According to the survey, monetary levies were borne by the Siberian migrants without great difficulty. Total arrears up to 1 January 1911 (in Turinsk to 1912) were 72,949 rubles or only 27.6 per cent of the total of a yearly levy.

The indebtedness of the migrants was not a serious matter. At the time of settlement, loans had been granted to 80.9 per cent of all migrants, at a rate not exceeding 165 rubles per family. Terms of repayment had been five years of exemption before repayment began, followed by ten years in which the loan should be completely paid off in equal annual payments. Already 11 per cent of the total loans had been repaid. The balance sheet stood as follows, in rubles per average household:[19]

	Loaned	Repaid
Region I	115	20
Region II	131	34
Region III	124	8
Region IV	146	5
All regions	127	14

[19] Ibid., p. 140.

There were certain other types of loans, of which food was apparently the most important. Of the total householders, 39.9 per cent had received an average of 41 poods of bread, and 22.5 per cent had been returned.

The condition of the budgets of the migrants received some attention. After "economic needs" and taxes were met, there remained on the average for each household, 361 rubles in Region I, 246 in II, 302 in III, 197 in IV. Out of these figures came expenses for food, averaging 210 rubles in Region I, 183 in II, 195 in III, 164 in IV. There finally was left a sum varying from 33 to 151 rubles, from which from 19 to 130 went for clothes and other minor expenses, leaving an absolute free remainder.[20] Kuznetsov figures that on an average for all four regions, expenses were accounted for 40.6 per cent by food, 57.5 per cent by household needs, and 1.9 per cent by levies of all kinds. Household needs included heat, light, repair of buildings, feed, seed, and purchase of cattle. It should be noted that these figures were taken from 90 cases in which the budgets of middle householders who had been settled at least three years were most carefully studied, rather than from broadcast questionnaires of some kind. The most striking fact which emerges from these data about expenses is the great degree of financial independence enjoyed by the migrants. To these people especially applies the phrase which Stolypin used to describe his ideal agriculturist rather than a type which he believed already prevalent in Russian society: these peasants were indeed "masters of their fate" in a manner true of few social groups in the twentieth century in any country.[21]

The picture as regards revenue was similar. The net profit per desiatina of plowland was in the four regions 13, 18, 12, and 4 rubles respectively, of hayland 6, 6.35, 5.75, and 5.50 rubles. On an average each household studied realized net profit from the sale of products in the first three regions 139, 99, and 57 rubles respectively. Each household could sell as market surplus, in Region I, about 150 poods of bread, 20 rubles worth of cattle, 70 rubles worth of milk; in Region II, about 100 poods of bread and 50 rubles worth of cattle; in Region III, about 50 poods of bread. If Kuznetsov's contention is correct that these particular households were smaller than the average, the economic situation was indeed a favorable one.

[20] *Ibid.*, p. 165.
[21] Stolypin used this phrase in a speech before the Duma on 5 December 1908.

The Capital of the Migrants in the Homeland and in Siberia

The figures obtained on capital were admitted to have only relative validity, though Kuznetsov deemed defects in both sets of figures, for the homeland and for Siberia, to have some compensating effect for the inevitably incomplete recollection of the migrants interrogated.

At home, the migrants had had 99,127 desiatinas of allotted and purchased land. Of this total, 49,559 or 50 per cent had been sold, 20,591 or 20.8 per cent rented, while 28,977 or 29.2 per cent reverted to the commune of their original home.[22] Of the portion of land which had been sold, data were available only on 17,071 desiatinas, for which 827,175 rubles were obtained. On this basis it could be calculated that for the entire amount the proceeds from sale must have been around 2,400,000 rubles. After the process of closing out and paying debts was complete, there remained 3,933,254 (this figure is given again as 3,339,254 in the survey) rubles to be taken with the migrants on their journey. Counting cash proceeds from sale of buildings and stock, as well as stock and implements brought, for the 16,487 households which had existed at least three years on the place of new settlement, an average of 239 rubles liquid assets had been available.

On an average 78 rubles was spent in transit, leaving 161 rubles capital at the moment of settlement. This totaled 3,301,517 rubles, of which cash accounted for 49 per cent and stock 51 per cent, for 20,456 households. Travel expenses thus amounted to about 32 per cent of the migrants' liquid assets.

As of 1911-1912, for 21,752 households, a total valuation was 12,301,852 rubles, on an average 566 rubles per household. Against this sum, 53,377 rubles of levies and 2,126,565 of loans, or a total of 2,179,942 rubles was outstanding, averaging 100 rubles per household. Subtracting this figure from 566, the valuation was thus 466 rubles per household, or 95 per cent (227 rubles) more than the average household had had at home. The time spent in Siberia for those studied ranged from three to eighteen years, on an average eleven years. The rise in capital since the time of settlement was still greater. The migrants began with a total of money, cattle, and stock realized averaging 161 rubles, and at the time of the survey their property not counting cash came to 466, or almost three times more than they had settled with.

[22] *Ibid.*, p. 148.

The greatest rise in capital was in Region I, where it was four times greater than at the time of settlement. The other regions enjoyed less favorable conditions but still capital had nearly doubled or more than doubled in all three.[23] Everywhere there had been a clear rise in capital, and even in the most difficult Region IV it had been definite over what the migrant had had at home.

Thus Kuznetsov's survey dramatically confirmed the more partial and casual conclusions, drawn by earlier official and private observers, that most of the migrants had rapidly achieved a position of prosperity and stability.

The Last Foreign Travelers

By the outbreak of the First World War much of the Trans-Siberian Railway had been in operation for almost twenty years. Some of the novelty had worn off, but some travelers were still writing up impressions of their journey. The travelers of the 1890's had mainly been struck by the volume of moving settlers. Although migration continued at a high level during the last years of Tsarist Siberia, the attention of the travelers was drawn more to the results of the great movement.

In their 1913 report on their trip, Richardson Wright and Bassett Digby kept their attention focused on the cities, but noted certain things about the countryside. For example, they were surprised by the prevalence of American harvesting machinery. "The American harvester can be seen in all parts of Siberia—as far north as Yakutsk and southward on the edge of the Gobi desert where camels draw the machines."[24] They carefully inspected one Siberian village, "Ookteechenskaia." Apparently on the basis of this they wrote that "in Siberia" one observed few middle-class tillers and "no prosperous farmers." By way of explanation, they declared, "Socialism is the answer"—meaning the commune.[25] One suspects here two conservatives. Although perceiving that there was little difference among Siberian villagers in economic status, they failed to realize that most villagers had substantially improved that status over that prevailing at home in European Russia, and they also exaggerated the effect of the Siberian commune—which was far from lively. They did note that the government cooperative credit system instituted for the farmers in 1895 had come to include 10,000 farmers' artels.[26]

[23] *Ibid.*, p. 153. See Table 18, Appendix I.
[24] Richardson L. Wright and Bassett Digby, *Through Siberia: an Empire in the Making*, New York, 1913, p. 11.
[25] *Ibid.*, p. 164.   [26] *Ibid.*, p. 169.

Whether or not they saw more socialism in this phenomenon, they regarded it as evidence of rural prosperity.

Philips Price, who made a journey with Douglas Carruthers and J. H. Miller for the Royal Geographical Society in 1910, was a good deal more careful in his observations. "For the greater part of a year," he wrote, "I was living in the midst of a new society passing through a fascinating phase of development. Siberia is now where Canada was a generation ago. Just as the English settler in Canada has become a Canadian, so the Russian settler in Siberia has become a Siberian. Siberia is beginning to discover her needs, is gradually forming a public opinion of her own, and is shaping her own policies, not infrequently definitely opposed to those of European Russia."[27]

Price first passed through the trans-Volga region, where, said he, the commune was "beginning gradually to die out, before the steady growth of peasant proprietorship."[28] Some hundred-odd miles beyond Cheliabinsk he encountered the first town of importance in Siberia, Kurgan, and in the vicinity "villages of recently arrived immigrants with clean new log-houses, covered with sheet-iron, painted red." Price found these a striking contrast to the mud-walled, straw-thatched houses of eastern European Russia.[29]

At Krasnoiarsk, the economic and administrative center of the region, he decided that there were "no real social barriers in Central Siberia between the rural agriculturists, the urban citizens, and the merchants. There are no divisions separating rural from urban society." He did expect "Capital and Labor" to develop there and "contest" as in western Europe.[30] From Achinsk he went by the post road on to Minusinsk. It was April, during the thaw. He saw where clearings had been made and plots surveyed, and observed immigrants constructing their houses, ready to plow as soon as the snow melted. The houses were log-frame, with boards for the roof, and were very clean inside. The peasants' food was typically eggs, rye and wheat bread, *shchi* (salt cabbage and mutton soup), and tea. Their food cost nothing but labor, and the same was true of most clothing. Expenditures were only for tea, tobacco, sugar, and some Moscow-manufactured cotton prints from which women's clothes were made.

[27] Price, *op.cit.*, pp. vii-viii. For Carruthers' account of the trip, see his *Unknown Mongolia: a Record of Travel and Exploration in North-West Mongolia and Dzungaria*, 2 vols; London, 1913.

[28] *Ibid.*, p. 5.

[29] *Ibid.*, p. 7.

[30] *Ibid.*, pp. 32-35.

Minusinsk appeared to him a typical Siberian provincial town. He talked to the county *nachal'nik*, appointed by the provincial governor, under whom civil officials administered both urban and peasant affairs. He met the inspector of mines for southern Yeniseisk province, who was a veteran of the battle of Plevna but who knew little about mines. The three best buildings in Minusinsk, he found, were the museum, the prison, and the vodka factory. He talked to several exiles, and "more than one" told Price he would remain in Siberia after his sentence expired. In Siberia, said Price, the exile system "is often rather an agent for the spreading of progressive ideas than for the suppression of revolutionary movements."[31] He noted that in 1900 punishment by exile for convicts and political prisoners had been abolished, but in 1904, when terrorism was increasing again, exile for political offenses was reestablished. It had come to be the practice to confine the criminals in the east, at Nerchinsk and Sakhalin, while the politicals were kept in West and Central Siberia. In 1906, 45,000 political exiles had come. In the year 1909 in Yeniseisk province alone over 50,000 politicals were serving sentence, though the majority of these, it was thought, would remain in Siberia after expiration of their terms.

Price spent some little time in a village of the upper Yenisei basin called Kushabar. It is interesting to compare his own study of the budget of one householder of central Siberia with the official statistics cited earlier. With 40 acres, this peasant sold grain and livestock yielding a 170-ruble annual gross return. Out of this income, he paid direct taxes of no more than 15 rubles (or 30 shillings).[32] The total direct taxes paid by the peasants of Yeniseisk province in 1907, Price reported, were 900,000 rubles, or only 3 shillings (1½ rubles) per head. Of course indirect taxes were also paid on tobacco, tea, and matches, but all these items cost only around 50 rubles per household per year, of which the tax accounted for but a small fraction.

Price was much impressed by the affluence as well as the spirit of the settler. As an Englishman, he took proper cognizance of the fact that his lodgings were clean. "In fact," he wrote, "the cleanliness and self-respect seemed to increase in direct proportion to the distance from civilization."[33] Some years back there had been a redivision of land, but not because of the grinding of the wheels of ancient

[31] *Ibid.*, p. 88. Compare Michie's observations, Chapter VI.
[32] *Ibid.*, p. 233.
[33] *Ibid.*, p. 96.

customs. New settlers had arrived, and the villagers decided they should not have all the new land so reshuffled it. Price concluded: "Here, then, was a 'socialistic' system—a system in which the little State owned the means of production—in process of change before the forces of 'Individualism' and the rights of private property. A movement the very antithesis of that towards which the proletariat of Western Europe are said to be trending. Which of these two movements is 'progress' and which is 'reaction'?"[34] To write such an observation in 1912 required no little insight and independence of mind.

[34] *Ibid.*, p. 127.

PART FIVE

THE FATE OF SIBERIAN MIGRATION

CHAPTER X

The End of Siberian Migration

The Siberian Population

The 1897 census had shown the population of Asiatic Russia to be 13,500,000. Estimates of provincial and regional statistical committees for 1911 gave a figure of 20,000,000. In a mere thirteen years, the total had increased by half.[1] The density of population remained very low. By 1911 in the Far East it was only .4 per square verst (total population, 855,000); in the Steppe it was 2.4 (population, 3,800,000); in Turkestan, 4.4 (6,500,000); in Siberia proper, it was 1 per square verst (8,500,000). However, only about one-tenth of the area of Siberia was inhabited by settled population, and in that zone the density was from 8 to 10 per square verst. This was the fertile strip, about 600 versts wide, in West and Central Siberia. Much of this area was near the railway: Kurgan county, Tobolsk, had a density of 16; Omsk county, Akmolinsk, had 9.8; Krasnoiarsk county, Yeniseisk, had 9.5. Some of it, however, was on rivers, like Barnaul county, Tomsk, which had a density of 11.5.

The Russian element (including Ukrainians) had increased its predominance. Its percentage of the total population was as follows:

Administrative Area	1897	1911
Siberia	82.0%	86.5%
Far East	63.3	74.0
Steppe	19 (approx.)	40.0
Turkestan	3.7	6.3

The proportion of Russians in Akmolinsk had risen from 33 to 58 per cent. In Tobolsk and Tomsk it stood near 95 per cent, in Yeniseisk 90 per cent, in Irkutsk 80 per cent, in Transbaikalia 70 per cent, in Yakutsk 7 per cent. The mark of the Great Migration was evident.

Since 1897, the overall population increase had been 46 per cent; the rural increase was 42 per cent, the urban 77 per cent. In West Siberia alone the cropped area had risen by 52 per cent in the years from 1907 to 1911. The sowing area of Asiatic Russia rose by

[1] N. V. Turchaninov, "Naselenie Aziatskoi Rossii. Statisticheskii ocherk," *Aziatskaia Rossiia,* Vol. I, pp. 64-68.

1,600,000 desiatinas from 1907 to 1910—40 per cent of the increase for the whole Empire (4,000,000). The increase of tillage and of cattle was almost twice as great as population growth. This meant a "development of productive forces never seen in Russia proper, where the productiveness of agriculture up till now is still in retard of the growth of population."[2]

Siberian prosperity had extended its effects to the homeland. The new migrant economy exported 50 million poods of grain, as compared with 10 million in 1899. It sent abroad 5,000,000 poods of butter, as against 400,000 in 1894. The percentage of Siberian meat out of all the supply in the markets of St. Petersburg and Moscow stood at from 45 per cent to 50 per cent, as against 10-12 per cent in 1903-1907. In 1900 the Trans-Siberian had carried 600,000 poods of meat; in 1911, 3,400,000.[3]

The 1897 census revealed the presence in Asiatic Russia of 1,400,000 people born in one of the fifty provinces of European Russia; in 1911 the comparable figure was estimated at more than 2,500,000. In the interval, about 2,000,000 desiatinas of the best lands of the best provinces had been given up by settlers bound for Siberia. In seven provinces alone (Chernigov, Kursk, Poltava, Samara, Voronezh, Ekaterinoslav, and Kharkov) almost 1,000,000 desiatinas was made available to the neighbors whom the migrants left behind.[4]

Siberian Land Settlement and the Commune

I. I. Popov cited approvingly Kaufman's characterization of governmental migration policy as "unprincipledness elevated to a principle." From his study of resettlement, Popov concluded that policy on both sides of the Urals had not reduced the agrarian problem, but was actually making it worse. His final words were, "Resolution of the agrarian problem in the interests of the peasants is inevitable," but not by setting up farms and draining off surplus population, but "in that direction in which the destruction of the First Duma pointed."[5] This was of course "Aesopean language" for revolution. Nevertheless Popov himself declared, "there is being realized a grandiose conception of reorganization of the whole land order of Siberia, a sort of social revolution, which must overturn the whole arrangement of agricultural life of Siberia, established by centuries as a result of climatic, topographical, territorial, agronomical and other peculiari-

[2] "Zemel'nye poriadki za Uralom," *ibid.*, p. 575.
[3] "Krest'ianskoe pereselenie i russkaia kolonizatsiia za Uralom," *ibid.*, p. 496.
[4] *Ibid.*, p. 493.   [5] I. I. Popov, *loc.cit.*, p. 267.

ties of Siberia."[6] Lamenting the destruction of the commune, admitting that the establishment of farms entailed a "social revolution," this revolutionary thus advanced a reactionary argument against reform.

The setting up of farms had to take place at the expense not only of the existing communes, but of the state ownership of land. Noting that except for the Russian Far East, the foreigner could acquire and hold land in Siberia only for the purposes of residence or business, M. P. Price wrote that "Siberia thus exhibits perhaps the most extensive scheme of land nationalization in the world."[7] In Asiatic Russia almost all land belonged formally to the state. Exceptions were only the land under the Cabinet of His Majesty (the personal property of the Emperor), the lands of the Cossack hosts, and as a rare exception grants to certain native groups and persons. Nothing like this extent of state ownership existed west of the Urals except in the Far North. According to *Aziatskaia Rossiia*, the explanation for it "must be sought in the relatively recent habitation of most of Russian Asia and in special geographic and economic conditions of this part of Russia, and in part even simply in a certain *retardation* of legislation on land rights compared with actual life. *The law and life sometimes go here in different paths*" (emphasis in the original).[8]

The region referred to was chiefly the migrant zone. In the Far North of Asiatic Russia there was no conception of landholding among the nomads, and the few Russians living among them lived not on the land but by trade. In the steppe region nomad economy likewise prevailed, although the incursion of migrants into its northern fringes was forcing the development of ideas of ownership among the natives, if only for purposes of self-defense. But in the fertile strip in the center, the idea of private ownership was rapidly taking root, in the face of the law which forbade it and of the commune which obstructed it.

Actual demarcation of land held by old-settler villages had been carried out by government surveyors, with participation of peasant or native representatives. Nominally this process had begun in 1835, actually in the 1870's; from 1908 the Resettlement Administration carried out the work itself. First a survey was made of existing landholdings. If the village holding did not reach the 15-desiatina norm, an increase up to that norm was permitted if free land was available.

[6] *Ibid.*, p. 263.
[7] M. P. Price, *op.cit.*, p. 236.
[8] "Zemel'nye poriadki za Uralom," *Aziatskaia Rossiia*, Vol. I, pp. 532-33.

If the holding exceeded the norm, the old-settler village could retain it, provided it admitted new members. Otherwise the permission of the Minister of Agriculture was needed. However, it appears that seldom was the village actually deprived of any land; usually migrants were admitted. The old-settler household thus retained an area of 40-50 desiatinas of usable land, far above the quantity it was usually prepared to work immediately.

A plan of boundaries was then drawn, and a forest allotment up to 3 desiatinas per man was marked out. The plan was considered by the village assembly and the peasant or native representatives, and then turned over to the land settlement commission, perhaps along with petitions for certain adjustments. The decisions of the commissions might be appealed to provincial or regional administrators and finally to the Governing Senate in St. Petersburg. In any case, transactions involving transfer or trade of lands went to the provincial administration. If the land settlement official disagreed with a decision taken there, the case went to the Minister of Agriculture, who was supposed to decide the matter in conjunction with the Minister of Interior or the Minister of the Imperial Court. In case of disagreement among the ministers, the case went to the Senate. The plan was then put into effect. Border markers were set up, and certificates of allotment (not title, since the state owned the land) were distributed in the village concerned.

This process of land demarcation established only the boundaries of villages. Readjustment of holdings by individual households took place by "voluntary" mutual agreement by the holders of allotment land. Naturally the kind of agreement reached depended upon the recognized custom in the village. The custom might and did change in a given village. However, there were several types of holding in the Siberian villages, and if the type changed, it occurred by common consent. V. V. Soldatov, on the basis of studies made in the Altai and in the Steppe region, found two basic forms of holdings, "free" and "equalized."[9] "Free" holding existed where there was a surplus of unoccupied land, and here each tiller used what land he liked and went "where the plow, scythe, and axe go," as the peasants put it. "Equalized" holding existed where land scarcity had developed; each tiller had the right to land corresponding to his capacity and needs, secured through periodic equalization usually on the basis of the size and strength of his family. When land scarcity appeared, a

[9] V. V. Soldatov, "Izmeneniia form obshchinnago zemlepol'zovaniia v Sibiri," *Voprosy kolonizatsii*, No. 7, 1910, p. 36.

village might pass from "free" to "equalized" holding, often gradually and by way of intermediate stages. Such stages included "squatter's" (*zakhvatnyi*) holding, wherein land was held for the tiller's lifetime or even hereditarily, but with the recognition and consent of the commune. The "squatter" had the right to use lands which he or his father had cleared and worked. When land became harder to obtain, "regulated squatting" might appear. Here land not used over a certain period of time might be taken by the commune; thus the claim had to be sustained not merely by the original labor of clearing, but also by continued working. The "equalized" form included periodic adjustments in holdings as the need arose. This would seem to be similar to the European Russian redistributory commune, but the appearance was misleading. As *Aziatskaia Rossiia* reported, "in Siberia in the general redivisions there is carried out no *transference* of allotments from their owners, which accompanies each redivision in the commune of European Russia. The fundamental principle of all redivisions in Siberia, with the most insignificant exceptions, is *the right of each householder to remain on his own old place, his 'stand.'* "[10] On looking more closely, Soldatov found that the "equalized" form existed only in a few areas, including thickly-settled counties of Tobolsk province adjoining European Russia (Kurgan and Tiumen) and here and there in Irkutsk and Trans-baikalia. Even in those localities the usual method was not to divide the land into scattered strips, but into sizeable portions. "Equalizing" them consisted of allotting smaller portions close to home to the poorer or less numerous family, larger portions more distant to the richer or more numerous one. "Equalized" holding represented the stage toward which the Siberian village tended to evolve *given the continuance of extensive farming*. However, this tendency might be offset by a variety of conditions, including custom and sheer stubbornness, and "equalized" holding had not developed in some of the most thickly settled areas of West and Central Siberia. A given village might indeed have several forms of holding existing side by side, one for meadows, another for plowland, and so forth. Meadows were often in short supply, and artificial grass-seeding was as yet almost unknown in Siberia, so sometimes the meadows alone might be "equalized." The economic logic of change in types of holding was not the same as what actually prevailed.

In fact, according to a government report, until the 1880's there was dominant "complete freedom in use of all resources, with the

[10] "Zemel'nye poriadki za Uralom," *Aziatskaia Rossiia*, Vol. 1, p. 559.

predominance of the squatter's or *khutor* form of economy";[11] in Soldatov's terminology, "free" holding. There had come to prevail throughout the larger part of Siberia, according to Soldatov, the system of "regularized squatting" for plowland. However, the most recent development was in the direction of something new: hereditary-household tenure. Often there was a change from the "squatting" form directly into this type of holding, "skipping" as it were the "equalized" form. As hereditary-household tenure developed, intensive agriculture with crop rotation often replaced the old extensive method. Soldatov concluded that the Siberian commune "is at present being shattered at its foundations."[12] In Siberia one finds thus a similar phenomenon to that already encountered on the frontier in European Russia. A. A. Kaufman concluded, in the words of K. Kocharovsky, "that despite the absence of serfdom and the relative freedom from administrative pressure the original individual holding of land by right of occupation had been changing, with the growing shortage of land, in the direction of increasingly communal and equalitarian forms of tenure; the unhampered evolution of landholding in Siberia appeared thus to reproduce the development of the land commune in Russia proper."[13]

Within limits, and up to a certain point of time, there is much to what Kaufman contended. Frederick Jackson Turner had written, "American social development has been continually beginning over again on the frontier."[14] In Russia is also found a sort of recapitulation of stages of agricultural change. However, the recapitulation was by no means as exact as Kaufman argued. It might be more accurately said that *as a result* of the greater freedom of the Siberian frontier, the peasant moved more rapidly from the stage of the carefree squatter through the period of making necessary adjustments with his new neighbors to the same opportunity which the European Russian farmer was also encountering and using: that of adoption of better farming methods on a plot of ground which was in fact (if not in law) his own to manage as he desired. Because this process occurred with such speed in Siberia, the old principle of *staroimochnost'*, or squatter's rights, was never forgotten, and it was reasserted in the emergence of hereditary-household tenure. Within little more than a generation, many Siberian villagers changed from "squatters"

---

[11] *Ibid.*, p. 557.   [12] Soldatov, *loc.cit.*, p. 52.

[13] K. Kocharovsky, "Alexandr Arkadievich Kaufman," *Encyclopedia of the Social Sciences* (1948), Vol. VIII, p. 550.

[14] Frederick Jackson Turner, *The Frontier in American History*, New York, 1920, p. 3.

to private landholders. In European Russia the same change took centuries to accomplish. The old conviction that a man's toil and sweat on the land earned him an indefeasible right to it had been enshrined in the proverb, "We are yours [i.e., the serf-owners'], but the land is ours." However, even after the end of serfdom, the land had passed not to the peasants directly, but to the commune, which was still heavily entangled in obligations to the state. Under Stolypin, the land west of the Urals was becoming peasant property at last. For the European Russian peasant, the commune had been weakening, and confirmation of title often involved little more than legalizing existing fact. It was the painful process of reshuffling the scattered strips and consolidating the farms which took time and trouble. In European Russia the state had not been directly in the way of private ownership since Emancipation, and from the time of the adoption of the Stolypin laws the state had supported private ownership firmly. In Siberia, the commune was also weakening, but the state lay directly in the path of private ownership.

As already noted, a law extending the homestead system to Siberia, along the lines of the Stolypin law of 14 June 1910, was introduced in the Duma. However, at the outbreak of World War I it had still to be acted upon. Accordingly, enclosure in Siberia could take place only on the initiative of private persons, unsanctioned and unsupported by the government. In old-settler villages, it was carried out by private surveying firms at the expense of the villagers. The government provided loans at the rate of around 35 kopeks per desiatina for surveying, though it is not clear whether this aid was wholly or partly intended for delimitation of village rather than individual boundaries as described earlier. In any case it appears that state loans were used for only a very small proportion of the surveying which was done as an immediate prelude to land settlement.[15]

Mainly through private effort and expense, then, from 1908 through 1913 land settlement was projected and plans were drawn up for the consolidation of 20,200,000 desiatinas. Boundaries were traced on 11,100,000, and work was finished on 6,010,000. This was out of a total area of 33,500,000 desiatinas held by old-settler villages. Bilimovich provides these figures for the progress of the work:[16]

---

[15] Only 1,000,000 desiatinas were surveyed by the aid of state loans. See "Zemel'-nye poriadki za Uralom," *Aziatskaia Rossiia*, Vol. I, p. 570.

[16] Alexander D. Bilimovich, "The Land Settlement," in *Russian Agriculture during the War*, New Haven, 1930, p. 341.

1908	118,500 des.
1909	366,500
1910	489,000
1911	585,000
1912	2,300,000
1913	2,151,000
	6,010,000 des.

Bilimovich declares that from 1912 onward consolidation was actually proceeding more rapidly in Siberia than in European Russia, "which is the more remarkable that in Siberia all the work was done on the initiative and at the expense of the peasantry." It will be recalled that land settlement occurred in European Russia in two steps: first, confirmation of title to the scattered strips as private property, second, enclosure (consolidation of the strips). In Siberia there was no legal way to confirm title, and *nevertheless* consolidation was proceeding at great speed. The phenomenon may throw some light on the issue of whether Stolypin, as certain critics have charged, "forced" the peasants of European Russia to set up farms. In Siberia the Stolypin laws did not apply, yet farms were appearing as fast, or even faster, than in European Russia where they did apply. It is unlikely that the Siberian farmer wanted the opposite of what his counterpart west of the Urals wanted, as it is comprehensible why in Siberia, where there was no ancient system of scattered strips, he was able to attain his desires with less effort.

About four-fifths of the 6,000,000-odd desiatinas was converted into farms (either *otrub* or *khutor*), and the *khutor* alone accounted for about one-fourth of the total consolidated. These consolidations were on old-settler land. As regards the migrant plots (we should remember that many migrants had entered old-settler villages), half the holdings allotted the settlers from 1911 onward consisted of enclosed plots. In the three years up to the beginning of 1914, some 2,100,000 desiatinas had been so allotted, and plans for the distribution of an additional 400,000 were ready, in accordance with the policy announced by Krivoshein and described in a previous chapter. Thus by early 1914 enclosure had encompassed a total of 8,500,000 desiatinas in Siberia, "the nucleus of a huge new country of khutors and otrubs."[17]

Though underestimating the lengths enclosure had already gone,

[17] *Idem.*

Aziatskaia Rossiia is basically correct in stating: "Today Siberia stands on the threshold of the introduction for all tillers of the rights of property in land, and islands of individuated private holding, scarcely noticeable, lying in seas of land taken by the holders without formal title, must form one common whole, falling under laws common to the whole Russian Empire on the right of property, ownership, and use of the real property of the state, communes, and private holders."[18]

The evolution of Siberian land tenure in the direction of private ownership might well have occurred in time without the Great Migration. Nevertheless, three articles in *Aziatskaia Rossiia* independently assert that the migrants contributed mightily to such evolution. "To no small degree the migrants from provinces with a land order firmly founded on private right [i.e., several western and Ukrainian provinces where the redistributory commune had never existed] accelerated the penetration into the legal order of the Siberian old-settler population of the new idea of private property."[19] Another writer says, "The migrants introduced into the concepts of civil law of the Siberian peasantry the idea of the actual economic possession of one's own land . . . and the inviolable permanence of tenure and liberation from any threat of equalization of once established meets and bounds."[20] Contends a third: "The migrants . . . brought with them from the motherland the aspiration to individual land use above all."[21] What this official publication was saying was that settlers who came from a region where there was *no legal* private property brought with them the *idea*, based on the experience, of private property, and successfully implanted it in another region where private property was unknown. No wonder there were allusions to the divorce of law from life!

Popov was certainly right to call this whole process "a sort of social revolution," but he was mistaken in denying that it was a revolution "in the interests of the peasants." It is difficult indeed to understand what the "direction in which the destruction of the First Duma pointed" might have to do with the problems of the Siberian settlers in 1914. Political revolution could offer them little. "Compulsory alienation" or seizure of landlord or state land—the revolutionary program in European Russia—was a meaningless slogan in Siberia. There were no landlords' lands at all to be seized,

---

[18] "Zemel'nye poriadki za Uralom," *Aziatskaia Rossiia*, Vol. I, p. 537.
[19] *Ibid.*, p. 533.   [20] "Sibirskie pereselentsy," *ibid.*, pp. 198-99.
[21] "Krest'ianskoe pereselenie i russkaia kolonizatsiia za Uralom," *ibid.*, p. 498.

and the settlers often had already more state land than they could use. Acquiring ample land did not solve their problems; it only made it easier for them to adopt better methods and diversify their agriculture and animal husbandry—and thereby to obtain real improvement. More land would certainly have helped the European Russian peasant, but there *was* little more, in either landlord or state hands. The real solution could not be found in practicing the same backward methods on slightly greater acreage; it could be reached only by using the land more efficiently. Siberian settlers were showing how that could be successfully done.

Throughout the Empire, peasant agriculture was being transformed into independent farming, and that economic change was accompanied by social consequences. A thaw was attacking the frozen agricultural system of communal tenure and extensive cultivation, as well as the apparent moral inertia of the Russian village. Siberia was leading the way, for those who had eyes to see. Stolypin saw, rejoiced, and yet pondered the menace of "rude democracy" in the east. His opponents would not see at all.

The First World War

In 1914 migration was still at a high level; 242,000 people passed over the Urals, and presumably a large part of this mass moved before the outbreak of war in the summer. In 1915 the figure fell to 28,000; in 1916 it was 11,000; in 1917, 6,000; in 1918, 64,000; in 1919 there was no migrant registration; in 1920, 85,000; in 1921, 71,000. The figure then dropped close to zero, rising again to strike a peak of 94,000 in 1925, to remain near there the following two years.[22] These official figures, as Obolensky notes, tell only a small part of the story.

The cataclysm of war set in motion masses of people beside which the Great Siberian Migration in its entirety was overshadowed. If one desires to measure the value of migration in purely quantitative terms, he ought to regard the war as a stupendous benefit. Over 7,000,000 soldiers were sent to the front and were there in 1917. Over 3,000,000 refugees were driven back from their homes by the German advance. In 1916 an attempt to mobilize natives for labor at the front was followed by a great uprising, and the consequent migration of some 300,000 Kazakh and Kirghiz refugees to Sinkiang. The rural exodus was marked, not only by the movement of peasant soldiers to the front, but by their attraction to industrial cities for

[22] V. V. Obolensky (Osinsky), *op.cit.*, pp. 127-28.

war industry, which employed some 2,000,000 workers by 1916.[23]

The immediate effect of the war was thus to relieve pressure on the land to a tremendous extent. Those left on the land were called upon for maximum efforts, and their productivity is widely reported to have increased notably. Antsiferov suggests that the wartime prohibition of liquor contributed to the rise in productivity,[24] but broader economic factors were operating. While no less than 2,600,-000 horses and considerable numbers of oxen were taken away for military use, and the import of agricultural machinery and fertilizer fell to nothing, it was the gentry who felt these deprivations far more than peasants. In 1915 the peasants actually sowed more land than before the war.[25] Then and later the fact was that peasant enterprise, which depended chiefly on the tillers' own labor, was able to survive economic dislocation far better than the capitalist farms of the gentry. If it had not been for some 430,000 war prisoners available as laborers for the gentry, their plight might have been insupportable. Antsiferov writes of peasant farming that "it not only remained unshaken but went on developing further" as a result of the war.[26] The pressure for resettlement naturally slackened. Transportation was not available anyhow because of wartime needs, but there was also much less demand for it on the part of settlers.

In 1917 the pressure returned with a rush. The disintegration of the army was well under way, and officers and men alike started a movement back to the rural areas, though a considerable proportion of both were soon absorbed into the armies which fought the Civil War on both sides. The mass movement back to the land threatened, as Lenin noted, the total disintegration of the Russian proletariat. Part of this movement was a migration of some 175,000 settlers over the Urals in the first third of 1918;[27] another part of it was directed southward. These facts led Kulischer to assert that the Bolsheviks were victorious only where the advance of their armies coincided with the movement of migration.[28] It is true that in the west they were driven back, while in the south and east they were victorious. The peasants who at first supported the Whites to safeguard their property soon went into opposition for the same motive, and "the ensuing peasant revolt spread over all western Siberia."[29] Kulischer correctly notes that land division was no issue in Siberia, since there

[23] Eugene M. Kulischer, *Europe on the Move. War and Population Changes, 1917-47*, New York, 1948, Ch. 3.
[24] See Antsiferov, *loc.cit.*, p. 120.   [25] *Ibid.*, p. 117.   [26] *Ibid.*, p. 295.
[27] Obolensky, *op.cit.*, p. 128.   [28] Kulischer, *op.cit.*, p. 35ff.   [29] *Ibid.*, p. 41.

were no gentry lands to divide, and yet the antagonism between White leaders and peasants was serious. To explain this antagonism would take us beyond the scope of this book, but it seems certain that the indecisive attitude of the Whites toward the property rights of the peasants of Siberia—who legally had no property rights at all!—and of the rest of Russia played an important role.

The disappearance of a battle line by 1920 opened the way to a continuance of the eastward movement on a larger scale. It is estimated that in the following three years 500,000 irregular colonists moved alongside the 160,000 who migrated under the terms of a Bolshevik decree on resettlement.[30] Kulischer comments accurately that while earlier migrants were attracted by the subsistence potentials of Siberia, these people came because of the actual means of subsistence which were to be found in Russian Asia.

Kulischer reports that after a strong but temporary reflux of migrants in a westerly direction caused by the great famine of 1922-1923, the direction once again shifted to Siberia. "Migration in 1925-1928 was but a resumption of prewar trends."[31] He wrote, "It remained largely a movement of peasants who liquidated their farms and went off, together with their families, mainly to lands beyond the Urals, to devote themselves anew to agriculture."[32] Two-thirds of the migrants (perhaps 400,000 people) went to Siberia, which was designated by a decree of 6 June 1925 as an area for colonization. Only in 1930 was individual colonization prohibited.

Thus the end of smallholding in Russia, brought about by Soviet collectivization, accompanied the termination of the freedom to migrate. The government no longer permitted the peasant to work out his own destiny. Knowing what we do about the persistence of the desire to own land and cattle, and the influence of this desire in bringing about the compromise measure which permitted individual possession of gardens and livestock in the collective farms, we may likewise suspect that the urge to resettle in search of a better life has not vanished. The peasant in the Soviet Union cannot be "the master of his fate," but nevertheless the central authorities of the Communist Party have learned to their chagrin that the peasant still has economic and moral weapons with which even they must reckon.

[30] *Ibid.*, p. 43. [31] *Ibid.*, p. 84. [32] *Ibid.*, p. 82.

CHAPTER XI

Conclusion

"Perhaps Siberia may yet become what she is potentially already—the Canada of the East—the home of a great self-governing people, free to educate themselves, to direct in their own way and for their own benefit as well as that of the Russian Empire the development of the great resources of a country rich in minerals both 'precious' and 'useful,' in fact first in the world in gold mines; abounding in fine timber; spread with wide fields, growing wider every year, of grain and hemp; with vast grazing lands; with vaster tracts teeming with every kind of fur-bearing animal; and peopled by a hardy stock of democratically-minded Europeans, trained to self-reliance and resourcefulness in no easy school."—M. A. Czaplicka, *My Siberian Year*, London, n.d., pp. 305-06.

Causes and Effects of Migration

What attracted the migrants to Siberia? The quest for land and freedom. What did they find there? More of both than they had ever known before. Often the settler gave his reason for departure as "lack of land," but if that is the only thing he sought he could often have had it at home by renting. Of course hard work and money were needed to make a land rental successful, but not only toil and cash were required of a prospective migrant, but also a break with his whole past and that of his ancestors. Mamin-Sibiriak expressed the feeling of an escapee from exile, who returns to his village, in regaining the only life he had known: "He longed for freedom, for open air, like every living being, and for him this freedom was to be found there in his own village. Now the world of the village appeared before his eyes in all its surroundings of toil, as it was constructed by his forefathers—nothing here was superfluous, each screw had its place, but the sundered individual was only a negligible particle of the great living whole and only within this whole did he have sense and meaning, like a thread in a fabric or a link in a chain. Each peasant fitted into this order and only through this order did he know what was good and evil; he rejoiced, mourned, hoped, wept, prayed, and, above all, felt himself to be at home."[1]

[1] D. N. Mamin-Sibiriak, "Lëtnye," in *Izbrannye sochineniia*, Moscow-Leningrad, 1949, p. 623.

239

To break away from a life in which the peasant felt secure and safe, whatever his wants, required more than simply the desire for a few more desiatinas of land. For millions of peasants, freedom was *not* to be found in their native village, and the opportunity to seek it even thousands of miles away compelled them to uproot themselves and risk everything for its sake. To separate "economic" freedom from "political" freedom is not warranted either in trying to analyze man's aspirations or in attempting to build a good state and society. Oppression and misery had never managed to extinguish in the peasant the desire for both "land and liberty"—the chance to care for his family decently and to call his soul his own.

The peasant's desire to seek afield for land in part reflected the crisis in communal land tenure and the three-course system of land use in south-central Russia. The growing density of population had rendered these institutions obsolete and inadequate to feed either the Russian village or the city. The Siberian migration showed the individual peasant family the way to realize its goals. For the Russian peasantry as a whole, migration had a double significance. It furnished the homeland a useful, and for the overcrowded central provinces perhaps an indispensable, catalyst for the successful execution of land settlement. It also created in Siberia a dramatic example of how rapid agricultural improvement could occur and what social and economic benefits it might produce.

The peasant's search for freedom was in part a consequence of his having already been relieved of the bondage of serfdom. He learned what a degree of independence could be like, and was eager for more. The breakdown of the legally stratified class system inaugurated by Alexander II's Great Reforms gave the peasant a chance to develop a sense of citizenship which he had hitherto experienced in only a very limited fashion within the village commune, where the power of the landlord—not to mention the state—was ever present. In European Russia, the destruction of class barriers— as in western Europe since the French Revolution—had deprived the upper classes of certain privileges and had given the lower classes more. Migration had a rather different effect. At first the prerogative of the lower and "protected" class of peasants, by its success migration attracted members of the "upper" classes, who sought to obtain the benefits of being a peasant (though by the last years of Tsarism, "farmer" may be a better word for the Siberian settler). In Siberia, the peasant learned that he could bend the law and officialdom to recognize and provide for his own needs; he even found it possible, as our evidence has repeatedly suggested, to evade the hand of the government entirely. There could be nothing servile about a man who managed to complete Siberian migration successfully.

The effects of Siberian migration, it was asserted at the outset, were in certain ways comparable to those of the American frontier movement. Turner believed that they included the development of a "composite nationality" of differing ethnic stocks, stimulation of a "nationalizing tendency" simultaneous with the creation of what he called "sections," and the encouragement of democracy and individualism.[2]

The mixing of ethnic groups which occurred in Siberia was of less dramatic dimensions than in America's melting pot, but it is still noteworthy. First of all, a considerable amount of intermarriage between Russians and the Siberian natives took place. While some of the Old Believers and other old-settlers kept strictly to themselves and preserved their old Russian characteristics, nevertheless children of Buriat-Russian marriages, "swarthy, blackhaired and black-eyed" with or without Mongoloid fold, were numerous enough to be given the special name *Karymy*. Sometimes Yakut-Russian marriages resulted in partial Yakutization of the children. For example, note the hero in Korolenko's story *Makar's Dream*, who spoke Yakut almost exclusively but who nevertheless lived in the unshakable belief that "he was a Russian peasant of Chalgan, and not a nomad Yakut."[3] In the steppe region there were also numerous unions between Kazakhs and Russians, whose offspring were often largely Russified.[4]

More important numerically than mingling with natives was the amount of intermingling of Russians from different regions. Our data on individual settlements have already suggested the conclusion that "group settlement, wherein migrants from one province, county, or township, establish a whole village in one place, is a phenomenon only of the most recent time and is in general a rarity." In all parts of Siberia there were villages with settlers who came from ten or fifteen different provinces. True, there was a tendency of settlers to seek out geographical and climatic conditions in Siberia comparable to those to which they had been accustomed at home—a tendency observed in other migrations as well. Still in Siberia there was to

---

[2] Turner, *The Frontier in American History*, New York, 1920, p. 1ff.

[3] Vladimir Korolenko, *Makar's Dream and Other Stories*, trans. by Marian Fell, New York, 1916, pp. 3-4.

[4] "Sibirskie pereselentsy," *Aziatskaia Rossiia*, Vol. I, p. 185.

be found "a kaleidoscope of intermingling in Asia of the representatives of all Russia."[5] Russians lived among, if they did not marry, natives. Great Russians, Belorussians, and Ukrainians, from Kiev and Kazan, Perm and Podolia, Viatka and Vitebsk, mingled, dwelt side by side, and intermarried.

These phenomena had a linguistic side. According to W. K. Matthews: "Inter-Slavonic dialectal miscegenation began when speakers of Central and South Russian as well as White Russians and Ukrainians arrived in Siberia in the eighteenth century, and it has continued with the rising tide of immigration which accompanied the opening of railway communication in the 1890's and especially since the exploitation of mineral deposits in Siberia since 1917. . . . It would seem that the majority of 'Siberians' (*sibirjaki*) to-day speak a Russian in which *akan'je* preponderates, so that the *okan'je-akan'je* dichotomy, characteristic of European Russian, no longer applies to Siberian. This is due not merely to the presence of Central and South Russian speakers in very considerable numbers, but to the levelling effects of Literary Russian."[6]

Again the intermixture of various Russian types took place at the same time as the flavor of native influence was being added. Matthews pointed to the existence of "certain characteristically Siberian developments" such as glycolalia (*sladojazyčije*), found chiefly among women; displacement of liquids by *j* (as for example *khojosho* for *khorosho*); and noted that since this phonetic phenomenon was found in dialects influenced by such Paleoasiatic languages as Yukagir, Koriak, and Chukchi, some investigators regarded it as of alien origin. Matthews asserts, "Such an origin can certainly be attributed to part of the great wealth of regional words which make the vocabulary of Siberian Russian almost as distinctive as that of American English. . . . Alien influences have also been noted in the 'singing intonation' of Siberian Russia and especially in the sharp, emphatic rising tone used in Western Siberia to express intense emotion."[7] Matthews ascribed the same cause to "marked variations in stressing which may be heard in Siberian dialects" such as *dochká* instead of *dóchka* (daughter), *ópasno* for *opásno* (dangerous), and so forth. Thus Siberian speech came to exhibit both a synthesis of European Russian features and an admixture of native influences;

---

[5] *Ibid.*, p. 190.
[6] W. K. Matthews; *The Structure and Development of Russian*, Cambridge, Eng., 1953, pp. 104-05.
[7] *Ibid.*, p. 106.

that is, it was at the same time more national and more regional than European Russian speech.

Siberia likewise developed both strong national and strong regional feeling. *Aziatskaia Rossiia* ascribes to the migrants the creation of "that inner living and close tie which has been established between Russia proper and that most distant of its frontier regions, to the extent that they have been settled by migrants from the central provinces. Feeling far from the homeland with especial straining towards her, spiritual nearness, and unity, the migrants there also act as living and convinced conductors of a common faith in the wholeness and indivisibility of our fatherland from the banks of the Neva to the heights of the Pamirs, the impassable crests of the Tian Shan, the border windings of the Amur and the far-off coast of the Pacific Ocean, where all—in Asia, as in Europe, our one Russian land—constitutes one great and inalienable possession of our people."[8] In this case the lyric qualities of nationalism are produced by the educated man who is writing. Though the migrant might not verbalize his feelings thus or even share those expressed fully, it seems plausible that he often may have become conscious of the expanses and potentialities of his country, even of being a Russian, in a manner quite new to him and hitherto utterly foreign to his experience.

That did not mean the settlers were indifferent to the distinctiveness of the region to which they had come. As in America, nationalism and sectionalism both developed powerfully. The aspirations of the *sibiriak*, his expression of regional needs and uniqueness, and the growth of ambitions for regional autonomy or even independence, cannot be explored here, though a considerable literature on the subject may be consulted.[9] The opportunities which arose for Siberian autonomism and the successes and mishaps of attempts to exploit them during the Civil War must likewise be deferred for examination elsewhere, although in many ways those events make a climax to the whole story of the Great Migration. Despite the fact that the Soviets did not feel the need for even nominal recognition of Siberian regionalism—since the Siberians did not make up a minority "nationality"—it is possible that such aspirations may one day be heard again.

Finally, what may one say of the development of democracy and individualism in Siberia? Democracy in the sense of popular par-

[8] *Aziatskaia Rossiia*, Vol. I, p. 199.
[9] See the forthcoming studies in Siberian sectionalism by Professor Victor Erlich of the University of Washington.

ticipation in government had not been fully attained. On the village level there had long been self-government, as in European Russia. Although the Siberian commune was nearly defunct as a manager of agriculture, the village assembly was a functioning organ of democracy, subject to far less outside interference in Siberia, where there was no gentry, than in the homeland. As for representative government based on suffrage, Albert J. Beveridge once asked some Siberian peasants through an interpreter, " 'Did they want to vote?' Why, they did that now. Did not all of them, even the women who were widows, have a free voice in their communes, etc.?" But to his question whether they wanted to take part in government in the sense of making laws and the like, they replied in the negative.[10] Part of this attitude doubtless belonged to the widely observed indifference of peasants to urban politics which comes from the lack of acquaintanceship with it; the explanation may partly have been that in Siberia the laws interfered so little with the lives of the peasants, while "making laws" had a vague connotation of encouraging officials to skulk about villages making trouble. Nevertheless, Beveridge's report dates from 1903, and beginning in 1906 Siberians, perhaps including Beveridge's apolitical informants, voted for deputies to the Duma. As noted earlier, there was certainly mounting agitation for county and provincial self-government in the form of the zemstvo, though how widespread this demand was would be difficult to establish.

Some writers on Siberia used the word "democracy" to mean chiefly social and economic equality. Commenting on the failure of the law of 8 July 1901, which envisaged sale of land to private capitalists east of the Urals, Pavlovsky writes, "Hence, as before, Siberia remained wholly democratic, a country of peasant farmers settled on State-owned land."[11] By "democratic" Pavlovsky means nothing pertaining to government, but rather he refers to the economic order of factual smallholding and the attitudes of equality which attended it. Compare Turchaninov: "The class composition of the population beyond the Urals is extremely homogeneous. Russian Siberia is at the present time a solid 'peasant sea.' "

Turchaninov continued, "Representing, in the person of the old-settlers, the descendants of daring escapees from Russia proper, having moved here under harsh conditions sometimes even prior to the conquest of the region, and in the person of the recent settlers,

---

[10] Albert J. Beveridge, *The Russian Advance*, New York and London, 1903, p. 222.
[11] Pavlovsky, *op.cit.*, p. 173.

the most energetic and enterprising representatives of their milieu—
for only such migrants become firmly acclimatized and strike root
in the new regions—the Siberian peasants indeed differ from the
remaining mass of the Russian peasantry . . . in their greater stead-
fastness . . . in the struggle with [nature] . . . their greater mobility
and readiness to accept every kind of innovation. . . ."[12]

The anthropologist Czaplicka puts it this way: "the word 'peasant'
for the Sibiriak does not call up the associations that it does in
Russia—the recollection of serfdom, of subjection to landowners
and clergy, of a position of humility at the very foot of a social ladder
whose rungs are not so much steps as barriers. The 'peasant' in
Siberia feels himself a citizen rather. He knows that he is the owner
of the country. For, with the exception of the population of the towns
—only 6 per cent of the whole—who form a class of 'burghers,' the
clergy and the civil servants, most of whom are newcomers to
Siberia, the Sibiriaks are all 'peasants.' "[13]

The equality of the Siberian frontier did not exclude feelings of
self-sufficiency and the spirit of initiative. The Siberian peasant,
according to *Aziatskaia Rossiia,* accepted complex machines of whose
very existence he had been unaware in the homeland, and came to
accept and act on the aid and advice of the local agronomist in trying
new methods. The settler showed "an exceptional capacity for self-
help, by means of cooperatives, credit unions, and other types of
unions and societies."[14] The growth of the Siberian cooperatives was
impressive enough to deserve a full-length study of its own. The
most dramatic development of all—the emergence of the individual
family homestead in Siberia at the expense of the commune and in
the face of the legal universality of state ownership—has already
been traced. Economic and social individualism were far advanced,
and some of the political interest and experience necessary to a functioning democratic government were at hand. There could be no
democracy in the full and true sense while the autocratic state remained, but that the Siberian population was in many respects prepared for democracy seems a reasonable supposition.

Two developments in journalism may serve to indicate one aspect
of the results which migration was helping bring about among
Russia's common people. A popular monthly magazine was appear-

[12] N. V. Turchaninov, "Naselenie Aziatskoi Rossii," *Aziatskaia Rossiia,* Vol. I,
pp. 74-75.
[13] M. A. Czaplicka, *My Siberian Year,* London, n.d., pp. 248-49.
[14] "Sibirskie pereselentsy," *Aziatskaia Rossiia,* Vol. I, pp. 198-99.

ing in St. Petersburg called *Khutor*, for which 1911 was to be the sixth year of publication. Edited by the agronomist P. N. Elagin, the magazine described itself as "the most widely distributed agricultural journal."[15] Its advertisement ran, "The correct practical agricultural knowledge furnished you by the magazine *Khutor* will help you to increase substantially the yield of your enterprise . . . [the magazine has the] objective of disseminating practically useful information on agriculture of the type chiefly useful for small enterprises." This publication, in the fashion of American advertising, offered as an inducement to subscribers free seeds and plans of farm buildings. Its price was two rubles per year. The magazine was evidently intended for the emerging independent peasants of the whole Empire—including Siberia, since its advertisement appeared in *Questions of Colonization*, much of whose concern was for Russian Asia. A still more surprising journalistic enterprise was a weekly called *The Peasant of the Altai*, which in 1914 was offering subscriptions for the fourth year of publication, in the city of Barnaul. The subject matter was described as including agriculture, cattle-raising, dairying, bee-keeping and truck gardening, crafts, factory industry and commerce, education, public health, veterinary medicine, cooperation and credit, and needs of regional and village government.[16] The settler of the Altai region—one of the chief targets of the whole migration—might indeed be either directly or indirectly concerned with all these topics. We cannot determine how many subscribers this journal boasted, nor how many it might have interested had literacy been more widespread. Nevertheless, one may feel confident that the readers of this magazine in the midst of Tsarist Asia would not find our assertions about the social and economic consequences of migration particularly startling.

The Fate of the Russian Peasantry

Antsiferov contends that in Russia "at the end of the nineteenth and the beginning of the twentieth centuries all agricultural development was in the direction of the improvement and extension of peasant farming."[17] Within peasant farming, Pavlovsky declares, "the individualist movement in the Russian village, of which enclosures were the manifestation, carried all before it, because it answered the most urgent needs of the peasant farmer."[18] These

---

[15] See advertisement of *Khutor* in cover pages of *Voprosy kolonizatsii*, No. 9, 1911.
[16] Advertisement of *Altaiskii Krest'ianin* is opposite p. 517 of Pt. IV of *Sibirskii Torgovo-Promyshlennyi Ezhegodnik, 1914-1915.*
[17] Antsiferov, *loc.cit.*, p. 25.   [18] Pavlovsky, *op.cit.*, p. 320.

conclusions may be unduly categorical. If many of the gentry were going bankrupt and selling out, others were adapting themselves to capitalist farming methods. If the enclosure movement was in general proceeding speedily and successfully, there were areas where it lagged and met resistance. Peasant farming might not have come to take over every last farm in Russia, and some farms might have remained for some time unenclosed. The more important issue is whether the gains of peasant farming and the progress of enclosure were opening up new perspectives of diversification of agricultural enterprise, new levels of prosperity, new horizons of individual and social development. All evidence suggests that they were doing so.

Nowhere was this more apparent than in Russian Asia. Not only was this true of changes in agricultural production, land tenure, and land use, but it also applied to the subsidiaries of agriculture—especially dairying and meat production—while industry was growing in the old Ural manufacturing area and the new area which would later be called the Kuznets basin. Peasant enterprise was dominant in Siberia; the kind of farming in which the peasant, depending wholly or chiefly on the labor of his own family, produced in part for home consumption and in part for market, was the prevalent type. But it was not the only kind of economic activity, nor was it desirable that it should be so, for either economic or social reasons. For those who lived by it, Siberian peasant enterprise provided a better standard of living than the tiller had known under any other conditions. The degree of economic and psychological self-sufficiency which the Siberian peasant enjoyed served as an example to his fellows west of the Urals whose problems were greater, even if partial solutions were in sight. The Siberian frontier offered new opportunity from which the entire Russian peasantry could benefit either directly or indirectly, by migration or observation.

Peshekhonov had written that "the resolution of the agrarian problem in Russia can begin in Siberia."[19] We have tried to suggest that such resolution depended not only on finding more land, in the homeland or Siberia, but more fundamentally on changes in institutions, habits, and attitudes. The roots of the necessary changes may be sought in western Russia, where enclosure and diversification of agriculture were starting to spread eastward. They may be found in Siberia, where the attitudes of agrarian individualism first became plainly discernible, and where land settlement and diversification spread fastest of all, among a free-minded peasantry. Or, they may be

[19] Cited by Popov, *loc.cit.*, p. 260.

found in the minds of the peasants, who had never forgotten their conviction that "land and liberty" were their just due. The acceptance of part of this claim by the government of Stolypin was an important landmark in the whole series of changes. Stolypin, who grew up in Kovno in the west and as prime minister visited Siberia, had some grasp of the magnitude of the transformation which the Russian peasants were undergoing or might, with encouragement, undergo.

Free farming in Siberia had suggested democracy to Stolypin, and he feared it. To a young U.S. army captain with the AEF in Siberia, named Frederick F. Moore, it suggested something similar, which he welcomed. Moore wrote, "I know Siberia as a land of peasants, rather than as a place where I met governmental chiefs and heard the discussion of international policies."[20] "The problem of Siberia is the peasant-minded population . . . whether working in cities or in the wilderness."[21] He thought that this population was mentally static, and exhibited "ignorance, credulity, stupidity, and cruelty."[22] And yet he believed "that the only hope which Russia has for regeneration, no matter how long it may take to do the work, lies in the peasant class."[23] What Moore wanted both in Russia and at home, he declared, was that peasant-minded people should have comfort and justice and enjoy conditions wherein, when an individual revealed ability, he should get his chance. "My ideal is not a nation of peasants by any means. But I do insist that a large mass of our own population prefers to be peasant-minded, and fights against being anything else."[24] He shrewdly noted that social origin was no determinant of beliefs; having encountered somewhere the old populist heroine, Catherine Breshko-Breshkovskaia, he observed that she was of the peasant class but was "not peasant-minded."

"Peasant-mindedness"—that is, agrarian or any other type of individualism—was not widely favored in Russia around the turn of the century. We have noted that for somewhat different reasons most government officials as well as the intelligentsia clung to the commune up to the Revolution of 1905. The government had regarded the commune as a bulwark against revolution; the intelligentsia had looked upon it as a harbinger of the future socialism. Until 1905, the majority of bureaucrats tended to agree with the view expressed in 1847 by Baron Haxthausen, who called the Russian commune to the attention of Europe: "The prophets of social

[20] Frederick F. Moore, *Siberia To-day*, New York and London, 1919, Preface.
[21] *Ibid.*, p. 258. [22] *Ibid.*, p. 265. [23] *Ibid.*, p. 269. [24] *Ibid.*, p. 270.

revolution are up in arms against wealth and private property; the abolition of hereditary rights and the equal distribution of land are the watchwords of the revolutionaries. In Russia such a revolution is impossible, because there the utopian dreams of western revolutionaries have fully materialized."[25]

That the commune rendered revolution impossible was shown to be a false assumption. The government learned that lesson fully in 1905, and although Witte and others had suggested that the policy should be to support replacement of the commune by homesteads, it remained for Stolypin to make the decision and obtain the consent of the Emperor to implement it. During the ensuing decade, for the first time the government and the intelligentsia opposed each other on the issue of the commune—though they had long been so deeply divided on other more pressing issues that they had scarcely noticed their fundamental agreement on that one.

For the governmental change of front, it was the peasant who was ultimately responsible. The reality of the emergence of homesteads, beginning modestly in the west of Russia, and the tremendous acceleration of migration, embracing the whole Russian East in its sweep, suggested to the government a feasible alternative to the commune. Both the western homesteaders and the eastern migrants had often acted in defiance of the law. We have already traced how a policy of free migration and support of homesteads was belatedly adopted, in the program of Stolypin and Krivoshein and the practice of the Ministry of Agriculture and the Resettlement Administration. The example of his neighbors in the west and the experience of his fellows who went east brought the peasant new opportunities. These opportunities were seized upon by the government and exploited fully, in the hope of avoiding revolution, but also in an attempt to secure to the Russian people such prosperity and happiness as was possible.

The intelligentsia remained for the most part unconvinced. Although they might be persuaded that the Stolypin policy was yielding results, they still felt that it was in essence a trick of Tsarism, an application of the autocratic knout to the downtrodden, intended to confuse them about their real interests. Stolypin wrote in 1904, "The government for the peasants is a means to the achievement of certain land reforms; for the 'third element' [the zemstvo-employed professional men, i.e., the form in which Stolypin had to con-

---

[25] Haxthausen, *Studien über die inneren Zustände Russlands,* quoted by Bilimovich, *loc.cit.,* p. 314.

tend with the intelligentsia while he was governor of Saratov] the government is power, that is, the objective which they seek to attain."[26] In the February Revolution power fell into the hands of the intelligentsia, who opposed the further progress of land settlement —in part because it had been the policy of the fallen monarchy, in part because they had always opposed it for ideological reasons.

The Octobrists and Nationalists in the Duma and Imperial Council had given the policy of land settlement serious consideration, in opposition to both extreme Left and extreme Right. Both of these parties, which were identified with the Duma and the monarchy, were swept away in March. The Kadet Shingarev became Minister of Agriculture in the spring, and he pushed through an act which abolished the Land Settlement Commissions and suspended the Stolypin legislation. Professor Posnikov was appointed chairman of the new Central Land Committee; he was likewise an opponent of the Stolypin policy. An official statement of the Provisional Government declared, "private ownership of land must cease."[27] The spontaneous land confiscation of late 1917 followed, which realized the common feature of all the opposition party land programs, seizure of gentry and state land[28]—whose underlying assumption was that "lack of land" was the root of the agrarian problem, rather than outmoded types of land tenure and use. The leaders of the February Revolution cannot be blamed for the confiscations of the autumn, which disturbed their labors and undermined their hold on state power. But they had for years fostered the illusion that the ownership of land by the gentry and the state was the chief obstacle to peasant betterment, and they ought not to have been surprised when the peasants illegally seized the lands which the moderate socialists endlessly delayed expropriating by law.

The peasants seized the land—often lying idle because of the wartime shortage of labor available to the gentry—not because it was in their considered judgment the solution of their problems, but simply because it seemed the best thing to do at the moment. The new government cried freedom, freedom, but had proclaimed the imminent end of private property and the abolition of the homestead policy, and offered nothing in their place. Soon enough the peasant found that seizing gentry lands was no solution. There was no more land to be divided, now that the "Black Partition" of old revolutionary tradi-

[26] "K istorii agrarnoi reformy Stolypina," *Krasnyi Arkhiv*, Vol. 4 (17), 1926, p. 87.
[27] Quoted by Bilimovich, *loc.cit.*, p. 372.   [28] See Chapter VIII above.

tion had finally come to pass. The real roots of the problem were now much easier to see and act upon.

By 1921 a Soviet publication admitted that to settle on an enclosed holding was now "the ambition of every peasant farmer," and that land settlement had been spontaneously resumed on a large scale. Taking note that "drastic steps are taken to counteract any tendency to form enclosed holdings," this publication confessed that "these measures frequently failed to achieve the desired result."[29]

Professor Max Sering, one of the Germans who had studied land settlement most closely, summed up: "The truth is that the Socialist revolution has ended in pure individualism. . . . The great achievement of Bolshevik rule has been the creation of a peasant class intensely conscious of the value of private ownership of land. Both in Greater Russia and in the Ukraine, according to all available information, the peasants have become 'fanatical owners,' as a result of the partition of large estates and of the struggle they have had to maintain their own holdings. . . . The peasants have not, in fact, obtained much more land than would in any case have passed into their hands as a result of the transfer of landed property in progress before the Revolution. The fact that they have obtained that land free of payment does not seem to them a very important advantage. More than once they have expressed a desire to pay for it, feeling that by so doing they would secure a legal title to their holdings."[30]

Even the Soviet publication cited referred to "the peasants' incontestable claim, founded on economic needs, to be granted a legal title to their land."[31] That did not mean that the Communists had suddenly become apostles of individualism. Those were still the early days when it was possible to publish dissenting views on Soviet soil. The Communists had already sought to begin the liquidation of smallholding in the period of "War Communism." Though they confessed temporary failure by adopting the New Economic Policy, they made no secret of the fact that they intended to try again. Under the NEP the Russian peasant once again was in search of a better life by way of smallholding.

Then, beginning in 1929-1930, the Communists launched an all-out attack on economic and psychological individualism in agriculture as well as in industry, and throughout Russian society and culture. The attack succeeded in collectivizing the majority of the peasants,

[29] *O Zemle*, Vol. 1, p. 77, quoted by Bilimovich, *loc.cit.*, p. 381.
[30] Quoted by Bilimovich, *loc.cit.*, pp. 382-83.
[31] *O Zemle*, Vol. 1, p. 73, quoted by Bilimovich, *loc.cit.*, p. 383.

but the resistance was fierce enough to compel the Communists to leave the tiller his own garden plot and livestock. The tiller keeps them to this day, though the Communists have repeatedly indicated that as long as he does there remains unfinished business for them in Russian agriculture.

It was the freedom to farm which the Soviets first attacked, although years passed before they could substantially destroy it, while they were also crushing the freedom of the worker to bargain and the freedom of the intellectual to speak and write. If the Soviet government has succeeded in building "the new Soviet man," the story of Russian agricultural individualism, of which the Great Siberian Migration forms an essential part, is at an end. If it has not succeeded, the brightest chapters of the story may remain one day to be written.

APPENDIX I

TABLE 11

Origin of Siberia-bound Migrants Registered at Cheliabinsk, 1887-1893
(Source: A. A. Kaufman, "Pereselenie," *Entsiklopedicheskii Slovar'*)

Province	No. of Families	Per Cent of Peasant Population of the Province
Kursk	10,785	2.8
Tambov	6,796	2.3
Voronezh	5,558	1.5
Viatka	5,356	1.6
Samara	5,072	1.5
Perm	4,547	1.1
Poltava	3,643	1.0
Riazan	3,139	1.3
Saratov	2,635	0.9
Kazan	2,598	0.8
Penza	2,472	1.2
Kharkov	2,360	0.8
Chernigov	2,179	0.7

Also Orel, Simbirsk, Nizhny Novgorod sent more than 1,000 families, 4 others 500-1,000; 10, 100-500; 14, less than 100. Total registered, 67,041.

TABLE 12

Origin of Siberia-bound Migrants Registered at Tomsk, 1884-1893
(Source: Kaufman, *loc.cit.*)

The Tomsk migrant point, for the decade from 1884 to 1893, registered 50,416 families, the 11 provinces sending most being

Kursk	7,769
Tambov	4,140
Poltava	2,164
Viatka	2,116
Perm	1,844
Voronezh	1,419
Chernigov	1,198
Samara	1,135
Kharkov	1,079
Kazan	1,002
Tobolsk	892
Total registered	50,416

TABLE 13

Provinces of Birth of European-Russian Born Living in Siberia, 1897
(Source: N. V. Turchaninov, "Naselenie Aziatskoi Rossii," in
Aziatskaia Rossiia, Vol. I, p. 68, based on 1897 census figures.)

Province of Birth	Number of Persons
Perm	116,000
Poltava	105,000
Kursk	95,500
Tambov	93,000
Voronezh	92,000
Chernigov	82,000
Samara	80,000
Viatka	75,500
Penza	56,500
Riazan	47,000
Orenburg	45,500
Orel	43,500
Saratov	43,000
Kharkov	36,500
Kazan	36,000

Total of European-Russian born, 1,400,000, out of a total of
5,341,745 Russian population of Asiatic Russia.

TABLE 14

Origin of Siberian Migrants by Regions of European Russia, 1885-1914
(Source: Obolensky, *Mezhdunarodnye i mezhdukontinental'nye migratsii*, p. 90.)

Years	1885-1889	1890-1894	1895-1899	1900-1904	1905-1909	1910-1914	For 30 Years
Black-earth center	70.0%	78.0%	65.0%	44.0%	46.0%	36.0%	49.0%
Western	2.0	0.4	12.0	29.0	25.0	16.0	19.0
Southern steppe and Caucasus	—	0.2	5.0	15.0	14.0	27.0	15.0
Eastern	27.0	22.0	14.0	8.0	9.0	16.0	13.0
Remainder	0.5	—	4.0	4.0	6.0	6.0	4.0
Total in 1,000's of migrants	84	283	659	447	1,838	1,069	4,380

TABLE 15

Land Held by Migrants Surveyed by Kuznetsov
(Source: *Sbornik statisticheskikh svedenii ob ekonomicheskom
polozhenii pereselentsev v Sibiri*, Vol. 1, p. 18.)
The average family questioned held:

Regions of Siberia	At Home	In Siberia
Steppe	3.6 des.	35.3 des.
Lesostep of West Siberia	5.0	39.9
Lesostep of East Siberia	4.8	40.0
Forest	4.9	37.5
All Regions	4.5 des.	38.3 des.

TABLE 16

Land Worked by Number of Years of Migrant Residence, among
Migrants Surveyed by Kuznetsov
(Source: *Ibid.,* pp. 21-23.)

Duration of Migrant Residence	Region I (Steppe)	Overall Average
More than 18 years	22.2 (des.)	20.6 (des.)
18-8 years	21.5	18.1
7-4 years	22.4	13.9
3 years	20.8	13.0
Less than 3 years	14.3	9.2
Average for all	21.1	14.4

TABLE 17

Average Holding and Rental of Migrants Surveyed by Kuznetsov,
Comparing Richest Group with Remainder
(Source: *Ibid.,* p. 126.)

	4,187 Richest Households	23,005 (The Rest)
Average per household of plow and hayland in des.	34.2	11.2
Of this total was rented	10.0	1.3
Plowland	3.4	—
Hayland	6.6	1.3

TABLE 18

Capital Held by Migrants Surveyed by Kuznetsov
(Source: *Ibid.*, p. 153.)

Capital	Present Value	Net	Time of Settlement	At Home	% of Inc. At Home	Over Capital at Time of Settlement
Region I	745	665	162	196	239	303%
Region II	753	440	188	293	50	134
Region III	511	417	168	250	67	148
Region IV	365	241	143	203	19	69
All Regions	566	466	161	239	95	189%

APPENDIX II

Heads of Certain Ministries of the Russian Empire

Prime Ministers

1905 (Oct.)	S. Iu. Witte
1906 (May)	I. L. Goremykin
1906 (July)	P. A. Stolypin
1911 (Sept.)	V. N. Kokovtsev
1914 (Feb.)	I. L. Goremykin
1916 (Feb.)	B. V. Sturmer
1916 (Nov.)	A. F. Trepov
1917 (Jan.)	N. D. Golitsyn
1917 (Mar.)	G. E. Lvov

Interior

1803	V. P. Kochubey
1807	A. B. Kurakin
1811	O. P. Kozodavlev
1819	V. P. Kochubey
1825	V. S. Lanskoy
1828	A. A. Zakevsky
1832	D. N. Bludov
1839	A. G. Stroganov
1842	L. A. Perovsky
1853	D. G. Bibikov
1855	S. S. Lanskoy
1861	P. A. Valuev
1868	A. E. Timashev
1878	L. S. Makov
1880	M. T. Loris-Melikov
1881	N. P. Ignatiev
1882	D. A. Tolstoy
1889	I. N. Durnovo
1895	I. L. Goremykin
1899	D. S. Sipiagin
1902	V. K. von Plehve
1904	P. D. Sviatopolk-Mirsky
1905 (Feb.)	A. G. Bulygin
1905 (Nov.)	P. N. Durnovo

1906 (May)	P. A. Stolypin
1911	A. A. Makarov
1913	N. A. Maklakov
1915 (Sept.)	N. B. Shcherbatov
1915 (Oct.)	A. A. Khvostov
1916 (Mar.)	B. V. Sturmer
1916 (Sept.)	A. D. Protopovov
1917 (Mar.)	G. E. Lvov

Foreign Affairs

1802	A. R. Vorontsov
1807	N. P. Rumiantsev
1815	I. A. Veidemeier
1817	K. V. Nesselrode
1856	A. M. Gorchakov
1882	N. K. Giers
1895	A. B. Lobanov-Rostovsky
1896	M. N. Muraviev
1900	V. N. Lamsdorf
1906	A. P. Izvolsky
1910	S. D. Sazonov
1916 (July)	B. V. Sturmer
1916 (Nov.)	N. N. Pokrovsky
1917 (Mar.)	P. N. Miliukov

Finance

1802	A. I. Vasiliev
1807	F. A. Golubtsov
1810	D. A. Guriev
1823	E. F. Kankrin
1844	F. P. Vronchenko
1852	P. F. Brok
1858	A. M. Kniazhevich
1862	M. Kh. Reitern
1878	S. A. Greig
1880	A. A. Abaza
1881	N. Kh. Bunge

1887	I. A. Vyshnegrad-sky	
1892	S. Iu. Witte	
1903 (Aug.)	E. D. Pleske	
1904 (Nov.)	V. N. Kokovtsev	
1905 (Oct.)	I. P. Shipov	
1906 (May)	V. N. Kokovtsev	
1914 (Jan.)	P. L. Bark	

Ways of Communication

(ministers 1811-1868 not shown)

1868	V. A. Bobrinsky
1871	A. P. Bobrinsky
1874	K. N. Posiet
1888	G. E. Pauker
1889	A. Ia. von Hub-benet
1892	S. Iu. Witte
1892	A. K. Krivoshein
1894	M. I. Khilkov
1905	K. S. Nemeshaev
1906	N. K. Schaffhau-sen-Schönberg och Schaufuss
1909	S. V. Rukhlov
1915	A. F. Trepov

Agriculture

(officially designated by three successive names, as follows:
State Domains

1837	P. D. Kiselev
1856	V. A. Sheremetiev
1857	M. N. Muraviev
1862	A. A. Zelenoy
1872	P. A. Valuev
1879	A. A. Liven
1881	N. P. Ignatiev
1881	M. N. Ostrovsky
1893	A. S. Ermolov

Agriculture and State Domains

1894	A. S. Ermolov

Chief Administration of Land
Settlement and Agriculture

1905	N. N. Kutler
1906 (Feb.)	A. P. Nikolsky
1906 (April)	A. S. Stishinsky
1906 (July)	B. A. Vasilchikov
1908	A. V. Krivoshein
1915	A. N. Naumov
1917 (Mar.)	A. I. Shingarev

259

APPENDIX III

Administrative Divisions of Asiatic Russia in 1914

(Source: G. K. Gins, "Administrativnoe i sudebnoe ustroistvo gubernii i oblastei Aziatskoi Rossii," *Aziatskaia Rossiia*, Vol. 1.)

1. Tobolsk province. Capital, Tobolsk.
   Uezds: Tobolsk, Tiumensk, Ialutorovsk, Kurgansk, Ishimsk, Tiukalinsk, Tarsk, Turinsk, Berezovsk, and Surgutsk.
2. Tomsk province. Capital, Tomsk.
   Uezds: Tomsk, Kainsk, Kuznetsk, Barnaulsk, Biisk, Mariinsk, and Zmeinogorsk.
3. Governor-Generalship of Irkutsk. Capital, Irkutsk.
   a. Yeniseisk province. Capital, Krasnoiarsk.
      Uezds: Krasnoiarsk, Yeniseisk, Achinsk, Minusinsk, Kansk, and Usinsk frontier region.
   b. Irkutsk province. Capital, Irkutsk.
      Uezds: Irkutsk, Verkholensk, Balagansk, Nizhneudinsk, and Kirensk.
   c. Transbaikalia region. Capital, Chita.
      Uezds: Verkhneudinsk, Barguzinsk, Nerchinsko-zavodsk, Selenginsk, Troitskosavsk, Nerchinsk, and Akshinsk.
   d. Yakutsk region. Capital, Yakutsk.
      Okrugs: Yakutsk, Olekminsk, Viluisk, Verkhoiansk, and Kolymsk.
4. Governor-Generalship of the Amur. Capital, Khabarovsk.
   a. Amur region. Capital, Blagoveshchensk. Amur uezd and okrug of Amur Cossack host.
   b. Maritime region. Capital, Vladivostok. Uezds: Nikolaevsk, Khabarovsk, Udsk, Nikolsk-Ussuriisk, Imansk, Olginsk, and okrug of Ussuri Cossack host.
   c. Kamchatka region. Uezds: Petropavlovsk, Okhotsk, Gizhiginsk, Anadyrsk, Chukotsk, and Komandorskie islands.
   d. Sakhalin region. Sections (*uchastki*): Aleksandrovsk and Tymovsk.
5. Governor-Generalship of the Steppe. Capital, Omsk.
   a. Akmolinsk region. Uezds: Omsk, Petropavlovsk, Kokchetavsk, Akmolinsk, and Atbasarsk.
   b. Semipalatinsk region. Uezds: Semipalatinsk, Pavlodarsk, Karkaralinsk, Ust-Kamenogorsk, and Zaisansk.
6. Governor-Generalship of Turkestan. Capital, Tashkent.
   a. Syr Daria region. Amu Daria *otdel* and uezds: Kazalinsk, Perovsk, Chimkentsk, Aulieatinsk, and Tashkentsk.

b. Samarkand region. Uezds: Samarkandsk, Katta-Kurgansk, Khodzhensk, and Dzhizaksk.

c. Fergana region. Uezds: Kokandsk, Skobelevsk, Andizhansk, Namagansk, and Oshsk.

d. Transcaspian region. Uezds: Mangyshlaksk, Krasnovodsk, Askhabadsk, Tedzhensk, and Mervsk.

e. Semireche region. Uezds: Vernensk, Kopalsk, Lepsinsk, Przhevalsk, Pishpeksk, and Dzharkentsk.

7. Uralsk region. Uezds: Uralsk, Lbishchensk, Gurievsk, and Temirsk.

8. Turgaisk region. Uezds: Aktiubinsk, Kustanaisk, Irgizsk, and Turgaisk.

APPENDIX IV

Dates of Russian Rulers, 1613-1917
(House of Romanov)

1613-1645	Michael	1741-1761	Elizabeth
1645-1676	Alexis	1761-1762	Peter III
1676-1682	Fedor II	1762-1796	Catherine II
1682-1725	Peter I	1796-1801	Paul
(1682-1696,	Ivan V, co-Tsar)	1801-1825	Alexander I
1725-1727	Catherine I	1825-1855	Nicholas I
1727-1730	Peter II	1855-1881	Alexander II
1730-1740	Anna	1881-1894	Alexander III
1740-1741	Ivan VI	1894-1917	Nicholas II

Key to Administrative Divisions (see next page)

(G—guberniia   Ob—oblast   Ok—okrug   U—uezd)

GRAND DUCHY OF FINLAND
1. Uleaborg — G
2. Vasa — G
3. Kuopio — G
4. Abo-Bjorneborg — G
5. Tavastehus — G
6. St. Michel — G
7. Nyland — G
8. Viborg — G

VISTULA PROVINCES
9. Suwalki — G
10. Lomza — G
11. Plock — G
12. Warsaw — G
13. Kalisz — G
14. Piotrkow — G
15. Siedlce — G
16. Radom — G
17. Kielce — G
18. Lublin — G

EUROPEAN RUSSIA
19. Estland — G
20. Lifland — G
21. Kurland — G
22. Kovno — G
23. Vilna — G
24. Grodno — G
25. Minsk — G
26. Volhynia — G
27. Podolia — G
28. Bessarabia — G
29. Kherson — G
30. Kiev — G
31. Mogilev — G
32. Vitebsk — G
33. Pskov — G
34. St. Petersburg — G
35. Olonets — G
36. Novgorod — G
37. Tver — G
38. Smolensk — G
39. Kaluga — G
40. Orel — G
41. Chernigov — G
42. Kursk — G
43. Poltava — G
44. Kharkov — G
45. Ekaterinoslav — G
46. Taurida — G
47. Voronezh — G
48. Tambov — G
49. Tula — G
50. Riazan — G
51. Moscow — G
52. Vladimir — G
53. Yaroslavl — G
54. Kostroma — G
55. Vologda — G
56. Arkhangelsk — G
57. Viatka — G
58. Perm — G
59. Nizhny Novgorod — G
60. Kazan — G
61. Ufa — G
62. Orenburg — G
63. Samara — G
64. Simbirsk — G
65. Penza — G
66. Saratov — G

67. Don — Ob
68. Astrakhan — G

CAUCASUS
69. Kuban — Ob
70. Stavropol — G
71. Terek — Ob
72. Black Sea — Ob
73. Kutais — G
74. Tiflis — G
75. Daghestan — Ob
76. Kars — Ob
77. Elizavetpol — G
78. Erivan — G
79. Baku — G

CENTRAL ASIA
80. Uralsk — Ob
  80a. Uralsk — U
  80b. Lbishchensk — U
  80c. Guriev — U
  80d. Temir — U
81. Turgai — Ob
  81a. Kustanai — U
  81b. Irgiz — U
  81c. Turgai — U
  81d. Aktiubinsk — U
82. Akmolinsk — Ob
  82a. Petropavlovsk — U
  82b. Kokchetav — U
  82c. Omsk — U
  82d. Atbasar — U
  82e. Akmolinsk — U
83. Semipalatinsk — Ob
  83a. Pavlodar — U
  83b. Semipalatinsk — U
  83c. Karkaralinsk — U
  83d. Ust-Kameno-
    gorsk — U
  83e. Zaisan — U
84. Transcaspian — Ob
  84a. Mangyshlaksk — U
  84b. Krasnovodsk — U
  84c. Ashkhabad — U
  84d. Tedzhen — U
  84e. Merv — U
85. Syr Daria — Ob
  85a. Kazalinsk — U
  85b. Perovsk — U
  85c. Chimkent — U
  85d. Aulieatinsk — U
  85e. Tashkent — U
  85f. Amu Daria <u>otdel</u>
86. Semirechensk — Ob
  86a. Lepsinsk — U
  86b. Kopal — U
  86c. Vernyi — U
  86d. Pishpek — U
  86e. Dzharkent — U
  86f. Przhevalsk — U
87. Samarkand — Ob
  87a. Katta-Kurgan — U
  87b. Samarkand — U
  87c. Dzhizak — U
  87d. Khodzhent — U
88. Fergana — Ob
  88a. Namagan — U
  88b. Kokand — U
  88c. Andizhan — U
  88d. Skobelev — U
  88e. Osh — U

89. Khiva
90. Bukhara

SIBERIA
91. Tobolsk — G
  91a. Berezov — U
  91b. Turinsk — U
  91c. Tobolsk — U
  91d. Surgut — U
  91e. Ialutorovsk — U
  91f. Tiumen — U
  91g. Kurgan — U
  91h. Ishim — U
  91j. Tara — U
  91k. Tiukalinsk — U
92. Tomsk — G
  92a. Tomsk — U
  92b. Kainsk — U
  92c. Barnaul — U
  92d. Kuznetsk — U
  92e. Zmeinogorsk — U
  92f. Biisk — U
  92g. Mariinsk — U
93. Yeniseisk — G
  93a. Yeniseisk — U
  93b. Achinsk — U
  93c. Krasnoiarsk — U
  93d. Minusinsk — U
  93e. Kansk — U
  93f. Usinsk
    frontier region
94. Irkutsk — G
  94a. Kirensk — U
  94b. Nizhneudinsk — U
  94c. Balagansk — U
  94d. Verkholensk — U
  94e. Irkutsk — U
95. Yakutsk — Ob
  95a. Verkhoiansk — Ok
  95b. Kolymsk — Ok
  95c. Viliuisk — Ok
  95d. Yakutsk — Ok
  95e. Olekminsk — Ok
96. Maritime — Ob
  96a. Nikolaevsk — U
  96b. Khabarovsk — U
  96c. Olginsk — U
  96d. Imansk — U
  96e. Nikolsk-
    Ussuriisky — U
97. Transbaikalia — Ob
  97a. Barguzin — U
  97b. Selenginsk — U
  97c. Verkhneu-
    dinsk — U
  97d. Chita — U
  97e. Nerchinsk — U
  97f. Nerchinsko-
    zavod — U
  97g. Troitskosavsk — U
  97h. Aksha — U
98. Amur — Ob
99. Kamchatka — Ob
  99a. Chukotsk — U
  99b. Anadyrsk — U
  99c. Gizhiginsk — U
  99d. Petropavlovsk — U
  99e. Okhotsk — U
100. Sakhalin Island

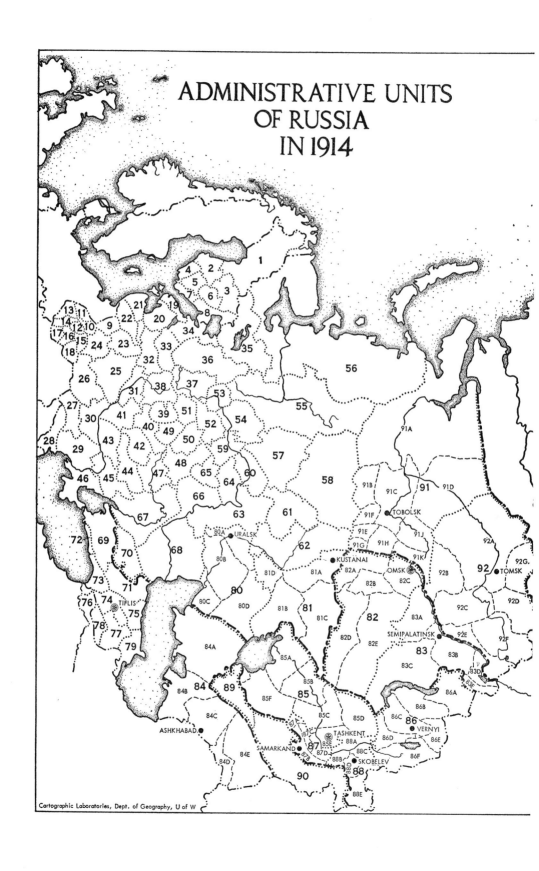

ADMINISTRATIVE UNITS
OF RUSSIA
IN 1914

Cartographic Laboratories, Dept. of Geography, U of W

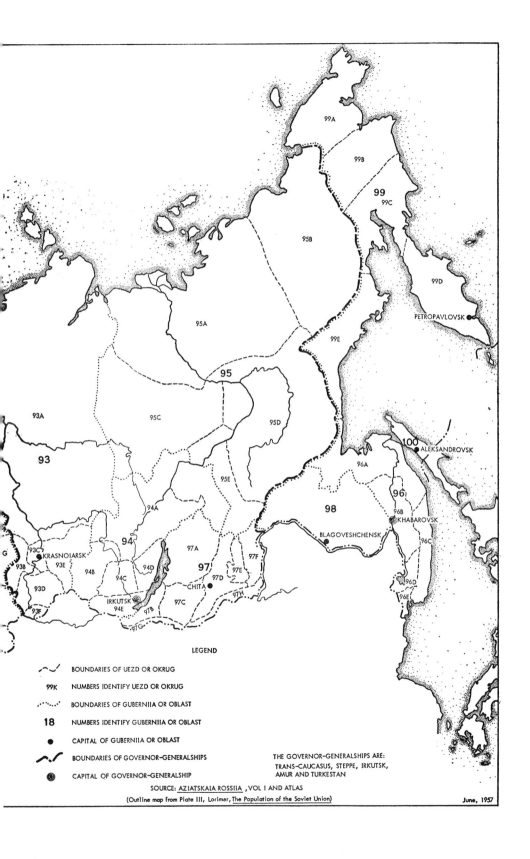

LEGEND

~~/	BOUNDARIES OF UEZD OR OKRUG
99K	NUMBERS IDENTIFY UEZD OR OKRUG
·····.·	BOUNDARIES OF GUBERNIIA OR OBLAST
18	NUMBERS IDENTIFY GUBERNIIA OR OBLAST
●	CAPITAL OF GUBERNIIA OR OBLAST
~~/	BOUNDARIES OF GOVERNOR-GENERALSHIPS
◉	CAPITAL OF GOVERNOR-GENERALSHIP

THE GOVERNOR-GENERALSHIPS ARE:
TRANS-CAUCASUS, STEPPE, IRKUTSK,
AMUR AND TURKESTAN

SOURCE: AZIATSKAIA ROSSIIA , VOL I AND ATLAS

(Outline map from Plate III, Lorimer, The Population of the Soviet Union)

June, 1957

BIBLIOGRAPHY

This study touches on several aspects of Russian development in addition to migration, and on certain aspects of migration which transcend the limits of Russian history. An exhaustive bibliography for these matters would not be warranted here. For the most complete bibliography on Russia in the period concerned—which as it happens gives great weight to Asiatic Russia—see Kerner, Robert J. *Northeastern Asia: a Selected Bibliography.* 2 vols. Berkeley, 1939. Vol. II.

The chief reference works used were:

Bol'shaia Sovetskaia Entsiklopediia. 1st ed. Moscow, 1926—.

Encyclopedia of the Social Sciences. New York, 1930-1935. 15 vols.

Entsiklopedicheskii Slovar' (Brockhaus-Efron). St. Petersburg, 1890-1904. 41 vols.

Entsiklopedicheskii Slovar' Russkogo Bibliograficheskogo Instituta Granat. Moscow, 1911-1929?. 11th ed. 52 vols.

Sibirskaia Sovetskaia Entsiklopediia. 3 vols. (A-N) Moscow, 1929-1932.

The books and articles listed below include all those works available to the writer on Siberian migration during the period in question, as well as those which provide background material and discussion of related problems which were found to be of greatest use or were cited in the text.

Andrievich, V. K. *Istoriia Sibiri.* Chast' I. Period ot drevneishikh vremen do ustanovleniia glavenstva goroda Tobol'ska i osnovaniia Irkutskago ostroga. Chast' II. Period s 1660 goda do votsareniia Imperatritsy Elizavety Petrovny. St. Petersburg, 1889.

Antsiferov, Alexis N., Bilimovich, Alexander D., and others. *Russian Agriculture During the War.* New Haven, 1930.

Aulagnon, Claudius. *La Sibérie Économique, considérée plus spéciale-ment dans sa partie Cisbaikalienne.* Paris, 1901.

Aziatskaia Rossiia. Izdanie Pereselencheskago Upravleniia Glavnago Upravleniia Zemleustroistva i Zemledeliia. 3 vols. and Atlas. St. Petersburg, 1914.

Balzak, S. S., Feigin, Ya. G., Vasyutin, V. F., eds. *Economic Geography of the U.S.S.R.* New York, 1949.

Barry, Arthur John. *Lecture on the Great Siberian Railway.* London, 1900.

Beveridge, Albert J. *The Russian Advance.* New York and London, 1903.

Bok, M. P. *Vospominaniia o moem otse P. A. Stolypine.* New York, 1953.

Bookwalter, John W. *Siberia and Central Asia.* 2nd ed., New York, 1899.

Bordeaux, Albert. *Sibérie: Notes de Voyage et de Séjour 1902-1903.* Paris, 1904.

Borodin, George. *Soviet and Tsarist Siberia.* London, 1943.

Bowman, Isaiah. *The Pioneer Fringe.* Ed. by G. M. Wrigley. New York, 1931.

Brutskus, B. D. *Agrarnyi vopros i agrarnaia politika.* St. Petersburg, 1922.

Butsinsky, P. N. *Zaselenie Sibiri i byt pervykh eia nasel'nikov.* Kharkov, 1889.

Carruthers, Douglas. *Unknown Mongolia; a Record of Travel and Exploration in Northwest-Mongolia and Dsungaria.* 2 vols. London, 1913.

Cary, Clarence. *The Trans-Siberian Route.* New York, 1902.

Chasles, Pierre. "Les réformes agraires et l'évolution des classes rurales en Russie." *Revue économique internationale.* October 1913.

Chelintsev, A. N. *Sel'sko-khoziaistvennaia geografiia Rossii.*

Clark, Rev. Francis E. *A New Way Around an Old World.* New York and London, 1901.

Cleinow, Georg. *Neu-Sibirien: eine Studie zum Aufmarsch der Sowjetmacht in Asien.* Berlin, 1928.

Cottrell, Charles Herbert. *Recollections of Siberia, in the Years 1840 and 1841.* London, 1842.

Courant, Maurice. *La Sibérie: Colonie Russe jusqu'à la Construction du Transsibérien.* Paris, 1920.

Curtin, Jeremiah. *A Journey in Southern Siberia.* Boston, 1909.

Czaplicka, M. A. *My Siberian Year.* London, n.d.

Dallin, David J. *The Rise of Russia in Asia.* New Haven, 1949.

Deutsch, Leo. *Sixteen Years in Siberia.* Trans. by Helen Chisholm. London, 1905.

Dmitriev-Mamonov, A. I., and Zdziarski, A. F., eds. *Guide to the Great Siberian Railway.* Trans. by L. Kukol-Yasnopolsky. St. Petersburg, 1900.

Dolgoroukoff, W. A. *Guide à Travers la Sibérie et les Territoires Russes en Asie Centrale. Année Troisième.* Tomsk, 1898-1899.

Druzhinin, N. M. *Gosudarstvennye krest'iane i reforma P. D. Kiseleva.* Tom I. Predposylki i sushchnost' reformy. Responsible editor, Academician B. D. Grekov. Moscow-Leningrad, 1946.

Dubrovsky, S. *"Stolypinskaia reforma."* Leningrad, 1925.

Erman, Adolph. *Travels in Siberia.* Trans. from German by W. D. Cooley. 2 vols. Philadelphia, 1850.

Fischer, Emil S. *Overland via the Trans-Siberian Railway.* Tientsin, 1908.

Fisher, Raymond H. *The Russian Fur Trade, 1550-1700.* Berkeley, 1943.

Fraser, John Foster. *The Real Siberia.* London, 1902.

Golder, F. A. *Russian Expansion on the Pacific, 1641-1850.* Cleveland, 1914.

Golovachev, D. "Pereselentsy v 1892 godu." *Vestnik Evropy.* August 1893.

Goodrich, Joseph King. *Russia in Europe and Asia.* Chicago, 1912.

Gosudarstvennaia Duma. Stenograficheskie otchety. 1906-1917.

Gurko, V. I. *Features and Figures of the Past; Government and Opinion in the Reign of Nicholas II.* Ed. by J. E. Wallace Sterling, Xenia Joukoff Eudin, H. H. Fisher. Trans. by Laura Matveev. Stanford, 1939.

Hansen, Marcus Lee. *The Atlantic Migration, 1607-1860.* Cambridge (Mass.), 1945.

Heller, Otto. *Sibirien: ein Anderes Amerika.* Berlin, 1930.

Henderson, Daniel. *From the Volga to the Yukon; the Story of the Russian March to Alaska and California, Paralleling our Own Westward Trek to the Pacific.* New York, 1945.

Iadrintsev, N. "Polozhenie pereselentsev v Sibiri." *Vestnik Evropy.* August, 1881.

Izgoev, A. S. *Russkoe obshchestvo i revoliutsiia.* Moscow, 1910.

Jasny, Naum. *The Socialized Agriculture of the USSR.* Stanford, 1949.

Jochelson, Waldemar. *Peoples of Asiatic Russia.* New York, 1928.

Kabo, R. M. *Goroda zapadnoi Sibiri.* Moscow, 1949.

Kaufman, A. A. "Pereselenie," *Entsiklopedicheskii Slovar'*, Vol. XXIII. St. Petersburg, 1898.

Kaufman, A. A. *Pereselenie i kolonizatsiia.* St. Petersburg, 1905.

Kaufman, A. A. *Sbornik statei.* Moscow, 1915.

Kennan, George. *Siberia and the Exile System.* 2 vols. New York, 1891.

Kerner, Robert J. *The Urge to the Sea: the Course of Russian History.* Berkeley, 1942.

Knox, Thomas W. *Overland through Asia.* Hartford, 1870.

Kofod, A. A. *Khutorskoe razselenie.* St. Petersburg, 1907.

Kolarz, Walter. *The Peoples of the Soviet Far East.* New York, 1954.

Kosinsky, V. A. *Osnovnyia tendentsii v mobilizatsii zemel'noi sobstvennosti i ikh sotsial'no-ekonomicheskie faktory. Mobilizatsiia zemel'noi sobstvennosti.* Prague, 1925.

Koulomzine, A. N. de. *Le Transsibérien.* Traduit du Russe par Jules Legras. Paris, 1904.

Kovalevsky, M. W. de. *La Russie à la fin du 19e Siècle.* Paris, 1900.

Kramar, Karel. *Die russische Krisis.* Trans. by Alfred Schebek. Munich and Leipzig, 1925.

Krypton, Constantine. *The Northern Sea Route: Its Place in Russian Economic History before 1917.* New York, 1953.

Kubijowytsch, W. *Siedlungsgeschichte, Bevölkerungsverteilung und*

Bevölkerungsbewegung der Ukraine. (Trans. by Dr. O. Kossmann and B. Kentrschnynskyj from *Geographie der Ukraine und benachbarten Gebiete*, by W. Kubijowytsch, original apparently in Ukrainian, Lemberg, 1938.) Berlin, 1943.

Kulischer, Eugene M. *Europe on the Move: War and Population Changes, 1917-47.* New York, 1948.

Kulischer, Eugene M. "Recent Migration in the Soviet Union." *American Sociological Review.* June 1944.

Lanoye, Fd. de. *La Sibérie d'après les Voyageurs les Plus Récents.* Paris, 1868.

Lansdell, Henry. *Through Siberia.* London, 1883.

Lantzeff, George V. *Siberia in the Seventeenth Century.* Berkeley, 1943.

Laserson, Max M. *The American Impact on Russia, Diplomatic and Ideological, 1784-1917.* New York, 1950.

Lebedeff, Boris. "The Abolition of the Russian 'Mir.'" *Contemporary Review.* Vol. CIII, No. 565. January 1913.

Legras, Jules. *En Sibérie.* Paris, 1899.

Legras, Jules. "Souvenirs sur P.-A. Stolypine." *La Vie des Peuples.* Vol. VII, No. 28. 10 August 1922.

Lengyel, Emil. *Siberia.* New York, 1943.

Lenin, Vladimir I. *Sochineniia.* 4th ed. Moscow-Leningrad, 1941-1950. 35 vols.

Leroy-Beaulieu, Paul. *De la colonisation chez les peuples modernes.* 6th ed. 1908.

Leroy-Beaulieu, Pierre (son of the above). *The Awakening of the East: Siberia-Japan-China.* Trans. by Richard Davey. New York, 1900.

Liashchenko, Peter I. *History of the National Economy of Russia to the 1917 Revolution.* Trans. by L. M. Herman. New York, 1949.

Lorimer, Frank. *The Population of the Soviet Union: History and Prospects.* Geneva, 1946.

Lozovoi, Ia. G. "Voprosy pereseleniia i kolonizatsii Sibiri." *Vol'naia Sibir'.* Vol. III, 1928.

Lynch, George. *The Path of Empire.* London, 1903.

Makarov, N. *Krest'ianskoe khoziaistvo i ego evoliutsiia.* Vol. I. Moscow, 1920.

Maklakov, V. "The Agrarian Problem in Russia before the Revolution." *Russian Review.* Vol. 9, No. 1, January 1950.

Maklakov, V. A. *Vtoraia Gosudarstvennaia Duma.* Paris, n.d.

Manuilov, A. "Agrarian Reform in Russia." *Russian Review* (London), Vol. I, No. 4, 1912.

Masuda, Tomiji. "Colonization of Siberia by Russian Peasants After the Emancipation." *Waseda Journal of Political Science and Economics.* Special Number in Commemoration of the Septuagenary Anniversary of the Founding of the University. Tokyo, 1952.

269

Matthews, W. K. *The Structure and Development of Russian.* Cambridge (Eng.), 1953.

Meakin, Annette M. B. *A Ribbon of Iron.* Westminster and New York, n.d.

Michie, Alexander. *The Siberian Overland Route from Peking to Petersburg.* London, 1864.

Miliukov, P. N. *Ocherki po istorii russkoi kul'tury.* 3 vols. Paris, 1930-1937.

Moore, Frederick F. *Siberia To-day.* New York and London, 1919.

Nasha zheleznodorozhnaia politika po dokumentam arkhiva Komiteta Ministrov. Istoricheskii ocherk sostavlennyi Nachal'nikom Otdeleniia Kantseliarii Komiteta Ministrov N. A. Kislinskim, pod glavnuiu redaktsieiu Stats-Sekretaria Kulomzina. 4 vols. St. Petersburg, 1902.

Niemojowski, Ludwik. *Siberian Pictures.* Edited, from the Polish, by Major Szulczewski. 2 vols. London, 1883.

Oganovsky, N. P. *Individualizatsiia zemlevladeniia v Rossii i eia posledstviia.* Moscow, 1917.

Pares, Bernard. "Conversations with Mr. Stolypin." *Russian Review* (London), Vol. II, No. 1, 1913.

Pares, Bernard. "The New Land Settlement in Russia." *Russian Review* (London), Vol. I, No. 1, 1912.

Pavlovsky, George. *Agricultural Russia on the Eve of the Revolution.* London, 1930.

Penrose, R. A. F., Jr. *The Last Stand of the Old Siberia.* Philadelphia, 1922.

Pioneer Settlement. Cooperative Studies by Twenty-Six Authors. Ed. by W. L. G. Joerg. New York, 1932.

Pokrovsky, M. N. *A Brief History of Russia.* 2 vols. Trans. by D. S. Mirsky. London, 1933.

Polnoe sobranie zakonov Rossiiskoi Imperii. Sobranie vtoroe (1825-1881), St. Petersburg, 1830-1884. 55 vols. *Sobranie tretie (1881-1913),* St. Petersburg, 1885-1916. 33 vols.

Popov, I. I. "Pereselenie krest'ian i zemleustroistvo Sibiri." *Velikaia Reforma.* 6 vols. Vol. VI. Moscow, 1911.

Price, M. P. *Siberia.* London, 1912.

Raeff, Marc. *Siberia and the Reforms of 1822.* Seattle, 1956.

Robinson, Geroid Tanquary. *Rural Russia under the Old Regime.* New York, 1949.

Rokitiansky, Nicholas John. *Stolypin Agrarian Reform.* M.A. thesis, Stanford, 1950.

Savickij, Nicolas. "P. A. Stolypin." *Le Monde Slave.* November and December 1933.

Sbornik statisticheskikh svedenii ob ekonomicheskom polozhenii pereselentsev v Sibiri. Materialy po obsledovaniiu tipichnykh pereselencheskikh poselkov, sobrannye i razrabotannye pod rukovodstvom i redaktsieiu V. K. Kuznetsova. Pereselencheskoe Upravlenie GUZIZ. 2 vols. St. Petersburg, 1912.

Schultz, Arved. *Sibirien: eine Landeskunde.* Breslau, 1923.

Semenov, M. P. de. *La Russie Extra-Européenne et Polaire.* Paris, 1900.

Semenov-Tian-Shansky, V. P., ed. *Rossiia. Polnoe geograficheskoe opisanie nashego otechestva.* Vol. XVI, *Zapadnaia Sibir'.* St. Petersburg, 1907.

Seraphim, Hans Jürgen. *Die landliche Besiedlung Westsibiriens durch Russland.* Jena, 1923.

Seton-Watson, Hugh. *The Decline of Imperial Russia.* New York, 1952.

Shidlovsky, Sergius. "The Imperial Duma and Land Settlement." *Russian Review* (London), Vol. I, No. I, 1912.

Shoemaker, Michael Myers. *The Great Siberian Railway from St. Petersburg to Pekin.* New York, 1903.

Shunkov, V. I. *Ocherki po istorii kolonizatsii Sibiri v XVII-nachale XVIII vekov.* Moscow-Leningrad, 1946.

Sibirskie voprosy. St. Petersburg. No. 1, 1905.

Sibirskii Torgovo-Promyshlennyi Ezhegodnik. 1914-1915 gg. Petrograd, n.d.

Sibirskoe pereselenie. St. Petersburg, 1896.

Sineokow, Vladimir. *La Colonisation Russe en Asie.* Paris, 1929.

Stadling, J. *Through Siberia.* London, 1901.

Statesman's Handbook for Russia. Ed. by the Chancery of the Committee of Ministers. Vol. I. St. Petersburg, 1896.

Stolypin, A. *P. A. Stolypin, 1862-1911.* Paris, n.d.

(Stolypin, P. A.) "Iz perepiski P. A. Stolypina s Nikolaem Romanovym," *Krasnyi Arkhiv.* Vol. 5(30), 1928.

(Stolypin, P. A.) "K istorii agrarnoi reformy Stolypina," *Krasnyi Arkhiv.* Vol. 4(17), 1926.

(Stolypin, P. A.) "Perepiska N. A. Romanova i P. A. Stolypina," *Krasnyi Arkhiv.* Vol. 5, 1924.

(Stolypin, P. A., and Krivoshein, A. V.) *Poezdka v Sibir' i Povolzh'e.* Zapiska P. A. Stolypina i A. V. Krivosheina. St. Petersburg, 1911.

(Stolypin, P. A., and Krivoshein, A. V.) *Die Kolonisation Sibiriens.* Eine Denkschrift von P. A. Stolypin und A. W. Kriwoschein. Einzige berechtigte Ubersetzung von Carl Erich Gleye. Berlin, 1912.

Sumner, B. H. *Survey of Russian History.* 2nd ed. London, 1947.

Svatikov, S. G. *Rossiia i Sibir'.* (K istorii sibirskogo oblastnichestva v XIX v.) Prague, 1929.

Syromatnikov, Sergius. "Reminiscences of Stolypin." *Russian Review* (London), Vol. I, No. 2, 1912.

Taft, Marcus Lorenzo. *Strange Siberia.* New York and Cincinnati, 1911.

Timoshenko, Vladimir P. *Agricultural Russia and the Wheat Problem.* Stanford, 1932.

Trotsky, L. D. "O Sibiri." *Severnaia Aziia*, No. 3, 1927.

Tschajanow, Alexander. *Die Lehre von der bäuerlichen Wirtschaft.* Trans. from Russian by Friedrich Schlömer. Berlin, 1923.

Turner, Samuel. *Siberia: a Record of Travel, Climbing and Exploration.* London, 1905.

Tverskoi, P. A. "K istoricheskim materialam o pokoinom P. A. Stolypine." *Vestnik Evropy.* April 1912.

Vladimir (Zenone Volpicelli). *Russia on the Pacific and the Siberian Railway.* London, 1899.

Voprosy kolonizatsii. Periodicheskii sbornik. 14 vols. 1907-1914. (As nearly a complete file as possible was assembled by the writer on microfilm through the courtesy of several American libraries and the University Library of Helsinki. The following numbers were used: Nos. 1, 6, 7, 9, 12, 13, 14.)

Voroponov, F. "K pereselentsam. Iz putevykh zametok." *Vestnik Evropy.* June and July, 1887.

V. V. (Voshchinin, V. P.) *Pereselencheskii vopros v Gosudarstvennoi Dume III sozyva.* St. Petersburg, 1912.

Vsemirnaia Vystavka 1900 g. v Parizhe. Komitet Sibirskoi Zheleznoi Dorogi. *Kolonizatsiia Sibiri v sviazi s obshchim pereselencheskim voprosom.* St. Petersburg, 1900.

Vsepoddanneishii Otchet Stats-Sekretaria Kulomzina po poezdke v Sibir' dlia oznakomleniia s polozheniem pereselencheskago dela. 2 vols. St. Petersburg, 1896.

Vysochaishe uchrezhdennoe Osoboe Soveshchanie o nuzhdakh sel'skokhoziaistvennoi promyshlennosti. Svod trudov mestnykh komitetov po 49 guberniiam Evropeiskoi Rossii. *Krest'ianskoe zemlepol'zovanie.* Compiled by A. A. Rittikh. St. Petersburg, 1903.

———. *Zemlevladenie.* Compiled by I. V. Sosnovsky. St. Petersburg, 1904.

Walsh, Warren B. "Political Parties in the Russian Dumas." *Journal of Modern History.* June 1950.

Weidle, Wladimir. *Russia: Absent and Present.* Trans. by A. Gordon Smith. London, 1952.

Windt, Harry de. *Siberia As It Is.* London, 1892.

Wright, George Frederick. *Asiatic Russia.* 2 vols. New York, 1902.

Wright, Richardson L., and Digby, Bassett. *Through Siberia: an Empire in the Making.* New York, 1913.

Young, C. Walter. "Chinese Immigration and Colonization in Manchuria." *Pioneer Settlement.* New York, 1932.

Zenzinov, Vladimir. *The Road to Oblivion.* New York, 1931.

INDEX

Date Due